T0270549

HERETIC

Also by Catherine Nixey

The Darkening Age

CATHERINE NIXEY

HERETIC

Jesus Christ
and the Other Sons of God

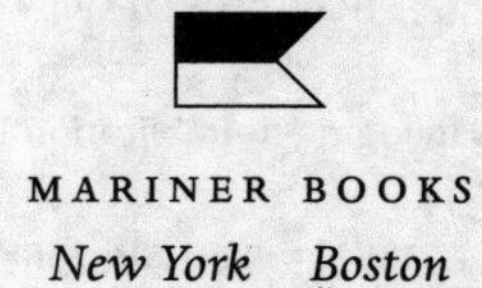

MARINER BOOKS
New York Boston

HarperCollins books may be purchased for educational, business, or sales promotional use. For information, please email the Special Markets Department at SPsales@harpercollins.com.

Originally published as *Heresy* in the United Kingdom in 2024 by Picador.

FIRST US EDITION

Library of Congress Cataloging-in-Publication Data has been applied for.

ISBN 978-0-358-65291-5

24 25 26 27 28 LBC 5 4 3 2 1

To P.J.J.N.,

For making me laugh.

'And when the Lord saw her, he had compassion on her and said to her, "Do not weep." Then he came up and touched the bier, and the bearers stood still. And he said, "Young man, I say to you, arise." And the dead man sat up and began to speak, and Jesus gave him to his mother.'

Luke 7:13–15, ESV

'Apollonius said, "Put the bier down, for I will end your crying over the girl." . . . Apollonius, after merely touching her and saying something secretly, woke the bride from her apparent death. The girl spoke, and went back to her father's house.'

Life of Apollonius of Tyana, IV.45

'Probably a crab would be filled with a sense of personal outrage if it could hear us class it without ado or apology as a crustacean, and thus dispose of it. "I am no such thing," it would say; "I am MYSELF, MYSELF alone."'

William James, *The Varieties of Religious Experience* (1902)

Contents

List of Illustrations

Photographic credits are shown in italics.

Prologue

'Christian children all must be / Mild, obedient, good as He.'

'Once in Royal David's City',
19th-century hymn

'He is killing our children'

A parent laments the behaviour of Jesus,
Infancy Gospel of Thomas, *c.* 2nd century AD

Even when Jesus was small, the villagers realized there was something unusual about him. Perhaps it was because he showed a certain confidence – bordering on arrogance – in the way he spoke to adults. Or perhaps it was due to the way his parents, Mary and Joseph, treated him: with a respect that at times seemed to verge on anxiety.

Or perhaps it was because he killed people.

Jesus' miracles hadn't started in a terrible way. Indeed, the first miracle, which would be spoken of for centuries everywhere from Alexandria to Arabia, was one of great charm. One Sabbath day, when he was just five years old, Jesus was playing alongside other village children in the ford of a brook. As young children love to do, he was diverting the rushing water into pools. Once the pool had been formed, the water cleared.

Yet, if one looked closely, there was something slightly strange about the way the water was behaving. It was not obeying the laws of nature as it ran and flowed and cleared. It was instead obeying the command of this boy: he gave the word, and the water changed its course.

Tiring of that game, Jesus began another. Taking some of the soft clay from the muddy edges of the water, he started to sculpt it into little sparrows, twelve in all. At that moment a man happened to walk past and saw what he was doing. Angry that Jesus was profaning the Sabbath in this way, the man went to Joseph and reported what he had seen. Joseph came to the boy. Why, he asked him, was he doing 'on the Sabbath things which it is not lawful to do?' Jesus didn't answer Joseph directly. Instead, he clapped his hands and cried out, 'Be gone!' to the sparrows.[1] And, chirping, the sparrows flew away.

Had the events of that day stopped there, they would have been remarkable enough. But they did not.

A young boy who had been watching all this came forward, took a willow stick, broke the dams that Jesus had created and let the waters out. Jesus turned on him in a fury. 'You insolent, godless ignoramus!' he said. 'What harm did the pools and the water do to you?' In a rage, Jesus carried on. 'Behold,' he said. 'Now you also shall wither like a tree, and shall bear neither leaves nor root nor fruit.'[2] The curse was opaque, but its effects were clear. For, immediately, that once healthy little boy became withered and deformed.

Worse was to come.

Not long after the incident at the stream, Jesus was passing through his village when another small boy ran past and bumped him on the shoulder. It may have been an accident; it may not. Either way, Jesus was once again angered and uttered an ominously oblique curse. 'You shall not go further on your way.'[3] His meaning became clear a moment later: the little boy fell down dead.

These are the words of the *Infancy Gospel of Thomas*.

Introduction

Each midwinter, in chapels and churches and cathedrals, it begins.

A single, small voice breaks the silence. 'Once in Royal David's city,' it sings, 'Stood a lowly cattle shed.' The carol goes on, telling a story so well known it hardly needs repeating. It is the story of how, in that lowly stable, a maiden (gentle, mild) laid her baby in a manger; and of how that baby became a boy (obedient, good); and of how that boy was in truth a saviour – the saviour – who now sits in heaven.

To listen to it is, as anyone who has heard it will know, a moving experience – almost less for its words than for how they are performed. For it opens with that child's voice, smooth as a pebble, bright as a star and all alone. As it moves into the second verse, the solo is joined by voices from the choir; and then finally the whole congregation joins in, a great swelling surge of sound, and the single note becomes a chorus and the message is in the mouths of all: Jesus has come. Christianity is here.

The history of Christianity – the tale of how this tiny insignificant sect came to dominate the West – is often told in similarly stirring terms. In this story, Christianity begins as a single voice – the voice of Jesus. It then gathers around it a small chorus – a fisherman here, a tax-collector there – before even more people are drawn to it, won over by the message of how that boy became a man who healed the blind, cured the lame, was crucified and rose again. First tens of people start to believe, then hundreds, then thousands, then millions, until, in one miraculous, triumphant moment, the Roman Empire itself converts and the fate of the world is changed.

This story is familiar not merely because we have been told it, but because Christianity infuses the art and architecture of the West: it spans the ceiling of the Sistine Chapel; it thunders through Handel's triumphant *Messiah* and it weaves through the lines of Milton and Dante and Donne. It has changed things both big and small: it has shaped the skylines of our cities – for it raised the dome of St Peter's and the towers of Notre-Dame and spreads its outstretched arms over Rio de Janeiro – and it has put words into our mouths, for when we talk of lands of milk and honey, or thieves in the night, or of turning the other cheek – or, indeed, of putting words into our mouths – we are speaking phrases shaped by it. Even our calendar conforms to Christianity, since in the West we celebrate on saints' days, rest on Sundays and holiday at Christmas and at Easter. Time itself is measured out in a Christian tread. This, it seems, is a message written in stone and just as immovable.

Except this certainty is an illusion. The Gospel of John might begin with the magnificently lapidary line declaring that 'In the beginning was the word' – but in the beginning there was not one, singular 'word', or one single Christian message.* The idea is a nonsense. In the first centuries of Christianity, there were instead many words, many voices – many of which disagreed with each other vehemently, and at times violently, on almost every aspect of this story. Because, in the years after the life and death of Jesus, there was absolutely no consensus on who he had been, or what he had done, or why he mattered – or even whether he did matter. In the earliest centuries of Christianity there were indeed Christians who said that Jesus was meek and mild and gentle, but there were many other Christians who

---

* On the translation of this as 'word' (and why it might be inappropriate), see Chapter Five.

believed equally fervently in a saviour who blinded those who criticized him and murdered those who merely bothered him. And there were some Christians who happily believed in both.

Differences are to be found everywhere. Consider, for example, the story of Jesus' birth. While there were, it is true, early Christians who believed that Jesus had been born of Mary, a virgin, there were large numbers of others who said: bunkum. Jesus was simply a normal man, who had been fathered by Joseph, 'just as all men were generated from a man's seed and a woman.'[1] Other Christians entirely rejected the idea that a god would grow inside a mortal womb as mere men did – it was too undignified. Instead, they argued, Jesus had been pre-assembled in heaven, then arrived on earth when he came down 'from above and passed through the Virgin Mary like water through a pipe.'[2] Which was apparently considered a more decorous solution. And one extremely ancient text, which can be dated to the middle of the second century, explained in some detail how Jesus had impregnated his own mother himself.[3] In this somewhat surprising account, Jesus explains how he, in the likeness of an angel, appeared to his mother Mary, who laughed, and how he then entered her himself, and 'I, the Word, went into her and became flesh.'*[4]

The differences go on. For almost any aspect of Jesus that is 'known' in the West today, there were once alternatives. While some ancient Christians venerated a Jesus who – like the familiar Jesus of Sunday schools and sunbeams – advised his followers to suffer the little children to come unto him, other ancient Christians venerated a Jesus who warned his followers in the strongest possible terms not to have any children at all, because all children turn out to be either 'lunatics or half-withered or crippled or

* This is in many ways an entirely logical extension of the idea of what would become known as 'the Trinity': if God is indeed three in one – if he is at once God, and Jesus, and the Holy Ghost – then it seems reasonable to assume that, if God (somehow) made Mary pregnant, then Jesus was (somehow) involved too. It is a thought-provoking read.

deaf or dumb or paralytics or idiots.'[5] And while there were indeed some early Christians who believed, as Christians do today, in a Jesus who was crucified, there were others who considered that idea absurd, for why would a god allow himself to be crucified? These Christians were said – at least by their critics – to believe instead that Jesus had magically swapped his body with that of another man at the last moment, then stood opposite, 'laughing', as the other man died in agony.[6]

Almost every early Christian text offers a different view; a different strand to 'the' Christian story that is familiar today. The differences are dizzying. Take the Virgin Mary. Honey-haired and head bowed, for centuries Mary epitomized an ideal of feminine meekness. But she was not always such a milquetoast: one ancient telling of the Nativity includes a Mary whose vagina can, and at one point does, roast human flesh. The text that contains this tale is in many ways very beautiful. At the moment of the birth of Jesus, the world quite literally stops turning: birds are stilled in mid-air; a shepherd who has raised his arm to strike his sheep becomes frozen, arm aloft; even the stars pause their nightly procession across the sky. Then, shortly after the birth of Jesus, a woman arrives at the familiar Nativity scene, with its ox and its ass, and – in a slightly less familiar twist to this story – inserts her hand into Mary's vagina to test whether she really is a virgin. The woman's hand is immediately burned off. 'Woe,' says the woman, as well she might.[7]

But, perhaps most importantly, not all of the voices that could be heard in the darkness of these early centuries were Christian. Despite what Christian histories and sentimental Christian hymns might make modern minds think, Jesus did not arrive into a world that was spiritually silent – and certainly not into a world that was in any way short of prophets. On the contrary: read ancient satirists and there appears to have been a glut of men around at this time who claimed to be able to heal the blind, cure the lame – and who were similarly fond of making hair-raising predictions about the future. As a Greek critic called

Celsus tartly put it: there are 'others who go about begging [and] say that they are sons of God who have come from above'.[8]

To educated Greek and Roman minds, all of these so-called 'prophets' deserved not pious reverence but parody – and Greek and Roman writers duly parodied them mercilessly. 'It is an ordinary and common custom,' wrote Celsus, for these so-called prophets 'to say: "I am God (or a son of God, or a divine Spirit). And I have come."' Their irksome spiel was always the same: after declaring their divinity, they would go on to declare that, 'Already the world is being destroyed. And you, O men, are to perish because of your iniquities. But I wish to save you. And you shall see me returning again with heavenly power.'[9]

I still remember where I was sitting when I first read Celsus. It was a grey autumn afternoon, and I was in the British Library, and the readers around me were starting to switch on the lights above their desks. As I looked at the words on the yellowing page before me (to this day, Celsus is a far from fashionable author), I saw passages that seemed to me to be so rude, so sceptical, so shocking – so, frankly, funny – that they took my breath away. I had to resist the temptation to nudge the person next to me and say: Look. Did you know this?

I certainly didn't, and I had been brought up in a house that was quite religious. Before they met and married, my mother had been a nun and my father had been a monk – and, even when they left religious orders, they didn't leave religion behind entirely. We all went to church every Sunday, said grace before meals and prayers before bed. Each Christmas, I helped my mother put out our crib, with its little pink baby Jesus and its ox and its ass; each Lent, I gave up chocolate; each Halloween, I was piously scandalized by those who painted their faces and went trick-or-treating, a habit that I considered both wicked and American. Until I was well into my teens, I believed in God – and it wasn't until my late twenties that I would be confident enough to say that I actively did not. Although for much of that time, my idea of God was rather hazy: as a young child, I thought that

God was called Peter because, throughout Mass, we seemed to say, at intervals, 'Thanks Peter God.'

Even though I eventually gave it up, Catholicism had settled on me like dust, falling in places visible and invisible. Long after I stopped believing, I would come across corners of Catholicism in my mind that had lain unnoticed and undisturbed for years. When I was in my late teens, I learned that a friend of mine hadn't been baptized and, just for a moment, I was shocked that her parents could have been so careless: her name seemed to me to be less securely attached to her if it wasn't held on with holy water. A moment later, I felt shocked that I had been shocked – and yet I had been.

But, then again, it requires little to shock the child of a monk and a nun: I also used to feel alarmed when friends' parents played loud pop music in their cars, and even by people who wore jeans, which seemed to me startlingly modern. I am not proud of my prissiness; I simply note it. And, long after I stopped believing in the truth of the Christian God, I still believed in the truth of Christian history, and of how this religion had been received and spread. Which is why, when I started reading Celsus in the library on that dull autumn day, I was shocked once again – but this time by my own ignorance: how had I not known that in the ancient world people had said such things?

I started reading, and didn't stop. I now know that there are good reasons why I didn't know this – and why some people still don't. In certain circles – among those with an interest in the history of Christianity, for example – the views of writers like Celsus are widely known. But they certainly aren't familiar to everyone, and they are rarely taught in schools. This is not surprising. Simply because something is a historical fact – and that there were many different forms of ancient Christianities is such a fact – does not mean that it will become widely known. The historian E. H. Carr once wrote that historical facts are 'like fish swimming about in a vast and sometimes inaccessible ocean; and what the historian catches will depend, partly on chance, but mainly on what part of the ocean he chooses to fish in.'[10] For many centuries, Christian historians did not, typically, spend much time fishing in waters where they might find alternative saviours, or tales of a murderous Jesus – and they certainly rarely chose to serve these up to their readers.

In truth, the absence of these stories is also due, at least partially, to more sinister causes than that. Many of the stories in this book were buried, in some cases quite literally, when Christianity came to power in the fourth century. Under the influence of Christianity, the noisy, critical, quarrelsome habits of the Roman Empire started to change. As the thunderous words of one fourth-century law declared, public discussion of religion was, in this newly Christian world, to cease; while those who continued to 'contend' about religion in public would 'pay the penalty of high treason with their lives and blood.'[11]

Other laws appeared soon after. Within a few decades of Christianity coming to power, so-called 'heretics' started first to be deprived of certain legal rights, then of certain jobs, then of their places of worship and even, eventually, their homes. One typically aggressive ruling proclaimed that 'the polluted contagions of the heretics shall be expelled from the cities and driven forth from the villages.'[12] In this new world, heretical books (and indeed books that were merely critical of Christianity) were outlawed and burned, while heretics could find themselves pursued, at times violently. Within fifty years of Christianity coming to power, as one observer noted, 'many whole communities of those who are called "heretics" were actually butchered.'[13] This book will look at this story and at how, as the great Oxford historian G. E. M. de Ste. Croix put it, the Catholic Church became 'the greatest organized persecuting force in human history.'[14]

At the heart of many of these persecutions was the new Christian concept of 'heresy'. Heresy came to be closely associated with Christianity, but as a word it long predated it. 'Heresy' comes from the Greek word *haireo*, which means 'I choose'.* In the form 'heresy' – *haeresis*, in Greek – it merely meant something that was chosen; a 'choice'.[15] In the pre-Christian Greek world, 'heresy' had been a word with positive connotations – to use your intellect to make independent-minded choices was, then, considered a good thing. It did not retain that positive feel. Within the first century of the birth of this new religion, 'choice' for Christians had become no longer a praiseworthy attribute but a 'poison'. Heretics started to be spoken of not merely as people but as a disease to be 'cured', a gangrene to be 'cut out' and a pollution to be eliminated in order to purify the Christian body as a whole. As St Augustine – always a man with enviable mastery of metaphor – would later put it, heretics were those whom the church 'voids from itself like shit.'[16]

Though it is worth being cautious of the word heresy, chiefly because it pretends to a precision that it lacks. Books on this era have, for centuries, referred to 'the heretics' and 'the orthodox' as though these terms are absolute ones, with clear-cut and unmoving definitions. They are not; they are relative – little more than the religious equivalent of 'mine' and 'yours', or perhaps, in the context of history, of 'winner' and 'loser'. 'Everyone', as the philosopher John Locke later wrote, 'is orthodox to himself.'[17]

This book is called *Heretic*, though not all the beliefs it chronicles are heretical – far from it. Some were schismatic; some were merely disapproved of – and many of the more surprising stories recounted here were (despite occasional harrumphing from the Church) an accepted part of Christian worship for centuries. I have taken *Heretic* as the title less because of its Christian meaning than its original Greek one. For this is a book about choice, and how choice can be lost.

---

* Precisely speaking, it is in its middle voice, *haireomai*, that it means 'choose' – 'I take for myself' – but middle forms are a mouthful; so, above, I give the first-person active.

This can happen in far more subtle ways than is often thought. When most people think of heresy, and of how heresies are wiped out, they will tend to turn to moments of violence: to slaughtered villages and ferocious laws; to tongues that are cut out and hands cut off; to beatings and scalpings and killings. And this story does have many of those things, certainly – as it should: not only does such violence have an effect on beliefs, it also, at the distance of a millennium or two, makes for splendidly entertaining history.

But violence can also be a distraction. Thomas Carlyle objected to history 'written in hysterics' – and that should be guarded against here, too.[18] Many in the ancient world will have converted to Christianity for positive reasons. This new religion brought many benefits, both spiritual and material, to its adherents, since early Christians, like later ones, cared generously for the needy. And while some were forced to convert by violence or its threat, the number of such conversions will have been small. Few societies, and certainly few ancient societies, can staff the violent repression of belief on a large scale. Certainly Rome could not: even at its height, the empire was administered so lightly that there was, on average, one member of senior imperial staff per 330,000 inhabitants.[19]

Violence is, in fact, rarely necessary. Most people do not require being flogged with leaden weights to abandon their ideas; for most, the fear that they might lose their job, or that they might merely lose a friend, is enough to make them change their beliefs – or at least stop talking about them. 'You may talk of the tyranny of Nero and Tiberius; but the real tyranny is the tyranny of your next-door neighbour,' as Walter Bagehot, the Victorian journalist and editor, wrote. 'Public opinion is a permeating influence, and it exacts obedience to itself.'[20] This, then, is a book about heresy and about how beliefs and ideas are violently silenced. But it is also about the ways in which people silence themselves. It is about the far more insidious ways in which things become first unwritable, then unsayable and finally unthinkable.

This book will itself do some things that are, in the world of history, if not heretical then mildly frowned upon. For one thing, it will unapologetically consider Christianity alongside other classical religions. To do this is relatively unusual (though much less so than it once was). For centuries, there was almost a gentlemen's agreement between classicists and theologians that the Greek and Roman gods, which fell into the categories of 'history' and 'mythology' (and, tacitly, of 'absurdity'), should be dealt with by classicists; while the Christian God and his followers, which fell into the category of true religion, should be dealt with by theologians.

This reluctance to bracket Christianity with other ancient religions is understandable. As the pioneering psychologist William James observed when he gave a series of lectures on religious belief, 'we instinctively recoil from seeing an object to which our emotions and affections are committed handled by the intellect as any other object is handled.'[21] But it is also poor history. Theologians and classicists might shelve their books in different corners of different libraries, but the classical world was far more promiscuous: a statue of Orpheus might, so one ancient author said, stand happily alongside one of Jesus; the name of Helios might appear alongside that of Christ in a single spell.[22] This book will mirror that ancient approach and mingle and compare Christian habits and non-Christian ones. Christianity was uniquely successful; it was not – despite its later claims – unique.

This book will also move briskly: it will skip across centuries and leap across continents – and it will do so without apology. Christianity spread with extraordinary rapidity across the known world, and its consequences would last for many centuries; to give even a sense of this it is necessary to be nippy. This book will therefore head to ancient Syria and listen to a spellbinding Syrian ode in which the Holy Spirit milks the breasts of a

Christian God who is far less masculine than the one most now know.[23] It will travel to Africa to listen to an Ethiopic Christian text that records how Jesus resurrected a cockerel from a chicken dinner and sent the bird into the sky for a thousand years. It will leap forward in time, too, to watch as 'crusaders' gather on the bend in a river in medieval France, then surge into a small town and slaughter every man, woman and child who they find sheltering in a cathedral, because some of them – not all, but only some – were heretics.

This book asks not only for your attention but for your imagination. It asks you to go to that moment of silence at the start of that carol and to imagine not just that there were other voices in the darkness, but that there was a time – a time long, long ago – when those other voices actually mattered. It is hard to make this imaginative leap: well aware that almost all those other voices would be wiped out in Europe, historians have tended to grant them oblivion in the pages of history, too. But they were there, these voices – and they did matter. In some places, they still do.

In late 1950, the explorer Wilfred Thesiger arrived in Iraq and travelled to its marshlands. He was bewitched by what he found. There, he saw people living a life that had hardly changed in 2,000 years. He also found a people who practised a religion that looked a little like Christianity: its followers believed in God, and in Adam, and in John the Baptist. But this religion was also very different, for these people believed that Jesus was not a saviour but a fraud and a malevolent sorcerer. To this day, in Ethiopia, many Christians still read that text about the resurrected cockerel; in India, Christians were influenced by a text that told how Jesus sold one of his followers into slavery.

The form of Christianity that survived in the West argued, for centuries, that its victory over its rivals was natural and preordained. It was nothing of the kind. Other forms of Christianity, and other ancient religions that closely resembled it, survived for centuries elsewhere. Had history tilted slightly differently, they might have survived in Europe, too. They did not. One kind of Christianity won in the West, then crushed its rivals out of existence. One single form of Christianity enjoyed serendipity and called it destiny. It was not. It could all, so very easily, have been different.

Although, in some ways, these early differences did not wholly die out. Many of those early iterations of Christianity are now largely forgotten – but they are not gone. Just as long-buried ancient walls leave lines in modern wheat fields, so these ancient beliefs have marked modern Christianity in ways big and small. Gospels and stories that would later seem shocking to modern readers were, for centuries, central to the calendar, readings and thought of the Church; many have infused the art and thinking of Western Christianity. Look carefully, listen closely, and you can hear whispers of them to this day. They are there in the poetry of Milton and in the damned of Dante; they are there in the paintings of Giotto, and they are there in the Christmas images that we in the West celebrate still.

Of course, I had little idea of this when, as a child, I set out that crib with my mother. Each year, we put out Mary and Joseph, and the three wise men. And, each year, we put out the ox and the donkey on which Mary had ridden. Our crib, we were certain, was correct: the perfect representation of the story of the birth of Jesus, as told in the Bible. And yet the ox and the donkey – seen in so many cards and carols and paintings – are not mentioned in the Bible. They are mentioned instead in another ancient gospel – a gospel in which, at the moment of the birth of Jesus, the world stopped turning, and the vagina of the Virgin Mary burned off another woman's hand.

Author's Note

There are many, many stories in this book and the reader might wonder: which was correct? It is important to state at the beginning that this book will take no position on this question. It will absolutely not attempt to adjudicate over which of these stories – of murderous Jesuses, or Marys with miraculous powers – is more plausible. These texts are not of interest to the historian because they are believable – all break the laws of nature merrily and frequently – but because they were (and in some cases still are) believed. To dismiss them because their theology or message seems implausible would make this a work of theology, not history.

The reader might also wonder which of these narratives, in the beginning, was more popular and important. These are hard questions. Many of these stories would go on to be very popular indeed: some would be read across several continents for several centuries. But their popularity took time to develop. This book looks at the early stages in the evolution of a religion and – as in the early evolution of any species – the absolute numbers involved are tiny.

Simply because a species becomes all-conquering does not mean it was always so. The gospel narratives known today were popular from the beginning. But so too were others. Evolution is unpredictable. At times, the ancestors of *Homo sapiens* teetered close to extinction. The race, after all, is not always to the swift nor the battle to the strong. Time and chance happen to them all. The religions that humans have embraced have risen and fallen with similar rapidity and unpredictability. In the first century AD, it would not have been immediately obvious which form of which ancient religion would eventually outcompete all the others. Of course religious believers – then and now – would beg to differ. They usually know which religion is best: their own. The early followers of Christ knew this clearly. But then so too did many followers of Zeus and Mithras. To the disinterested observer, the matter is much less clear.

Which of these Christian stories was more popular? The simple answer is that, in the earliest years, none was very popular at all. One (very rough) estimate puts the total number of Christians in the year 100 AD at around seven thousand. The number of fully literate Christians able to read these stories has also been estimated and it is smaller still: perhaps under a hundred. This is clearly a wild guess (or in academic parlance, a heuristic) but it is telling nonetheless.

Few, in the first centuries of Christianity, would have been able to confidently predict which of its stories would win out over all the others. But eventually, time and chance had their say and the race was won by some of them. We know those stories, still, today. This book is the story of the others.

Where possible, this book will avoid using such freighted terms as 'heretic' and 'heretical' and 'orthodox' and 'pagan'. When they are used, they will often be in inverted commas – though, since context often applies its own inverted commas, and since relentless use of quotation marks can start to feel fussy, they will not always be used; if they are not there, they can and should merely be assumed.

This book does not touch on early Christianity's relationship to Judaism. An excellent introduction to this topic remains Géza Vermes's *Jesus the Jew*. Nor does this book touch, except tangentially, on the early Church's ferocious rhetoric against Jewish people, nor the anti-Jewish laws and edicts that Christian rulers often passed and enforced against Jewish people in these centuries, for that vast topic would deserve a book to itself. However, for those who are interested, reading the Theodosian Code is not a bad place to start.

Chapter One

ANTICHRIST

'Apsethus is a god'

Greek parrots proclaim the arrival of yet another deity,
Libya, *c.* 2nd century AD

His birth had been miraculous. In the reign of Caesar Augustus, as the first millennium began, in a town in the east of the Roman Empire, a woman fell pregnant. While her belly was swollen with her child, a divine being appeared to her and spoke to her – though she was not at all afraid. She asked the heavenly vision who her son would be, and he replied that her child would be a god. Not merely the son of a god – but a god himself, made flesh and born from the womb of a mortal woman.[1]

And indeed, when this boy was born, heaven itself seemed to acclaim him. For a bolt of lightning appeared, poised in the heavens above his birthplace, before disappearing upwards. 'The gods', one of his followers later wrote, 'were giving a signal and an omen of his brilliance.'[2]

His life offered stranger things yet. As the boy grew into a man, people started to come to him. Some came because they had heard the stories of his miraculous birth and were curious; others perhaps were attracted by his unusual appearance. Despite being beautiful, he dressed in a way that was simple to the point of eccentric, growing his hair long, wearing plain linen robes and going about barefoot.

Some came to hear him speak: he was so charismatic that, when he arrived in a city, even workmen left what they were doing and came to follow him. Others came to ask him for healing: they had heard that he could drive away demons, drive pains from men and even – or so some said – raise the dead.

The scene of this man's most astonishing miracle had begun unremarkably enough. He was in Rome, and it was a dull and miserable day. It was raining, and a sickness had been sweeping the city; people everywhere were coughing and talking with rasping voices. Even the emperor himself had been affected.

At around this time, this man set out on a walk. As he went, he noticed a funeral procession making its way through the rain, following the body of a young girl. The girl was from one of the grandest families in the city, and today should have been one of joy for them, as it was her wedding day. But, in the very hour of her marriage, she had died. Now, instead of dancing through the streets in celebration, the two families were walking through the drizzle, united only by grief. It was said that the whole city mourned with the groom as he went.

Seeing their sorrow, the man approached immediately. Put the body down, he said, 'For I will end your crying over the girl.'[3] He asked the mourners what her name was. The crowd, uncertain what was going on, assumed he was about to perform a funeral oration. Instead, he approached the corpse and, 'merely touching her and saying something secretly, woke the bride from her apparent death.' She instantly revived. 'The girl spoke, and went back to her father's house.'[4]

Some scorned such stories as superstitious claptrap. But others saw, and they believed – not merely that he had performed these miracles, but that his mother's vision had been true. They believed that this long-haired healer was indeed a god in human form: a healing god born of a mortal woman. The man himself had even once declared: 'I am not mortal'.[5] One later writer suggested that his biography should be called, 'A Visit of God to Mankind'.[6]

Stories about this man spread far and fast; people flocked to his shrines. He rapidly became one of the most popular wonder-workers in the Roman Empire. Indeed, he became so popular that soon, or so it was said, even the imperial family itself started to worship him.[7]

And his name was Apollonius of Tyana. Or, as the Christians would later call him, he was an 'antichrist'.[8]

*

The poet Milton had been clear. The moment of Christ's birth had brought instant defeat upon the gods of the Roman Empire. On that very morning, those ancient Roman gods and goddesses, those demigods and nymphs, had heard the news and, realizing they were beaten, had simply fled the earth. In the groves and the hills and the woods of Italy, wrote Milton, 'A voice of weeping . . . and loud lament' was heard as the old deities fled, in terror.[9] Christ had come: heaven and earth had been transformed.

This is an idea that would linger in poetry and in prose. The Enlightenment historian Edward Gibbon argued that Christ's birth didn't merely begin the Christian religion – it marked the start of all true religious belief in the ancient world. The Romans had been far too clever, Gibbon wrote, to believe in their own ridiculous gods – in lecherous, philandering Jupiter and sulky Juno and all the others – and had looked upon these gods with 'secret contempt'. It had only been with the arrival of Jesus that the Romans really started believing in religion, for finally they had received a 'genuine revelation, fitted to inspire the most rational esteem and conviction.'[10] As late as the twentieth century, a children's history book, *A Little History of the World* by E. H. Gombrich, would feel able to confidently explain to its readers that, in Christianity, the Romans heard 'something that was entirely new, something that had never been heard before'.[11] The message is clear: the ancient world had been waiting for its saviour.

The idea is charming – and it is untrue. Read ancient texts carefully, without the distorting fog of two millennia of Christian thought, and it becomes clear that the benighted pagan world was not, after all, waiting for its saviour. If anything, it seemed to think it was suffering from an overabundance of such men; and almost nothing about Christianity struck any ancient observers as the slightest bit novel. Christians claimed that Jesus was the son of a god and had been born of a virgin? Well, as ancient authors briskly pointed out, that was hardly a unique claim. Such stories had been told of the healing god Asclepius (whose father was Apollo and whose mother had been a mere mortal); Apollonius (whose father was the god Proteus and whose mother was mortal); and Pythagoras (father: Apollo; mother: mortal); as well as the less-than-virtuous Alexander the Great (whose divine father was rumoured to have impregnated his mother in the form of a snake).[12] As irritated ancient critics pointed out, the list was long.

Far from greeting the tales of Jesus with breathless awe, the reaction of most ancient intellectuals seems to have been one of contempt, or boredom, mingled with barely concealed mirth. Little about this new sect escaped criticism of ancient observers. Christian parables were 'fictitious' garbage, wrote a scornful third-century philosopher named Porphyry; they were no more than 'little imaginative stories' that were 'replete with stupidity' and written in a 'comical and unconvincing' style, while Christian metaphors were 'dubious little saying[s]' and Christian theology was, he thought, idiotic.[13] Ancient authors had similarly little time for Christian promises that the end of the world was nigh (it manifestly wasn't) and that all Christians would be resurrected after their deaths (they clearly wouldn't). The Christian apologist C. S. Lewis once wrote that Jesus must have been either a liar, or a lunatic, or truly God.[14] The cynical pagan world was very clear which of these three it thought him to be – and it certainly wasn't the latter.

Christianity, it is true, did offer some religious novelties. Its habit of ceremonially drinking the 'body' and 'blood' of its saviour was one, but this was, to say the least, not greeted with wholehearted enthusiasm by ancient observers. When Greeks and Romans heard about it, their reaction was less Gibbon's 'rational esteem' than utter revulsion. This is, wrote Porphyry, an intensely strange idea: 'that a man should taste human flesh, and drink the blood of the same tribe's members and race – and by doing so he should partake of eternal life.'[15] Porphyry professed himself confused by the whole thing. 'What does this . . .

mean?' he asked. Was it meant allegorically? If so, it was both baffling and revolting – 'bestial and absurd' – and unpleasant even to think about. Even the 'fragrance of this story demoralises the soul by upsetting it with unpleasant things.'[16] True, this habit wasn't a total novelty: there had always been those who believed that human blood had miraculous powers. Pliny the Elder had written with disgust of how some would hurry into the arena to drink the blood of gladiators, as if it contained life itself.[17] But this odd idea could surely appeal to almost no one – and, added Porphyry with typical intellectual disdain, still less to any man who had had the advantage of a good education.

One of the things that irked ancient observers most about the new Christian cult that had appeared in their midst was not merely that its followers claimed Christ performed miracles, or that he had divine qualities. It was that they seemed to consider this in any way special. Why, asked the irritated Celsus, is it that all our stories are to be regarded as mere 'legends' while yours is to be regarded as 'noble and convincing'?[18] Christians, one Greek writer observed testily, claim that Christ was unique, but other men 'also performed wonders . . . in fact, they performed boundless wonders.'[19] Moreover, Christians placed baffling amounts of faith in texts that had clearly been written by uneducated hands. 'They talk of Jesus up hill and down dale,' one classical critic wrote, 'revering him for giving sight to the blind and doing some such miracles as these.'[20] But, he argued, 'the deeds of Jesus have been exaggerated' by his followers, who were hardly intellectuals, he added, but rather 'liars [and] yokels'.[21]

Jesus' prophecies – revered by his followers – were treated with similarly short shrift by sceptical Greeks and Romans. There are so many men 'who prophesy at the slightest excuse,' wrote Celsus.[22] Such people could be spotted both inside and outside temples, babbling about the end times. They 'wander about begging and roaming around cities and military camps; and they pretend to be moved as if giving some oracular utterance.'[23]

These doom-mongering prophets were common in the East,

Celsus went on – indeed, they were 'the most perfect type among the men in that region.' Their so-called 'prophecies' followed a familiar pattern (or so Celsus said). First, such men would claim divinity for themselves; then they would warn that the world was being destroyed; then they would add, 'Blessed is he who has worshipped me now! But I will cast everlasting fire upon all the rest, both on cities and on country places. And men who fail to realise the penalties in store for them will in vain repent and groan. But I will preserve for ever those who have been convinced by me.'[24] Even Christianity tacitly acknowledged that it had a large number of competitors – and frowned upon them. As the Gospel of Matthew warned, 'there shall arise false Christs, and false prophets, and shall shew great signs and wonders; insomuch that, if it were possible, they shall deceive the very elect.'[25]

It was all so confusing, Celsus archly complained. How on earth could one know which doom-monger to believe? 'If these people proclaim Jesus, and others proclaim someone else, and if they all have the common and glib slogan, "Believe if you want to be saved, or else away with you" – well then, what will those do who really want to be saved? Are they to throw dice in order to divine where they may turn, and whom they are to follow?'[26]

Porphyry was bothered by another aspect of the Christian story. If, to be saved, one had to believe in Christ, then why, Porphyry asked, did God leave it so late to send him? Why leave everyone who lived and died before Christ to roast in hell? 'What', Porphyry asked, 'have humans done in the many centuries before Christ? . . . Why has the so-called saviour made himself unavailable in all these centuries?'[27] What about all the poor people who had been born and died before Jesus came? Why not turn up a bit earlier? 'Was it necessary that he come at the end of days and not earlier', leaving 'an innumerable multitude of peoples', born before Jesus, to be damned? How can a supposedly 'compassionate and merciful God', Porphyry wondered in contempt, allow that?[28]

The Christian idea that the end of the world was nigh also

took a hammering from Porphyry. Surely no one, he wrote, 'is so uneducated or so stupid' as to believe in the absurd Christian view of what would happen in the end times. Besides, as he pointed out, the end of the world wasn't nigh at all. Christians had claimed that it would come when the gospel was known across the world. But, Porphyry wrote, 'every street on earth' knew the gospel these days, 'But the end is nowhere [in sight] and it will never come.'[29]

Later, when Christianity became first more confident, and then aggressive, it would start to reject the idea that it was similar to any of these other cults, or that Jesus had anything in common with other ancient healers or saviours – but, in the early days of its existence, it did not merely admit the similarities, but even traded on them: they offered plausible precedents for Christianity's own claims. 'When we say also that [Jesus] was produced without sexual union,' wrote the second-century Christian author Justin Martyr, 'and that He . . . was crucified and died, and rose again, and ascended into heaven, we propound nothing different from what you believe regarding those whom you esteem sons of Jupiter.'[30]

Justin was able to make such comparisons in part because – contrary to the imaginings of Milton and Gibbon – the ancient world had not been emptied of its gods the moment that Christ arrived on earth. On the contrary: ancient deities were still present in ancient minds, and still venerated by many. The Roman pantheon was far larger than is often remembered: there were not merely the famous gods who are remembered today – the Apollos and Junos and Jupiters – but countless lesser ones too.

Every human endeavour in the ancient world – from holding a meeting of the senate, to planting a crop, or even having sex – cast a divine shadow and had its associated deities. Indeed, as one critic later grumbled, sex seems to have been particularly well supplied by the divine. The bedrooms of the amorous were filled, one fifth-century Christian tutted, with a veritable 'swarm of deities' overseeing matters. The 'goddess Virginensis is present to unfasten the virgin's girdle'; then, once that was done, 'the god Subigus is present to ensure her husband will be able to subdue [the woman] successfully'; while 'the goddess Prema is there to press [the woman] down once she has submitted, so that she will not struggle . . .'[31] Romance might have been absent from Roman bedrooms; religion, clearly, was not.

And, in this quarrelsome and competitive pantheon, there were several deities who resembled Jesus – or rather, given that several predated him, it would be more precise to say that Jesus resembled them. The world of ancient Roman religion is often referred to as a marketplace and, as is common in marketplaces, many of the most successful products resembled each other closely. Not all of these divine figures filled precisely the same divine niche, nor did they perform precisely the same miracles: some claimed to be prophets; others were divinities; others worked wonders. But they did all share one characteristic, for all were roundly mocked by their more sceptical neighbours, who considered them cranks and charlatans.

Consider the second-century Apsethus, a supposed (and rather underwhelming) mystic from Libya, who was so keen to be recognized as a god that he trained parrots to flap around him squawking, 'Apsethus is a god.' His neighbours promptly captured the parrots and, in revenge, trained them to instead squawk a brisk but effective denunciation: 'Apsethus, having caged us, compelled us to say, Apsethus is a god.'[32] The Libyans, whose sense of humour later seems to have failed them, eventually decided to burn Apsethus alive. A prophet is often without honour in his home town.

As cynics observed, it didn't take much to get a new religion going in those days. A Greek satirist called Lucian wrote an acidulous account of a charlatan named Alexander, who popped up in the east of the Roman Empire at the start of the second century AD and started peddling a new religion there. His aim – at least according to Lucian – was less divine than very earthly indeed: as Lucian explains, Alexander had 'readily discerned that human life is swayed by two great tyrants, hope and fear.' Religion helped to tame both, and so Alexander realized that he 'would speedily enrich himself' if he set up a religion.[33]

Alexander had all the prophetic staples: he had a divine backstory (he was supposed to be the grandson of a god) and the looks (his eyes used to shine 'with a great glow of fervour and enthusiasm').[34] The only thing he was lacking were the proper prophetic locks: his hair wouldn't grow to quite the required length, so, Lucian writes, Alexander had to resort to hair extensions. This was done so skilfully that 'most people did not detect that [his hair] was not his own.'[35]

Once his look was complete, Alexander – a 'consummate rascal' – got going on his 'victims', as Lucian calls them, heading off to some backwards province in search of what Lucian considered to be the essential ingredient of a new religion – namely, 'fat-heads' and 'simpletons' who might be persuaded to become its followers. All a man had to do was turn up in some provincial backwater, Lucian wrote, start spouting rubbish, and the locals there would stare at him 'as if he were a god from heaven.'[36]

Lucian's Alexander is entertaining enough, but to modern eyes the most striking ancient wonder-worker of all is Apollonius, as so many of the stories told about him carry echoes – and more – of those told about Jesus. Even the year of his birth was similar to that of Jesus. The latter, it is estimated, was born at some point between 6 BC and 4 BC; Apollonius' birth date is similarly imprecise, but it is estimated that he was born somewhere between 4 BC or 3 BC and the 'early years' of the first century AD; though other historians – and this is a mark of how vague his history is – place his date as late as 30 or 40 AD.[37] It is possible, even probable, that their lives overlapped. And, as ancient critics of Christianity pointed out with gusto, the two men's lives were replete with similarity, from their births onwards.

At least one ancient author even seems to have made a laborious point-by-point comparison of the two men's lives. Precisely what this work said is not now known – like so many other writings that were critical of Christianity, it has largely been lost. But the briefest look at Jesus' life and Apollonius' shows just how easy such an attempt would have been, for in so many ways the two resemble each other so closely. Consider their births. When Apollonius of Tyana's mother was pregnant – or so his surviving biography claims – that divine being appeared to her, but she was unafraid, and was told she was pregnant with a god.[38] Similarly, an angel appeared to Jesus' mother Mary, 'And the angel said unto her, "Fear not, Mary: for thou hast found favour with God."' Mary too is told that she will conceive a son and that he will 'be great and will be called the Son of the Most High.'[39] In the gospels, Jesus' birth is marked by a 'star in the East'; Apollonius' is marked by a bolt of lightning in the sky.[40]

Their later lives offer other similarities. When both men get to adulthood, they start to lead a peripatetic existence, roaming about the countryside, preaching and gathering large numbers of followers. When Apollonius arrives in a town, we are told, 'not even workmen stayed at their crafts, but followed him.'[41] For Jesus, it is fishermen who leave their work. Come, follow me, says Jesus to the fishermen, and 'Immediately they left their nets and followed him.'[42]

Both Apollonius and Jesus raise the dead. Apollonius' miracle begins when he is walking in Rome and his attention is caught by that funeral procession and the girl's body being carried on a funeral bier (a form of ancient stretcher for the dead). In the gospels, Jesus' attention is drawn when, as 'he drew near to the gate of the town', he saw 'a man who had died was being carried out, the only son of his mother, and she was a widow, and a considerable crowd from the town was with her.'[43]

Apollonius tells the crowd to put her down and that he will end their tears. In the Bible, it is the mother who is approached by Jesus, but the message is similar: 'And when the Lord saw her, he had compassion on her and said to her, "Do not weep."'[44] Apollonius then approaches the body: by touching her, and whispering something inaudible, he wakes the dead girl and, we are told, she spoke and returned to her father's home. In the account in the Bible, Jesus 'came up and touched the bier.' He then spoke to the body: 'he said, "Young man, I say to you, arise." And the dead man sat up and began to speak, and Jesus gave him to his mother.'[45]

The similarities continue. Both Apollonius and Jesus end up irritating the authorities enough that they are put on trial by the Romans. In both narratives, the trials are a moment of high drama, as the potential punishment for each man is execution. And yet, Jesus and Apollonius go willingly to their trials – much to the distress of their closest followers and friends. A little before Apollonius' trial, one of his friends asks him if he will ever see him again. Apollonius assures him that he will. 'Alive?' asks the friend. Apollonius laughs. 'To my way of thinking, alive, but to yours, risen from the dead.'[46]

Both men, either in or around the time of their trials, are accused of pretending to be some form of divinity. Jesus is brought before the Jewish chief priests and the scribes, who ask, 'Are you the Son of God, then?'[47] Apollonius is asked, directly, in his trial, 'Why is it that men call you a god?' (He is also asked by his interrogator, who sounds momentarily more like an irritated 1960s father than a Roman, why he wears his hair so long.) In neither is a hard conviction given by the judge: in Jesus' trial, Pontius Pilate washes his hands of what is about to happen, saying, 'I am innocent of this man's blood.'[48] Apollonius is not found guilty for the odder reason that he simply disappears from the courtroom in a 'godlike and inexplicable' manner.[49] Jesus is executed; Apollonius vanishes.

Afterwards, both reappear to their followers, who doubt what they are seeing. In the narrative about Jesus, one of his disciples, Thomas ('Doubting Thomas', as he would become known), refuses to believe that he really is seeing his master, resurrected. Eventually, Jesus says to Thomas, 'Put your finger here, and see my hands; and put out your hand, and place it in my side. Do not disbelieve, but believe.'[50] In the case of

Apollonius, one of his followers similarly cannot believe that he is really looking at his beloved master, or that he really is alive. So Apollonius 'stretched out his hand and said: "Take hold of me, and if I evade you, then I am indeed a ghost . . . But if I resist your touch, then you shall [know] I am both alive and that I have not abandoned my body." '[51]

Quite how these similarities arose in the two stories is, to this day, unclear. Did the text of Apollonius copy that of the gospels? It is impossible to know. If the author of Apollonius' surviving biography knew about Christ, then he hides his knowledge well, as Jesus is not mentioned a single time in the text.[52] Did the gospels copy stories that were circulating about Apollonius? Again, it is impossible to say. Accurate dates for the composition of each text would bring some clarity, but the dates available are almost all frustratingly vague.

Both men were born around the same time and it is possible that they were contemporaries. But the question of who was written about first is unclear. The books in the Bible that tell the story of Jesus' life (the 'gospels') were written, it is thought, over a period between around AD 70 and AD 110 – in other words, at least a generation after Jesus' death. The only biography of Apollonius that survives today – there had been more, but they were lost, most probably in the ensuing centuries as Christian attitudes to Apollonius became increasingly aggressive – was written around AD 220. Clearly, then, the account of Apollonius was written much later: it is the obvious candidate for having copied the stories about Christ, rather than vice versa. Though it is not quite that simple. Apollonius' surviving biography was written later – but it is also clear that it relied on a much earlier, lengthy biography written by someone who claimed to be a younger contemporary of Apollonius.[53] What that work said is, of course, not known; it is impossible to tell if it resembled the biography that survives. But if the claim about an earlier work is true, then the first written account of Apollonius might date to around the same time as the first gospels. If.

But that is mere speculation. In the absence of any of those earlier works, one guess – and, given the vast losses of ancient literature, this debate, like so many, is one reduced to guesses – is that neither text precisely copied the other, but instead that both accounts arose in a world steeped in the same myths. Both texts, as one modern academic has put it, drew on 'a common stock of philosophical ideas, especially influenced by Stoicism, about what is a good and virtuous life'.[54] Moreover, time plays tricks on the modern reader. When we read Apollonius' biography today, we are chiefly struck by the similarities with the life, and particularly the trial and death, of Jesus. But, to an ancient reader, the far more obvious parallels would have been with the execution, trial and death of Socrates.

Milton imagined that the nymphs and gods of the old religion had fled at the moment of Christ's birth. But they had not. Apollonius and Christ were both born into a world in which the lame walked and the blind could see; in which mortals ascended to heaven and gods walked among men. The first century 'in the year of our Lord', as it came to be called, was in truth a century that was full of many lords, and saviours, and gods – both the one who became 'our Lord', in the West, and the many, many more who did not.

Chapter Two

TO HEAL THE BLIND AND CURE THE LAME

'This cock-and-bull story'

The Greek writer Celsus considers the Resurrection,
2nd century AD

You did not want to get sick in the Roman Empire. History remembers classical medicine as astonishingly advanced and, in many ways, it was. There were gynaecologists so skilled that they knew how to turn a baby in the womb to allow it to be born safely; doctors so skilled they could perform operations on still-beating hearts; and surgeons so dexterous they could even perform plastic surgery: one ancient text advises its readers on how to carry out a breast-reduction operation on a man – an operation considered necessary since, the text dolefully observed, such breasts 'bring the reproach of femininity'.[1]

We should not be misled. There was, it is true, a brilliance in the world of Greek and Roman medicine; but there was also ignorance, suffering and a vast catalogue of incurable, painful and often embarrassing conditions. Life expectancy at birth in antiquity was around twenty-five years.[2] Of those who made it past the first year of life, most would probably survive into their thirties and forties, but only 5 per cent made it to sixty.[3] Even for those who survived, life was often hard, since most diseases had no cure save for that provided by the body itself, or the grave. Those few Romans who were able to find and afford a physician may well have subsequently regretted it, since many ancient 'cures' were arguably more alarming than the ailment. 'The most efficacious remedies for diseases of the rectum are wool-grease,' wrote Pliny the Elder with confidence, before adding that this should be mixed with 'a dog's head, reduced to ashes; or a serpent's slough, with vinegar.'[4] Mingle with a touch of personal bravery, and then apply.

Childbirth was appallingly dangerous, for both mother and child. Alongside passages of supreme sophistication, an ancient gynaecological handbook offers advice on how to deploy a tool known as 'the embryo-slaughterer' during difficult births, for ancient doctors knew as well as modern ones that babies must be delivered, even if they could not be delivered alive. One memorable passage describes how best to pierce and then crush the skull of an unborn child while it is still in the womb, to allow it to be more easily extracted. For particularly stubborn births, this particular guide advises using hooks. As its calm, clinical prose explains, the labouring woman should be tied down to the bed and the hooks lubricated with olive oil, then inserted into the womb and attached anywhere on the baby that they might gain purchase – eye sockets, say, or the roof of the child's mouth, or its collarbones. And then the doctor should pull – hard.[5]

Small wonder, then, that when doctors' advice proved too expensive or too elusive – or too appalling – people turned elsewhere for help. For, when doctors failed, the gods might step in. Ancient holy men could not merely raise the dead, they were able to perform any number of lesser miracles, too. Jesus, or so his followers liked to say, was able to heal the sick, cure the lame and make the blind see. But, as Celsus and others pointed out, such claims were commonplace. Walk into any town in the east of the empire and there you could find any number of men who 'profess to do wonderful miracles' and 'who, for a few obols, make known their sacred lore in the middle of the marketplace and drive daemons out of men and blow away diseases' and even bring things back to life – or at least they made it look as though they had.[6]

It is hard to remember today, now that religion and healthcare have been split asunder by science into almost entirely separate realms, that in the ancient world they were intimately intertwined. Read the ancient poets, and they will tell you that Mount Olympus resounded with the noise of divine squabbles and heavenly seductions. Archaeology tells a very different story. Look at the prayers, petitions and offerings left in temple after temple and it seems far more likely that the cloudy reaches of

Olympus echoed instead with the pleas of the sick; with the sound of people begging the gods to smooth their leprous skin, heal their gouty knees, safely deliver their babies and, in one particularly anguished case, to heal a mysteriously injured 'member' whose owner was too embarrassed to go to a doctor. Dig through the remains of many ancient temples and you will find thousands of tiny models of body parts – of legs and wombs and breasts and feet and eyes – formed out of stone and clay: offerings left in the hope that the temple's divine inhabitants might see the troubles of this mortal clay and mend them.* A great deal of all ancient religion was little more than healthcare with a halo.

Modern readers often fail to notice this. European literature might have begun with a plague in the opening lines of the *Iliad*, but on the whole the spots and pimples, seizures and sicknesses of ordinary men and women did not trouble the pens of ancient historians.[7] Or indeed of modern ones: historians tend to prefer grander topics than a painful attack of piles or a troublesome bout of diarrhoea. But they were there, these illnesses, and they mattered. In truth, though historians disdain them, they also mattered to the grand sweep of history, too. Sickness could – and frequently did – lay low an army as effectively as the slings and arrows of the enemy. Indeed, the army need not even be that sick. Read letters from soldiers posted in the north of England in the first century AD and it becomes clear that a large proportion of them had been laid up in the sick bay by a condition they called 'blear-eye', a disease that caused the eyelids to become inflamed. Not something that features in the more martial narratives of Caesar or Tacitus.

The ancient fascination with medicine can be seen clearly in other genres that have managed to last the centuries. We have

* To this day, if you go to some Greek Orthodox churches, you will find shops outside selling images of body parts – arms, legs, eyes – on beaten metal for the faithful to buy and bring as offerings.

precious few texts from the Roman Empire: it is estimated that less than 1 per cent of all Latin literature survives today.[8] Those works that do remain hint at what captured the interest of the copiers – and medical texts loom large. It has been estimated that fully 10 per cent of the Greek literature that survives from before AD 350 are medical texts by the surgeon Galen.[9]

But the ancient heavens heard what the historians failed to, and many of the deities who thrived most successfully in this era were those connected with healing. Today, people tend chiefly to remember the healings of Jesus – and not without reason. These miracles played so prominent a part in the early Christian message that one historian of early Christianity, Adolf von Harnack, bluntly wrote that 'Christianity is a medical religion.'[10] But Christianity wasn't the only medical religion. This was a world that could glitter with miracles and be moved by the hand of heaven. One Greek text – from the third century BC – praises a divine 'gentle healer' for the 'diseases that thou didst wipe away, Lord, by laying on us thy gentle hands.'[11] One single ancient stone – inscribed in the fourth century BC – gives grateful thanks to a god from a group of supplicants who have variously had 'the sight of both eyes restored', had their lameness healed and been cured of paralysis.[12] Long before Jesus arrived on earth, there were many who took up their beds, and walked.*

Accounts in which the blind were healed and the lame walked were perennially popular – perhaps, a cynic might say, because they were easiest to fake. (Accounts in which amputated limbs regrew are rather harder to find in the historical record.) Some of these stories became particularly celebrated. In the first century AD, in the East, a prophecy started to circulate that said men would come from Judaea who would rule over the entire world.[13] Many came to believe that the prophecy had referred to

* Religious economists, incidentally, argue that this is precisely what one would expect to happen. As Rodney Stark puts it in *The Rise of Christianity*, in religion, 'successful new firms will simply be variants on the standard religious culture'.

the emperor Vespasian – not, it must be said, without reason, since he did.[14] Certainly he seems to have been touched by heavenly powers. One day, after he had visited a temple, two sick men approached him. One of the men was blind, the other lame, and they implored him to heal them.

Vespasian was reluctant; he was both sceptical that such a stunt would work and had a lot to lose and little to gain from attempting it. As the historian Suetonius records, 'he could scarcely believe that the thing would any how succeed, and therefore hesitated to venture on making the experiment.'[15] Vespasian was eventually jollied, or perhaps bullied, into it by the encouragement of his friends and, in public and before a large crowd, did as the men asked, touching the eyes of the blind man with his spittle, and touching the lame man's heel. His attempt 'was crowned with success in both cases'.[16] The blind man saw and the lame man walked. For an ancient event, this story is exceptionally well attested. It appears in Tacitus, Suetonius and Dio Cassius – and was clearly widespread in late AD 69 or early AD 70, when it (allegedly) happened.

It is notably similar to other stories told at the time – perhaps most famously in the story that Christians told of Jesus, which was probably written down at about the same time. In this, Jesus is approached by 'some people [who] brought to him a blind man and begged him to touch him.' Jesus, more willing than Vespasian to attempt such a thing, immediately helped: he took the blind man and 'spit on his eyes and laid his hands on him'. Initially, the blind man saw nothing, then 'he looked up and said, "I see people, but they look like trees, walking."' Then Jesus 'laid his hands on his eyes again; and he opened his eyes, his sight was restored, and he saw everything clearly.'[17] It has been suggested that the story of Jesus was tweaked to compete with that of Vespasian.

Christians were initially happy to admit similarities between their own healer and the healers of other religions. 'When we say that He made well the lame and the paralytic,' Justin Martyr wrote, 'and that he resurrected the dead, we seem to be mentioning deeds similar to and even identical with those which were said to have been performed by [the Greek god] Asclepius.'[18] Asclepius wasn't the only wonder-worker with whom Christian healers were compared – or perhaps confused. When St Paul and a companion arrived in a town and healed a lame man there, the crowd knew precisely what had happened. 'The gods have come down to us in the likeness of men!' they cried. St Paul and his companion were assumed to be, respectively, Hermes and Zeus in human form; so much so that the local priest of Zeus promptly brought wreaths to the city gates 'to offer sacrifice with the crowds.'[19]

It is Jesus' healing miracles that are remembered today; but in the ancient world his fame was far eclipsed by that of Asclepius. And, as ancient critics of Christianity didn't hesitate to point out, the similarities between the two men didn't stop merely at their miracles. Asclepius was also not merely a son of a god, but was said to be a god on earth: some believed he was none other than Apollo, made flesh in human form. The similarities went on: Asclepius, like Jesus, suffered a violent death, and was also deified and ascended into heaven. Devoted followers of Asclepius would describe him as being dressed in 'white raiment and with flowing hair' and as sitting, as one second-century-AD follower put it, 'enthroned in the sky'. He too was able to perform all the usual miracles: to make the mute speak and the blind see; to make withered hands work again; to smooth the skin of the leprous, raise the dead and heal the lame. Indeed, in one account, Asclepius, with Apollo's help, healed a lame man so successfully that, when a small boy stole his crutch, the man instantly got up and 'pursued him'.[20] He was so loved for his healings that his followers took to calling him 'Lord' and 'Saviour' and even 'Saviour of the human race'.[21]

Though Asclepius and Jesus were far from indistinguishable. While Asclepius did heal through mystical means and appear in shining raiment, he could also be pragmatic. In other inscriptions,

Asclepius often sounds less like a shimmering deity and more like a hearty games mistress, as he is recorded advising supplicants to go riding, take cold baths and walk barefoot for the good of their health. Nor did Asclepius disdain the lesser ailments in the medical dictionary. One woman who called upon the services of this god recorded that she was well satisfied that the divine saviour had assisted in ridding her of a tapeworm.[22] Another man declared himself to be Asclepius' servant when the saviour rid him of an abscess; another celebrated being cured of lice.[23] Descriptions of Asclepius' healings, even the effective ones, were not always related in an entirely ethereal manner. Take, for example, the account of the worshipper who dreamed that, as candles were brought into the temple of the god, he suddenly found 'that it was necessary for me to vomit'. And thus, as he records, 'I vomited.'[24] Not a reading to inspire unmixed religious awe.

And there were many healers, including Asclepius, who raised the dead. By the turn of the first millennium, when Jesus was born, the history of miraculous resurrections was, like so much else, a long one. Consider the story, recorded by Herodotus, of the fifth-century-BC god – or, depending on your viewpoint, utter charlatan – Salmoxis. This man had turned up among the Thracians ('a poor and backward people', sniffs Herodotus) and managed to convince them that he was a god. He had done this through a tortuously complicated project: he had first wooed local notables, wining them, dining them and teaching them 'that neither he nor they would ever die, but would go to a place where they would live in perpetual enjoyment of every blessing.'[25] This clearly was a touch implausible for even the dim-witted Thracians to believe, so Salmoxis had prepared a trick to 'prove' his claim. One day, he simply vanished and went into hiding, thus plunging his Thracian friends into mourning. Then, after a few years, he popped back up – apparently from the dead – and so 'in this way persuaded the Thracians that the doctrine he had taught was true.'[26] To this day, an underwhelmed Herodotus observes, these people believe they will never die, but that they will go to join Salmoxis.

By the first century AD, to be revived from death was such a common phenomenon that it even merited a section in one of the earliest encyclopaedias. Pliny the Elder's vast, thirty-seven-book *Natural History* had the ambitious aim of describing no less than 'the natural world, or life'. It managed to cover a great deal of it too: this energetic work details everything from metallurgy to art history to monkeys (they are possessed of 'wonderful shrewdness') and griffins (dubious, Pliny thinks), and even offers a rather bracing brand of anthropology (among the Arabs, Pliny writes, 'the one-half live by Robbery, and the other by Merchandise').[27] Many of Pliny's readers, incidentally, had rather narrower interests and, in the centuries that followed, superfluous chapters were shaved off to make separate and far more popular medical abridgements, such as the 'Physic of Pliny', which circulated widely in the Middle Ages.[28]

This early encyclopaedia also covered death – or apparent death. For, in chapter 53, the reader is offered the heading: 'Persons Who Have Come to Life Again After Being Laid Out For Burial'.[29] Here, Pliny offers a host of such stories, and speculates on possible explanations for how it had happened. The selection includes one story about a great doctor named Asclepiades, who had lived from the middle of the second to the middle of the first century BC.

This tale – which would be widely retold, for years – is an intriguing one. One day (as a later telling explained) Asclepiades had been walking back home from his country house when he saw a funeral procession making its way through the suburbs of the city. A huge mass of people in their funeral clothes had come out to pay their last respects to some dead person. The doctor went closer, curious either to see who was dead or perhaps in the hope of making 'some discovery in the interests of his profession.'[30] The corpse was obviously ready for the pyre: 'it was already sprinkled with perfumes, his face already daubed with fragrant ointment, his body already washed, already all but prepared for the flames'.[31]

And yet, as Asclepiades looked at it, he started 'carefully observing certain signs [and] he ran his hands several times over the man's body and found hidden life in it.'[32] Whereupon the doctor cried out, 'The man is alive, so throw away the torches, scatter the fire, dismantle the pyre, move the funeral banquet from the grave to the table.'[33] The doctor, 'having thus wrested him from the hands of the undertakers, brought him home like one restored from the underworld, and immediately used certain medicines to revive the life hiding in the recesses of the body.'[34] According to Pliny, the story made the doctor's name.[35] And perhaps it also fuelled a narrative trend.

This was a world that flickered with the supernatural: when one early Christian wanted to argue that Christ had indeed risen from the tomb, he turned to the phoenix to support his claim. Cannot the phoenix, which 'builds itself a nest of frankincense, and myrrh, and other spices', rise again from the dead? Can it not be resurrected? Well, then, this Christian argued: so too can Christians.[36] The Christian writer Origen made a similar argument. 'The unbelievers mock at the resurrection of Jesus Christ,' he wrote, but such stories were common. 'Several people are recorded to have returned even from their tombs, not only on the same day, but even on the day after. Why then is it amazing if [Jesus] who performed many miracles of a super-human nature . . . also had something extraordinary about his death so that, if he so wished, his soul might leave his body and, after performing certain services without it, might return to it again when it wished?'[37]

Not everyone was convinced. Celsus scathingly attacked the Christian resurrection and suggested that his followers who allegedly witnessed it were either 'deluded by . . . sorcery'; or had dreamed it all; or 'through wishful thinking had a hallucination due to some mistaken notion.' An experience, Celsus observed wearily, which 'has happened to thousands.' Though Celsus had another suggestion for how the story had arisen: the Christians had just made it up. It is, he wrote, 'more likely [that they] wanted to impress the others by telling this fantastic tale', and so invented the whole 'cock-and-bull story'.[38]

Such tales hint not only at the ancient hunger for healers, but also at the depth of everyone's ignorance on medical matters. It is salutary to remember that, for all the brilliance of Greek and Roman medicine, doctors nonetheless struggled to identify the difference between the seemingly obvious conditions of 'being dead' and 'being alive'. As medical texts warned, confusion on this point was easy, since diseases might present in such different ways. As the medical writer Celsus argued, with a dash of defensiveness, 'Nor, in the face of such a variety of temperaments, can human frailty avoid this.'[39]

In Egypt, tales were told of healers so skilled that they could not merely resurrect corpses, but even revive decapitated ones. In *The Golden Ass*, an eccentric novel by the North African writer Apuleius, the protagonist watches while yet another man is brought back to life by a local prophet.* The scene is, by now, a familiar one. Once again, an aristocratic corpse is being carried through the streets; once again, a large crowd has gathered. Once again, a prophet is in town – this time, a man named Zatchlas, from Egypt, who is 'a prophet of the first rank.' As one character explains, Zatchlas has agreed that, for 'a large fee', he will 'bring back the soul of the deceased from the Underworld for a short while and restore his body to life.'[40]

And so Zatchlas began his work, and 'laid some sort of herb on the corpse's mouth and another on his breast. Then turning eastwards he silently invoked the majesty of the rising sun,' which, as the narrator wryly observed, 'among the witnesses of this impressive performance excited expectations of a

* While the modern novel is widely considered to have begun with *Don Quixote*, there are several classical works that are considered (by classicists, at any rate) to be novels.

great miracle.'[41] And, sure enough, they got one. Immediately, 'The corpse's chest began to fill, its pulse to beat, its breath to come; it sat up and the young man spoke.' Though, in this particular case, the scene is rather less moving, as the dead man is annoyed that he has been raised from his slumber. 'Why, why,' grumbles the irritable former corpse, 'have you called me back for these few moments to life and its obligations'?[42]

This wealth of resurrection stories would be used as a weapon against Christianity when it started to claim that its saviour was in any way unique. Unique? Hardly, said Celsus. There were so many other almost identical stories of people who had come back to life or been to the underworld and back – not just Salmoxis, but Pythagoras, Orpheus, Heracles, Theseus . . . The list went on. 'How many others', Celsus asked with typical disdain, 'produce wonders like this to convince simple hearers whom they exploit by deceit?'[43] It was such a common trope that in the first century AD there was even a play that involved the resurrection of a character who, having apparently been killed by poison, then 'began to stir slightly, as though recovering from a profound sleep, and lifted its head and looked about.' Everyone in the theatre witnessing this resurrection – and the audience included the elderly Emperor Vespasian – was delighted and 'much moved'.[44] Their enthusiasm was by no means diminished by the fact that this particular resurrected character happened to be a dog.

Critics of Christianity didn't just attack the fact that such stories were commonplace; they also pointed out that they were ridiculous. Christians promised literal, bodily resurrection after death to their followers. Oh, really? asked the Greek critic Porphyry. How precisely is that going to work? Because, after people died, their bodies rotted away – and worse. Many people, argued Porphyry, 'have perished in the sea and their bodies have been consumed by fish, and many have been eaten by wild birds and animals.' Given that their bodies were now dispersed over such a wide area, and in so many animals, 'How then is it possible that those bodies should return?'[45]

Porphyry didn't stop there. Imagine, he went on, 'a man was ship wrecked, [then] mullets devoured his body. Next these were caught, and after they were eaten, those who ate them were killed and eaten by dogs. When the dogs died they were eaten by ravens and vultures who devoured them entirely. How could the bodies of the ship wrecked men, spent by these creatures, be brought together?' Porphyry, warming to his theme, goes on. Imagine that another man 'was consumed by fire, and another comes to an end in worms. How is it possible for [such a body] to return to its former substance?'[46] Childish questions, said injured Christians. God could arrange such things.

It has been suggested that the plethora of resurrection stories seen in this period may have been encouraged by the frequency of tomb thefts. Place a body in the tomb at this time and it was far from certain that it would stay there undisturbed. Numerous laws were promulgated in the Roman Empire against 'Those persons who violate [the homes] of the dead.'[47] It was not only the contents of tombs that were stolen – the treasures and gold – but the very fabric of the tombs themselves: the high-quality stone used in tombs made fine building material. Such laws appear to have been ineffectual, since one single ancient city offers fifty-one inscriptions warning against tomb-breaking, dating from between the first and the fourth century.[48] Bodies, from whatever religion, could not be certain that they would rest in peace.

A whiff of anxiety that this – a mere tomb robbery – is how Jesus' resurrection will be seen can be sensed in the Gospel of Matthew. This gospel makes much of the fact that not merely a stone is put in front of Jesus' tomb, but also a guard, 'lest his disciples go and steal him away', mutter the Pharisees, 'and tell the people, "He has risen from the dead",' as a 'fraud'.[49] Pilate, showing a surprising liberality with the soldiers of the Roman military, agrees to send some men to guard the tomb of the man he has just crucified. The echo of an ancient slur – that Jesus' body had merely been stolen – is detectable in those lines. In the Gospel of John, the first assumption of Mary Magdalene is that Jesus' body has been stolen.[50]

Trickery in and around tombs was so common that, by the first century AD, such antics had caught the eye of an ancient novelist. The oldest surviving novel in the West is an enjoyably ridiculous yarn called *Callirhoe*. In it, the hero believes his beloved to have died.* He arrives at her tomb in the early morning – only to find it empty and her body gone: 'When he arrived, he discovered that the stones had been moved and that the entrance was wide open. He was astonished at the sight and seized by a fearful bewilderment at what had happened.'[51] It is, as some have pointed out, similar to one of the accounts in the gospels in which Jesus' followers arrive at his tomb and, 'looking up, they saw that the stone had been rolled back – it was very large.' When they go into the tomb, the body has gone 'and they were alarmed.'[52] It has been tentatively suggested that the novel, which was written a few years before the assumed date of that particular gospel, might have had some influence on it.[53]

But, in this world, who wouldn't, at times, turn to the divine for a little help? Even rational men could, by grief or fear, be pushed from rationality into faith. The fact that medicine was so poor, and young death so common, made illness and loss no easier to bear. When the Roman statesman Cicero lost his daughter Tullia – she died shortly after giving birth – he was all but undone. The great orator had no words; the great speaker lost his voice. Instead, as he wrote in letters of pitiable grief, he now swam in silence: 'Early in the day I hide myself in a thick,

---

* He believes, incidentally, that she has died because he (or so he thinks) had kicked her to death a little earlier in a fit of rage (by good luck, she survived). Happily for him, his assault doesn't seem to dampen the passion of either of them and, by the end of the novel, they are reunited to live happily ever after.

thorny wood, and don't emerge till evening.' His only converse was now with books, though even that was 'interrupted by fits of weeping.' He promised that he would, eventually, struggle against those tears, but 'so far it is an unequal fight.'[54]

There are, wrote the Roman poet Virgil, in one of his most famous lines, 'tears of things': *lacrimae rerum*. It is a strange phrase: vague and awkward, but also – it was true. And who, however logical, when the mortal tears fell, would not feel tempted to turn to something else, something higher than themselves, to help with the pain? In those terrible dark days of walking and of weeping, Cicero considered setting up a shrine to Tullia – and he was quite explicit that it was to be a shrine, as if to a god. 'I want it to be a shrine,' he wrote; 'I am anxious to avoid its being taken for a tomb.' He wanted 'to get as near to deification as possible.'[55] There were tears of things. There was disease and death and uncertainty. But there was also, in the heavens, hope.

Chapter Three

THE FALSEHOODS OF THE MAGICIANS

'There is no one who doesn't fear being bound by curses.'

Pliny the Elder, *Natural History*, 28.4, 1st century AD

The Rome of the imagination is dazzling. In films and paintings and books, it is a place of glittering marble, a city of striking sophistication and beauty, a place of men with brilliant white togas and brilliant minds. To the modern eye, the grandeur that was Rome lies not merely in its buildings – in its straight roads and aqueducts and amphitheatres and efficient toilets – but also in its straight thinking. This is a city of eager erudition, a city whose richest men might acquire a library of well over a thousand scrolls. It is a city so voraciously intellectual that a man might, as Pliny the Elder did, instruct his assistant to walk around after him, reading out loud to him constantly from the scrolls that he carried in his hands (his gloved hands in winter): reading to him as he ate, as he lay in the sun, as he was rubbed down after his bath – reading, reading, reading, text after text, lest learning be lost for even a moment.[1] It is a city of architectural advances too, in which vast tumbledown areas are cleared to make way for projects of elegance and light, for gardens like the famous ones of Maecenas, with its elegant promenades and handsome landscaping, and – it is thought – the first heated swimming pool in Rome.

All that is true. But it is also not true. Rome was a city of light and brilliant intellectual advances, but it was also a city of darkness. Despite its daytime beauty, Rome could not overcome the night. Arguably, it never even tried to. There were no streetlights in this city and, after dusk fell, the towering blocks of flats – Augustus had limited their height to seventy feet, but laws were made to be broken – resulted in streets so dark that even an emperor could walk along them unnoticed, brawl in them unrecognized.[2] The rich man in his scarlet cloak could swirl through the streets with a long line of attendants carrying flickering brass lamps and torches – but even the wealthy weren't safe. Death at the hands of bandits was a common enough end that it had its own inscriptional shorthand on tombstones.[3] And while the rich had torches and attendants, the poor had to hurry on alone, their way lit only with a single guttering lamp, through streets stinking of piss and studded with shit, through the dripping arches of the aqueducts, through the dark. Through the fear.[4]

Because the Romans were afraid, very afraid, of the dark.[5] They were afraid of thieves and robbers and brigands, of cold iron and hard clubs. And above all they were afraid of ghosts. Look carefully and the fear can be seen, clearly, in their writings. Among the upright architectural treatises and the stirring tales of military victories in foreign lands, there are other works that speak not of conquered peoples but of unconquered terrors: of the terror of the dark, and of the ghosts of the night; the terror of pale shades that flit and of the shadowed tomb.[6] In the graveyards, wild figs grew, splitting open tombs with their roots.[7] In the shadows, cries were heard. Beneath those straight minds lay crooked fears, and beneath the white marble statues of the gardens of Maecenas lay white bones. For those famous gardens – a powerful symbol of growing Roman sophistication – had been built on a necropolis, on the mass graves of criminals and paupers. The corpses, so one poet hinted, had not quite been covered over.[8] And at night, into these places, the magic came.

For there was magic in Rome, in those days. Modern minds might not take such things seriously, but for the ancients magic was serious – deadly so. Roman poets immortalized it, Roman laws banned it, Roman mothers warned their children against it. Witches – or so the poet Horace said – crept into those gardens of Maecenas at night, with their pale faces and their unkempt hair and black robes, and their strange rites.[9] Some of these hags performed rites among the dead – pouring blood sacrifices to summon spirits, or to turn the path of the moon, or to control the fates. But many did even more horrifying work among the living. In another poem, Horace wrote of the most feared witches of all: the child-snatchers. These women had vipers for hair, it was said, and stones for hearts, and they would abduct a small boy and then they would kill him, even as his soft mouth begged for mercy.[10]

All ridiculous, of course – just Horace being silly. Or so Romans might tell themselves by day. But when darkness came – when the sun set, when shadows fell, when a child was lost – it was hard to see clearly what was ridiculous and what was not. 'A magical hand snatched me,' reads the epitaph on one ancient tombstone, erected for a four-year-old boy. Not just any boy, either, but a slave boy from the house of the Caesars themselves – and evidently a beloved one, as it would not have been cheap to commemorate him so. But, as his epitaph makes clear, love wasn't enough to save him from dark magic. There is 'cruelty everywhere', the stone warns. 'You parents,' its ominous inscription reads, 'Guard well your children / lest grief be fixed in your whole heart.'[11]

Many might laugh at all this – but even those who thought witches were nonsense knew that knives were real enough. You didn't need to believe in magic to believe in magical rites. And these rites, as educated Romans knew, could be appalling. Stillborn infants, records Pliny the Elder, were 'cut up limb by limb for the most abominable practices.'[12] The idea of this frightened people enough that, eventually, the law stepped in. 'If any man or woman shall undertake the crime of killing an infant,' ruled one later law, thought to have been formulated against magical practices, 'let all know that the guilty party shall be punished with death.'[13] The Christians weren't the only ones who believed that drinking human blood might have magical powers.

There were other fears, other spells – so many spells. And so many who claimed to be able to perform them. For, alongside its more familiar professions – its straight-backed centurions and its serpent-tongued orators; its engineers and its architects and its lawyers – Rome also had a large number of people who made their living through more disreputable means: through magic. They are less celebrated these days, but they were there, a rich seam of specialists who, for a price, would perform any magical service you required. Horace wrote about the witches and the hags, but it certainly wasn't just them. There were also the fortune-tellers and the exorcists, the diviners and the augurs and the haruspices, the astrologers and the enchanters and the poisoners and – or so the cynics would say – the priests. And, most famous of all, there were the magicians – or, to give them their Latin name: the magi.

The magi themselves would doubtless have baulked at being bracketed together with the hags and the chancers. In Persia, such men were a proper priestly caste: there, Herodotus wrote, the magi interpreted the dreams of kings and even had the power to offer human sacrifices. In Persia, the magi were men of status, practising something closer to what a modern eye would call religion rather than magic; though, such nice distinctions – insofar as they existed at all in the ancient world – were largely lost in translation. So, in the Rome of the first century AD, the word *magi* came to be widely used to mean little more than 'magicians', 'diviners' – or, at best, 'astronomers'– and to refer to any wonder-worker who came from the East. Perhaps they came from Persia, but ancient geography was vague and so you might also qualify as a magician if you came from Egypt or even from India – from any of those lands of spice and of strangeness and – at least in Roman minds – of powers beyond imagining.[14]

Precisely what magic Roman magicians had practised was, for a long time, not very clear to modern scholars. Rome officially disapproved of magic, and had done for centuries. Stand before the Twelve Tables, Rome's most ancient and august legal code – already almost half a millennium old when Christ was born – and there, in beaten bronze, among the sober statutes about land disputes and inheritance procedures and the right height to which one should prune fruit trees, it was possible to see other laws, far stranger laws: laws that ruled against anyone who 'enchants by singing an evil incantation' or against any miscreant who 'enchants away crops'.[15] It was almost more alarming that Rome outlawed magic than it would have been if it had ignored it: official disapproval denoted official anxiety. 'There is no one', wrote Pliny the Elder, 'who doesn't fear being bound by evil curses.'[16]

Most educated Greeks and Romans treated magicians with frank disdain. Pliny's writing drips with disapproval as he recounts 'the infamous lies that have been promulgated by the magicians'.[17] It wasn't just the Twelve Tables that issued penalties: the emperor Augustus himself had thousands of prophetic texts burned, and the punishments meted out to magicians could be horrifyingly vicious.[18] One Roman legal expert later noted that people who perform 'impious or nocturnal sacrifices, to enchant, curse, or bind anyone with a spell, are either crucified or thrown to beasts.'[19] Magicians themselves 'should be burned alive.'[20]

Once the Roman Empire embraced Christianity in the fourth century, laws against magic hardened even further. The Bible itself offered good precedent for rooting out magic: when St Paul visited Ephesus, he caused its inhabitants to be so seized with fear by his miracles that 'a number of those who had practiced magic arts brought their books together and burned them in the sight of all. And they counted the value of them and found it came to fifty thousand pieces of silver.'[21] No doubt the number is a vast exaggeration, but the point is clear: Christianity was happy to be associated with the extravagant burnings of incorrect books.

In later centuries, as Christianity consolidated then extended its power, magical texts were cracked down on further. House-to-house searches were conducted by fervent Christian brethren, who served their God by seeking out and burning unacceptable texts.[22] Many magical books were burned at such times – though the men lighting the bonfires were not careful bibliophiles, and volumes of philosophy and the liberal arts ended up in the flames too.[23] At particularly dangerous moments, intellectuals – terrified of the mere taint of magic – burned their own libraries themselves, lest the accusation of magic might attach itself to them.

The result of all this is that, today, evidence for ancient magic is scant. There was never a total absence of writings about magicians – text after text can be found disparaging magical practices, or despising them, or outlawing them. But there were no libraries by magicians themselves, no great compendiums of ancient lore. Most magical books that existed in ancient times had, as the translator and academic Hans Dieter Betz put it, 'disappeared as the result of systematic suppression and destruction.'[24] An entire genre of classical writing had been lost. Or so, for centuries, it seemed.

And then, in the first half of the nineteenth century, some unusual papyri started to turn up in the antiquities markets of Europe.

Chapter Four

SERPENT'S BLOOD AND EYE OF APE

'Take an eye of an ape or of a corpse that has died a violent death and a plant of peony.'

Tested spell for invisibility,
Greek Magical Papyri, I.247–50

The manuscripts were remarkable. Crumbling at the corners, ravaged by time, filled with odd drawings, these texts were like little that had been seen before. They were authorless and almost impossible to categorize. They were clearly ancient – they would later be dated to between the second century BC and the fifth century AD – but they were not like any ancient texts that were then known.[1] They were not history or philosophy, nor comedy or tragedy, nor poetry, nor medicine, nor indeed anything that classicists felt comfortable with.

On their frayed pages, words had been written into odd shapes and into patterns: into the forms of triangles, and inverted triangles, and circles; some had been written within sketches of headless humans; elsewhere, words had been written next to drawings of beetles.[2] The pages were peppered with strange shapes and symbols, and filled with words that looked like utter nonsense, eerie gibberish that went on for line after line, making no sense at all: 'IAO AOI OAI . . . OOOOOO AAAAAA . . . OAI . . .' ran one text. 'IAO AYO IOAI / PIPI OOO OO III AYO . . .' it continued.[3] The texts babbled meaninglessly, recording ancient chants that ring in your ear as you read them: 'EUPHORBA PHORBA PHORBOREOU PHORBA PHORBOR . . .'[4]

These texts were so ancient and so interesting that, when they were auctioned, the great museums and libraries of Europe – the Louvre and the British Museum, the Bibliothèque Nationale in Paris, the Staatliche Museen in Berlin – bought them swiftly. And they were so odd that, for a long time, these institutions more or less ignored them. They were categorized as mere 'curiosities', stored carefully in the collections and, for a time, forgotten about.

When scholars started to study them, tentatively at first and then with increased enthusiasm, what they found was astonishing. For, beneath the eyes of the translators, these odd texts conjured up a world that had been assumed lost: the world of the ancient magicians. Here, at last, were texts that spoke of magic, but not with scorn or satire, as Pliny had done, nor with fury, as Roman and Christian laws had done, but with reverence, belief – and a great deal of practical instruction. These works had been written for ancient magicians, and almost certainly by ancient magicians. They were, in short, spell books.

And what a world these spells created: a place in which the laws of nature could be bent and broken; in which diseases could be cured or caused at a word; in which the dead might sit up and speak. These papyri spoke of a world in which you could still the wind and solidify streams; where banquets might be summoned with a word; demons could disappear like smoke and men could become invisible at will. Theirs was a world in which you could – or so their spells promised – be carried into the air like a feather to ride on the curled clouds, or turn the waves of the sea solid so that 'you can run over them firmly'.[5]

Ancient spell manuscripts are eerily atmospheric. Some are stained with drops of wax – perhaps, it has been suggested, from the candles which were used with them in ceremonies.[6] Most of those that were found in that nineteenth-century cache probably once belonged to a single library – it has been suggested that they may have even belonged to a single, now long-forgotten, ancient 'magician'. Even today, they make for striking reading. The spells that these texts contain were described by the great classical scholar A. D. Nock as 'recipes for magical processes' – and they read like recipes, too, advising their readers, with the recipe book's usual certitude, how to take the unformed world and chop it up into measured and manageable amounts, adding a pinch of this and a dash of that, to ensure miraculous results.[7]

Take, advises one of these magical recipes, 'an eye of a night owl and a ball of dung rolled by a beetle.'[8] Take 'frankincense [and] old wine', advises another.[9] Take frankincense and myrrh, and more frankincense, says a third.[10] The ingredients go on, spell after spell, a blend of the homely and the holy, the exotic and the impossibly unattainable. Take cumin and cardamom, nightshade and bayberries; take cinnabar ink and a drowned cat; take serpent's blood and the soot of a goldsmith; take the plant of a peony and an eye of an ape.[11] Like many a modern cookery book, the ingredients lists are often unforgivingly esoteric, their exoticism adding to their mystique. Rarely do they demand only the stuff of the store-cupboard; instead, they ask for a bewildering mix of the common and the downright impossible: for storax and sage; for asphodel and opium; for myrrh, garlic and gall of gazelle. Blend it all in fragrant wine and begin . . .[12]

At times, like recipe books, the spells offer tacit acknowledgement that these ingredients might not be the easiest to source, and so – just as a modern recipe will demand za'atar, but allow thyme in extremis – they too offer alternatives. Though the substitutions are perhaps more trouble than the original. If one can't find the eye of an ape then, as one particular spell (a 'tested spell for invisibility') explains, it is also possible to use the eye of 'a corpse that has died a violent death.'[13] Another demands the 'material of a dog and a dappled goat', but adds, as a concession, that one might instead use matter 'of a virgin untimely dead'.[14] Ancient magicians must have been relieved.

Yet, what things could be achieved if the spells were done correctly. Many of them promise good health, some claiming to cure epileptic seizures, or to be for 'those possessed by daimons';*

* The English word *demon* comes from the Greek word *daimon*, but there is an imaginative gulf between the two, which is why translators often transliterate it rather than translating it. A 'daimon' could be an evil spirit – but it could also refer to more appealing ideas, such as one's own fortune or lot in life; or to the souls of great men from another era. The idea of demons as things that were reliably horned and horrible came later.

others promise to stop blood from a woman, or act as a failsafe pregnancy test, or cure swollen testicles; while another is simply 'for an erection'.[15] Some are mutedly modest in their aims, promising that they will restrain anger, or 'keep bugs out of the house', or allow you to win at dice.[16] Others are more ambitious. There are invisibility spells and spells for foreknowledge; there are spells to meet one's own daimon, guard against daimons and drive out daimons; there are spells that speak of lords and holy spirits, of angels and gods rising into heaven; and spells that allow you to meet a god and make a god obey your command and descend from heaven all in white.[17]

A strong vein of ancient religion runs throughout – but these texts do not abase themselves before the divine. Far from it. Instead, ancient deities are treated in their pages with a brusque practicality, and mixed and added and blended to this spell or that one, in much the same way as the spices are. There are spells that call upon Apollo, Artemis, Aphrodite, Zeus, Hermes, Helios and the god of the Hebrews; there are spells that blend Babylonian religion with Egyptian mysticism; or Greek religion with Jewish; there are even, as their modern translator puts it, 'a few sprinkles of Christianity.'[18] One spell promises that it will allow its practitioner to summon 'Apollonius of Tyana's old serving woman.'[19] Another (an 'excellent rite for driving out daimons') hails not only the God of Abraham, but also 'Jesus Chrestos'.[20] Another instructs its user to take the oil of unripe olives and the fruit pulp of the lotus and then to announce, 'I conjure you by the God of the Hebrews/Jesus'.[21] The most popular god is the Jewish God – for, as their translator, Betz, points out, 'Jewish magic was famous in antiquity.'[22]

These strange documents manage to be at once both other-worldly and almost painfully mundane. They speak, as so many ancient texts do, of physical misery and fear, of pain and illness, of sorrows and of death and of drowned children, of women unable to conceive, of men who have gone blind. They speak of sorrows that hope to be stayed by the hand of heaven – for they are unlikely to be stayed by anything else. In certain Christian writings, magic was demonized and it was demonic; it was outlawed and insulted. But, more truthfully, its greatest sin was that it was competition. The magician acted, for most, not as a dangerous summoner of demons, but as a miracle healer, writes Betz, as an 'all-purpose therapist and agent of worried, troubled, and troublesome souls.'[23] Magic had its dark moments, but – far more often, to judge by these spells – it was used to lighten the at times intolerable burdens of life. 'Magic', writes Betz, 'is the art that makes people who practice it feel better rather than worse, that provides the illusion of security to the insecure, the feeling of help to the helpless and the comfort of hope to the hopeless.'[24]

These books were not a total revelation. Ancient magical texts had been known before. Magical texts from other cultures, and particularly from Egypt, had been extensively studied and written about. In 1899, an Egyptologist named E. A. Wallis Budge published a book, titled *Egyptian Magic*, which dealt with magical works from Egypt. His conclusions in this work feel familiar. It is clear, Budge wrote, that the power of priests and magicians, in those days, 'was believed to be almost boundless'.[25] Such a man could do almost anything, and even command the weather itself. 'The powers of nature acknowledged his might, and wind and rain, storm and tempest, river and sea, and disease and death worked evil and ruin upon his foes.'[26] The sun in the sky and the waters on land changed at his command: 'waters forsaking their nature could be piled up in a heap, and even the sun's course in the heavens could be stayed by a word.'[27] An Egyptian magician was able, by saying the right words in the right tones, to 'heal the sick, and cast out the evil spirits which caused pain and suffering in those who were diseased, and restore the dead to life.'[28] He could even, Budge wrote, change the fate of the dead and 'transform the corruptible into an incorruptible body, wherein the soul might live to all eternity.'[29]

Budge was able to write about Egyptian magic relatively

early, and with relative ease. Egyptian magic, written in an 'oriental' language and in hieroglyphs, was reassuringly foreign: crudely speaking, odd magical practices recorded in exotic-looking scripts were more or less what the Victorian mind expected of what they considered to be irrational oriental nations. The study of ancient Greek magical texts was rather more fraught. In those newly discovered papyri were spells about casting out demons and healing the blind and turning oneself into a god, but not in any oriental language – but in Greek, the language of Pericles and of Aeschylus – and, even more uncomfortably, the language of the gospels. When a seminar was begun in the University of Heidelberg, in 1905, to teach students about the *Greek Magical Papyri*, it was therefore both a 'daring enterprise' and slightly covert. 'Magic', writes Betz, 'was so utterly despised by historians and philologists that the announcement of the seminar did not mention the word "magic" but was simply phrased as "Selected Pieces from the Greek Papyri." '[30]

Such awkwardness has ancient precedents. When Christianity had appeared in this world full of magic, and started to tell tales of its miraculous saviour, Greeks and Romans had instantly recognized precisely what they were dealing with: magic and sorcery. The works of Jesus, Celsus wrote, were on a level with 'the works of sorcerers.' And, Celsus wryly added, given 'these men do these wonders, ought we to think them sons of God?'[31] This accusation didn't just appear in Roman writings. In Jewish traditions, Jesus was remembered as many things (most of them unflattering), but a common accusation was that he was no more than a 'potent magician' possessed of great 'magical power'.[32] The fact that Jesus was supposed, as a child, to have spent some time in Egypt – a noted centre of ancient magic – only added to ancient suspicions about him. Celsus, for example, assumed that it was while Jesus was in Egypt that he 'tried his hand at certain magical powers on which the Egyptians pride themselves; he returned full of conceit because of these powers, and on account of them gave himself the title of God.'[33] In some texts of Mandaeism, another ancient religion that shares many beliefs with Christianity (it reveres Adam, and John the Baptist), Jesus was simply dismissed as 'the wizard Messiah, son of the spirit of the Lie'.[34]

Almost from the first moments of its existence, Christianity became engaged in a ferocious war about whether it was a religion – or whether it was merely magic, with pretensions. Ancient Christians fought back – though not perhaps in the way that modern minds might expect. They tended not to deny that other people in the ancient world performed miracles or exorcised demons – few Christians had any interest in denying that this was a world that thrilled to the supernatural. Instead, they merely claimed a competitive edge over these other wonder-workers: those who performed exorcisms in the name of Christ, they argued, were better than the other exorcists, who were frauds.

As the Christian author Justin bragged, Christians could be seen 'driving the possessing devils out of the men, though they could not be cured by all the other exorcists, and those who used incantations and drugs'.[35] One Christian text features a Jesus who argues, with an accountant's precision, that other magicians have been weakened by his arrival because 'I took from all of them a third of their power.'[36] In a similar vein of competitive quality-control, Augustine later argued that bad miracles were performed 'by practitioners of the art of wicked curiosity: the art which they call magic.'[37] Such wicked miracles depended on 'the fraudulent rites of demons.'[38] Christ's miracles, he argued, were better as they were 'performed through simple faith and pious trust, and not by means of incantations and charms.'[39]

This line of argument disgusted non-Christian observers with its inconsistency. 'Is it not a miserable argument to infer from the same works that [Jesus] is a god while they are sorcerers?' scoffed Celsus. 'Why should we conclude from these works that the others were any more wicked than [their] fellow?'[40]

Other classical authors chipped in to agree. Christians, they argued, were 'benighted fools', guilty of 'superficiality and gullibility' since they were 'led by a few illusions to declare Jesus a god'.[41]

Modern scholars have tended to be far more wary about comparing Jesus to magicians than the ancient world was. Or rather, for a time they were. Then, in the late seventies, the provocative and prodigiously talented scholar Morton Smith, then a professor of ancient history at Columbia University, wrote a book titled *Jesus the Magician*. In it, Smith made a simple argument: in the modern world, Jesus is remembered as the son of God, but that was not a widely held view in antiquity. Only Jesus' followers saw him that way; to the majority of other ancient observers, he was a magician – or, more precisely, to many, he was a charlatan.

As Smith put it: ' "Jesus the magician" was the figure seen by most ancient opponents of Jesus, while "Jesus the son of God" was the figure seen by that party of his followers which eventually triumphed.'[42] Smith argued that it was merely a quirk of fate and of history that had led to the latter view becoming dominant and the former being forgotten. The 'triumph of Christianity' was so total, so profound, so long-lasting, that the original and more widespread view of Jesus – that he was a magician and a charlatan – had not merely been forgotten, but, for centuries, actively suppressed. Ancient fragments in which Jesus is derided as a magician still do survive. But, as Smith observed in a typically arch aside, 'by some amazing oversight, New Testament scholarship says almost nothing about them.'[43] Instead, Smith wrote, 'modern scholars, trying to discover the historical Jesus behind the gospel legends, have generally paid no attention to the evidence for Jesus the magician and have taken only the gospels as their sources.'[44]

Smith argued that, given their natural prejudices, this was understandable – but it was poor history. A historical picture of Jesus based solely on uncritical texts written by his followers and ignoring those by his opponents has, Smith wrote, 'about as much historical value as a portrait of Charles de Gaulle or Mao Tse Tung drawn exclusively from Gaullist or Maoist publications. We must try to hear the other side too.'[45] And so, that is precisely what Smith did, laying out those texts that had called Jesus a magician – and comparing his miracles to those that the magicians had performed.

Christians said that Jesus was the son of God, and indeed a god himself? Well, just look at the magical papyri, argued Smith. Such claims were clearly absolutely standard practice in that period among magicians. 'I am thee and thou art I,' runs the incantation in one ancient magic spell, addressed to a god. 'Thy name is mine, my name is thine, for I am thy image.'[46] Jesus created magical meals almost from thin air? Well, making food appear from nothing was a staple of ancient magic – moreover, there were spells in the *Greek Magical Papyri* that offered a far larger menu than Jesus managed. One ancient spell promises that it will, via a magical assistant, not only provide fish and bread and wine, but also whatever 'you wish in the way of foods: olive oil, vinegar . . . and he will bring plenty of vegetables, whatever kind you wish.'[47] Not merely loaves and fishes, but side orders too.

Jesus walked on water? According to the papyri, this was a standard trick. A magical assistant can, one spell claims, 'quickly freeze rivers and seas', making it possible to run across the surface.[48] How about turning the water into wine, as Jesus did? This magical assistant can do that too – though, once again, he can go one better and not merely offer table wine but the vintage stuff, summoning 'costly wine, as is meet to cap a dinner splendidly.'[49] That such things were common is corroborated not merely by these texts, and by Celsus' scoffing at magical meals, but also by Lucian, who wrote a story in the second century about a magician who was believed to be able to 'soar through the air in broad daylight and walk on the water and go through fire slowly on foot'. Lucian's narrator went on to add a whole list of miraculous wonders that this supposed mystic performed: he was able to make people fall in love, he explained, and even call 'mouldy corpses to life'.[50] The usual things.

Curing people of demonic possession was another magical favourite. The gospels offer several accounts of Jesus driving out demons. In one of the most famous, Jesus comes across a man who lives in a graveyard and spends his days 'crying out and cutting himself with stones'. Jesus first commands the demon to 'Come out of the man, you unclean spirit!' before asking, 'What is your name?' The demon replies with the supremely eerie line: 'My name is Legion, for we are many.' After a little to-and-fro discussion between Jesus and the man, the demons are sent into a great herd of pigs, 'and the herd, numbering about two thousand, rushed down the steep bank into the sea and drowned'.[51]

Such spectacles were, however, hardly unique. Both the texts of the magical papyri (which are rich in spells that claim to be able to send daimons hither and thither) and the writings of ancient satirists support the idea that 'healing' through exorcism was a common trick in these years. The ever-cynical Lucian (whose writing, unsurprisingly, would later be put on the Catholic Church's Index of Prohibited Books) provides a typically sceptical account of one such 'healing'.

In his story, a magician stands over the prone and demon-possessed body of a patient, then asks him – or, more precisely, asks the demon possessing him – 'Whence came you into his body?' The patient, Lucian writes, 'is silent, but the spirit answers in Greek or in the language of whatever foreign country he comes from, telling how and whence he entered into the man.' At which moment, 'by adjuring the spirit and if he does not obey, threatening him, [the exorcist] drives him out.'[52] As Lucian records, the onlookers are impressed by such a feat. 'Indeed,' one says, 'I actually saw one [demon] coming out, black and smoky in colour'.[53] What keen eyes you must have, retorts his companion, dryly. You can see many things that 'make a very faint impression on the dull optics of us ordinary men.'[54]

Both ancient magic and ancient religion were atmospheric events: smoke, candles, wax drippings and a good dose of gibberish appear to have been as essential to the recipe as frankincense and myrrh. Lucian had as little patience with the enunciation of magical men as he did with their exorcisms. He records an account of one magician who promised to take some followers (or perhaps 'customers' is a better word, given his fat fee) on a trip to the underworld. As Lucian sardonically observes, this particular magician had all the essentials of a powerful magical man, namely 'grey hair and a very majestic beard' – and almost entirely inaudible speech.[55] When the magician started to perform the ceremony, it was hard to hear what he was saying because, as Lucian observed, 'like an incompetent announcer at the games, he spoke rapidly and indistinctly.'[56]

That particular mumbling incantation was followed by other magical rites – including a baptism (at midnight), the sprinkling of blood and the invoking of this god and that one – all seasoned, for extra drama, with 'a number of foreign-sounding, meaningless words of many syllables.'[57] When, well over a millennium later, critics of Catholicism would scorn Catholic rites as magical mumbo jumbo and accuse them of having inspired the patter of magicians (it was said that the Catholic phrase 'hoc est . . . corpus meum' – 'this is my body' – had been transubstantiated into the 'hocus pocus' of magicians), they were merely following a long tradition of elocutionary argument.*[58]

Often such criticisms of magical rites were accompanied by the slur that this was all being done for money. Ancient critics

---

* A wonderful description of an unintelligible religious ceremony is given by Salman Rushdie in his memoir, *Joseph Anton*. In it, soon after the fatwa has been issued against him, Rushdie goes to a memorial for Bruce Chatwin. 'The service at the Greek Orthodox Cathedral of St Sophia of the Archdiocese of Thyateira and Great Britain . . . was all sonorous, mysterious Greek. Its rituals were ornately Byzantine. Blah blah blah Bruce Chatwin, intoned the priests, blah blah Chatwin blah blah. They stood up, they sat down, they knelt, they stood and then sat again. The air was full of the stink of holy smoke.'

frequently accused magicians and healers of being after nothing but profit. The biography of Apollonius contains a section in which he attacks those prophets who trick their spectators with 'sham learning'. This trade, Apollonius says, 'consists entirely of money-grubbers. All their boasted devices they have invented for the sake of gain, and they hunt piles of money by inducing others, whatever they desire, to think them omnipotent.'[59] According to the Porphyry, many Christians were motivated less by love of God than love of money, for they converted 'rich little women' to their religion, then enjoyed their donations. Religion was, he implied, little more than a money-making ruse: 'Rustic and poor people', he wrote, 'performed miracles by magical arts since they possessed nothing whatsoever.'[60]

Satirists and critics might poke fun at the similarities between religion and magic, but for Christians the closeness between the two was far less comfortable. Look carefully at modern translations of ancient biblical texts and the long-standing Christian discomfort with the idea of magic can still be seen. For centuries, a certain Christian embarrassment lingered over all words to do with magic, and particularly over the translation of the vexed word *magus* or, in its plural, *magi*.[61] This is odd as, in one sense, it is not a hard word to translate. Perfectly good equivalent English words exist, for in most contexts it simply means 'sorcerer' or 'magician' – indeed, in many places in the Bible, it is translated as precisely those words.

However, when it comes to the tale of the men who arrive at the birth of Jesus, the words 'magicians' or 'sorcerers' are almost never used by English biblical translators. Instead, the King James Version and many others prefer the more august – but frankly tendentious – translation of 'wise men'. Behold, runs the famous line, 'there came wise men from the east to Jerusalem.'[62] Other versions leave the word untranslated, as the appealingly mysterious 'Magi'. But a much more accurate translation – and one that mirrors translations of this word elsewhere in the Bible – would be: 'Behold, there came sorcerers from the East' – or at the very least 'Behold, there came diviners'. That, however, was not the version that was finally settled on.*

However, to see Christianity and magic as existing merely in conflict is not quite correct, for it wasn't just in hostile texts that glimpses of magic could be seen. In ancient images, figures were often shown holding objects that were associated with them, to help identify them to the viewer. Jesus is often, for example, shown holding a scroll – because that attribute denotes his teaching. He is also – far less comfortably, for modern Christians – often shown holding a wand, which implied then precisely what it implied now. In Greek and Roman texts, wands had long been associated with magicians: Circe had held a wand when she transformed Odysseus' men into pigs; Mercury held a wand when he led the dead back to life. The *Greek Magical Papyri* also make reference to staffs and wands: one spell instructs its user to 'shift the aforementioned ebony staff, which you are holding in your left hand, to your right hand', in order for the magician to release a god.[63]

And, in early Christian art, Jesus holds a wand when he is performing miracles. In one fifth-century wooden panel, he holds one when he is changing water into wine and when he performs the miracle to multiply loaves; in a third-century image from the catacombs, he holds one when he raises Lazarus from the tomb. These are not unusual images. On the contrary: while the sign of the cross is almost entirely absent from early Western Christian art, wands are widely seen. After the scroll, as the art historian Thomas Mathews has pointed out, 'the wand is the most constant attribute of Christ in early Christian art.'[64]

Such images have caused considerable discomfort. Some Christian scholars have argued passionately that these early images of Jesus do not show a 'wand', but instead a 'staff', perhaps a staff of authority. The debate is heated – and largely

* In Ireland, the 'wise men' became the 'wise Druids' – in many ways a more fitting translation.

irresolvable, since it is an argument over what modern term to apply to an ancient object. But, whichever modern English word is used to describe what is seen, it is clear that, when Jesus carries out wonders, he is shown doing so with the aid of a long thin stick. As Mathews puts it, the wand (a word Mathews doesn't hesitate to use) 'is not incidental but a standard and necessary feature in Early Christian art . . . By carrying a wand, Jesus, too, has been made a magician. The implications of this are enormous.'[65]

Early Christian authorities might beg to differ. Augustine himself warned against people who looked for Christ and his apostles not in books but in pictures on the walls. And yet, in Arles and in Ravenna and in Rome, Christians worshipped before images of a Jesus who holds a long, thin staff in his hand as he causes bread to appear, wine to flow and Lazarus to rise from his tomb.

Chapter Five

THE PRODUCT OF INSANITY

'What can I do for you? . . . Why didn't you guard your virginity?'

Joseph loses patience with Mary,
Liber Requiei Mariae, c. 3rd century AD

The problem, as St Augustine knew well, was the vagina of the Virgin Mary. This is rarely considered in the modern world. Yet, for a time, Mary's vagina – or to be more precise, her hymen – was an issue of profound theological importance to Christianity, and that hymen's presence (or absence) was debated in the highest circles of the Church and written about by everyone from the most loathed of heretics to Augustine himself.[1]

The debate arose because this topic was not only one of great import, it was also one on which most gospels offered little help. The Christmas story is a story of a birth, but it is commonly told with biblical, rather than biological, simplicity. Of the four gospels found in modern Bibles, only two mention the actual birth of Jesus – and both do so briskly. The Gospel of Luke spends longer explaining the tax and travel arrangements of Mary and Joseph than it does on the moment of the birth itself, which is briefly dispatched in a single sentence.[2] The Gospel of Matthew is more laconic yet, merely recording with workmanlike brevity that Mary 'had given birth to a son.'[3]

But, in the early centuries of Christianity, there was a gospel that lingered long and lovingly over every aspect of the birth of Christ. This gospel, known today as the *Infancy Gospel of James*, tells the story of the birth of Jesus with a physical and psychological detail lacking in the better-known versions.* It offers

* This gospel, like many apocryphal gospels, has several names. By scholars, it is most commonly referred to as the *Protoevangelium of James*, but it is also known as the *Gospel of James*, and it has other titles, too. Every single one of its titles is, for one reason or another, unsatisfactory, so, for ease, I shall stick with the *Infancy Gospel of James* – chiefly because 'Protoevangelium' is a mouthful. In the West,

detailed descriptions of how Joseph felt when he discovered that his supposedly virginal Mary was already quite far gone (in short: not good) and considerable detail on the lead-up to the birth. It even contains an intimate account of the birth itself, which begins with Mary's contractions, involves the unexpected intervention of a midwife, and ends with a vaginal examination that is, in every sense, unorthodox.

Yet, while it is almost forgotten today, the *Infancy Gospel of James* was, for a time, one of the most popular and influential Christian gospels of all. It was read in churches in the East, for centuries, at important feasts – and even at Christmas.[4] Its sacred words have been woven into the liturgy, art and calendar of Christianity for centuries. At least 140 manuscripts survive in Greek alone, and the spread of languages into which it was translated includes Syriac, Ethiopic, Georgian, Sahidic and Armenian.[5] As one modern scholar put it, the 'sheer number . . . attests to the value placed on this text in the Christian tradition'.[6]

This book tilted the theology, the calendar and even the character of Christianity: the cult of the Virgin Mary, still evident today in the Catholic Church, is unthinkable without it. Together with later gospels in which it was absorbed, it even shaped the way the Nativity was represented. The famous image of Mary riding on a donkey is not present in any of the gospels contained within modern Bibles. This image, however, does appear, dramatically, in the *Infancy Gospel of James*. Similarly, if you have ever seen a Nativity scene in which the baby Jesus is watched over by an ox and an ass, or in which he is born in a cave, you are looking at its influence, for these appear not in the Bible but in the gospel into which the *Infancy Gospel of James* was later absorbed. These scenes infused the works of Giotto and were held in the blue and beaten gold of Byzantine mosaics.[7] It is, in the words of one modern theologian: 'hardly possible to overestimate the

its stories were better known through another gospel into which it was absorbed, with the equally off-putting title of the *Gospel of Pseudo-Matthew*.

influence of [this text] on subsequent church history.'[8] And it contains, at its heart, the story of how the Virgin Mary's vagina was capable of burning human flesh.

As the scene of the birth opens, Mary and Joseph are travelling towards Bethlehem, Mary sitting on a donkey. They have not travelled far when Mary tells Joseph to take her down from the animal because her contractions are beginning. Or, as she puts it, in a brief and dignified phrase, 'the child within me presses me to come forth.'[9] Joseph manages to find a cave in which Mary can give birth, and – an even greater stroke of luck – a Hebrew midwife to assist. While he is outside the cave and Mary is labouring within, he suddenly notices that the entire world has quite literally stopped. The birds of the heavens are held motionless in the sky; a nearby shepherd, who had been lifting his hand to smite his sheep with his staff, has frozen with his hand in mid-air; the river has stopped flowing; the stars have stopped moving. Jesus has been born.

The moment of stillness ends. The birth over, the world starts up again – and, as it does, controversy begins to churn. It is at this moment that the gospel takes an unexpected turn. Because, for reasons that are not entirely clear, another woman, named Salome (no relation to the better-known Salome in the Bible, though she shares with her a certain insubordinate air), turns up at the mouth of the cave. The midwife, running outside after the birth, tells Salome, in great excitement, 'I have a new sight to tell you about; a virgin has brought forth.'[10] Salome, not unreasonably, expresses a certain scepticism at this idea. 'As the Lord my God lives,' she says, 'unless I thrust in my finger, and search for the parts, I will not believe that a virgin has brought forth.'[11]

The midwife, not entirely to her credit, rises to the challenge. Get ready, she briskly tells Mary, 'for there is no small contention concerning you.'[12] Salome enters the cave, and then, without a moment's pause – or, indeed, permission – puts her finger into Mary's vagina. Quite what Mary's feelings are on this unexpected move are unrecorded, but the response of her vagina is unambiguous, for Salome's hand is suddenly burned off. Salome is appalled. 'Woe unto my iniquity and mine unbelief,' she laments, 'because I have tempted the living God, and lo, my hand falleth away from me in fire.'[13]

'In the beginning was the Word'. These words – the first words, of the first verse, of the first chapter of the Gospel of John – are an intimidating opening to a book. They confine eternity to a clause, complex philosophy to a word, and they are also, in truth, pretty confusing. That their English translation is not very good doesn't help matters. 'Word' is at best an unusual and at worst a very bad translation of the original Greek, *logos*, a richly dense word that does indeed mean 'word', but which also means everything from 'inward thought' to 'reason' itself. But, for all the confusion, one thing is clear: this line is singular. Singular in the sense of being unusual and singular in the sense of being very firmly not plural. This religion, this line seems to imply, will offer its believers the singular, lapidary word of the single, all-powerful God.

Almost two millennia later, the sense that the Bible offers the single, immovable word of a single deity remains. Step into any church – matting, seats and stone – and you will find the Bible up at the front – sometimes chained, as if for extra immobility, to its pulpit.[14] Bound in Bible black, it is itself binding: to swear an oath upon the Bible means swearing not only that your words are true, but also that they will not change. Its very language feels fixed: the words of the King James Version stud the English language still – magnificent and sometimes curious linguistic fossils.

Like fossils, these phrases were shaped by another world, an ancient world, in which milk and honey were paradise and a lost sheep a disaster; a world of dust and ashes, of serpents and scorpions, and of famine and sorrows – a world whose phrases taste, today, strange and foreign on the tongue. But then, these words felt old even when they were new. Time and time again, when the translators of King James wrestled Hebrew and Greek into English, they chose not to translate into easy modern prose, but to cling as close to the original text as possible. This was the word of God, and it was not to be meddled with for mere ease of understanding. English must change before this text, rather than vice versa. So the King James Version, with its heavy tread, was born.

But this apparent immobility is an illusion. The Bible is ancient, but it is not immovable. There was not, in the beginning, 'the Word', singular. There was not, in the earliest days, a single story, resonant and unchallenged. There were many words, many stories. There were, in the first three centuries of Christianity, Christianities that said there was one almighty God, as modern Christians would expect. There were also Christianities that said there were two divine powers – an evil one and a good one – and others who believed in hundreds of divine beings.[15] There were Christians who believed in bodily resurrection – and there were Christians who believed this was laughable claptrap. And, in the earliest centuries of Christianity, it was far from clear which of these beliefs was the 'right' one – or even that there was such a thing as a 'right' one.

Consider the virginity of the Virgin Mary. Today, this is one of the most familiar aspects of the entire Christian story. Those who have been brought up in a Christian society will know (or, at any rate, will have been told) that Mary was a virgin and that she was told by the Angel Gabriel that she was with child. They will know that Mary and Joseph travelled to Bethlehem, that Jesus was swaddled in cloths and placed in a manger, for there was no room in the inn.

But, in its early days, when Christianity smelt of revolution and dissent rather than authority and old stone, opinions on how Jesus had been conceived and born differed wildly. Some Christians, it is true, argued for the virgin birth. Others argued that

Jesus hadn't been born in any human sense at all: he merely put on and took off the appearance of mortality whenever he fancied, like a piece of clothing. He had previously, they argued, appeared on this earth as Adam – and occasionally he still did, turning up 'clothed with Adam's body'.[16] Other Christians argued that Jesus hadn't been pre-assembled in heaven, nor grown in Mary's womb, but had instead put himself together: 'On his way from heaven he came to earth,' argued one, 'and assembled his own body from the four elements.'[17]

Still other Christians offered wholly different accounts of the birth itself. In an unnerving text known as the *Latin Infancy Gospel*, the account of Jesus' birth is given in the first person, by the midwife. She records how, at the moment of his birth, Jesus 'shone brightly round about like the sun' and the whole cave became bright with his light. The midwife is shocked, and 'stood there stupefied and amazed, and fear seized me.' But, as she watched, 'the light itself, gradually withdrawing, became like a child, and in a moment became a child as children are customarily born. And I took courage and bent down and touched him, and took him up in my hands with great fear, and was seized with terror because he had no weight like other children who are born.' It becomes even more frightening, for, the next moment, Jesus 'smiled at me with the most sweet smile, and opened his eyes and looked sharply on me. And suddenly there came forth from his eyes a great light like a brilliant flash of lightning.'[18]

Perhaps most dangerously of all, there were large numbers of Christians who said Mary was no virgin, Joseph was no saint and there was nothing at all miraculous about this birth. Jesus, they argued, was simply a man: he was Joseph's son and Joseph had fathered him, 'just as all men were generated from a man's seed and a woman.'[19] Jesus 'is like all men' in his birth, but, as one Christian group argued, he was merely 'different in his life – in prudence, virtue and a life of righteousness.'[20] Or so it was said. Here, as always, it is worth being suspicious of ancient accounts of unorthodox Christians. Heretical and even merely erring Christian sects were so successfully stamped out that almost all the evidence that survives on them is in mere literary scraps: either quotations or descriptions in accounts by hostile Christians. And those accounts are not disinterested sociological observation but texts in a ferocious propaganda war. They should therefore be treated with considerable caution. But they are nonetheless useful – and their veracity can frequently be tested against other sources. Take the view that Joseph was the true father of Jesus: clearly it was widespread, since other Christians later stepped in to deal with such nonsense. As one later ruling explained, if anyone declared that Jesus came from the father, 'just as corporeal sons do according to emission and passion, let him be anathema.'[21]

The virgin birth was not only one of the most contested ideas within early Christianity, it was also one of the most roundly mocked outside it. Non-Christians treated the idea of a virgin birth not with reverence, but instead with much mirth and what one injured believer described as a 'scoffing spirit'.[22] The cynical Celsus suggested that Mary had been made pregnant by a soldier called Panthera (a name that, in Greek, sounds similar to the Greek word for 'virgin', which is *parthenos*). Jesus, embarrassed by his lowly background, had later 'fabricated the story of his birth from a virgin' to cover the shame of his uncertain paternity.[23] The Christian writer Tertullian admitted that people accused Jesus of being the 'son of a carpenter or a whore.'[24]

This particular story also recurs in Jewish literature. In the Talmud, there are tantalizing references to a man who some think is probably Jesus.* Here, Jesus' father is not Mary's husband, and he is certainly not God. Instead, Jesus is the child of Mary's

* It is only 'probably' because the man isn't named as Jesus – he is instead called 'Ben Pantera' or 'Ben Pandera' – the son of Pantera. He is, at other times, called 'Ben Stada'. The question of whether or not this man is Jesus is, as the Princeton scholar Peter Schäfer puts it, 'hotly disputed'.

lover, Pandera – a name that clearly sounds similar to Celsus' Panthera. As the Princeton professor of religion Peter Schäfer has written, the idea that the 'Holy Spirit' made Mary pregnant is here treated as 'nothing but a cover-up of the truth'.[25] Instead, this text argues that Mary 'had a secret lover and that her child was just a bastard like any other bastard. Joseph's suspicion . . . was absolutely warranted: Mary had indeed been unfaithful to him.'[26] This alternative ancient narrative goes further: Jesus is described not as a messiah, but instead as a 'fool' who brought forth 'witchcraft from Egypt.'[27] The idea that Jesus was the son of a Pantera, or Pandera, or Panthera hung about for centuries – in one case, a Christian author entirely misunderstood and added Panthera into the Holy Family, explaining that he was the paternal grandfather of Jesus.[28]

If some Jews and non-Christians found it hard to believe the story of the virgin birth, so too did many Christians. The idea that Mary was a virgin is mentioned in only two of the four gospels in the Bible, while the idea that she remained a virgin throughout her life is, to put it mildly, harder still to find within the pages of the New Testament. The Gospel of Matthew, for example, notes that Joseph knew Mary not 'until she had given birth to a son.'[29] It takes a certain sort of creative textual analysis to read that sentence as meaning 'never'. Yet more creativity is required to overcome the fact that all four gospel accounts of Jesus' life refer to him having brothers (and, in some places, refer to sisters, too). This was the kind of creativity theologians were well able to supply, and the perpetual virginity of Mary is held as dogma in the modern Catholic Church.[30]

The problem of whether or not Mary was a virgin was even more complex in the early centuries of Christianity than is often realized. Today, when people discuss the possibility of a 'virgin birth', what they tend to be discussing is merely a 'virgin conception'. But, for ancient writers, both conception and birth presented difficulties. This is because what it means to be a virgin has changed, subtly. To describe someone as a virgin in the modern era has, typically, been a simple statement of personal history: it has meant that that person has never had penetrative sex. Two thousand years ago, virginity was not merely a historical state, but a physical one: it meant that a woman had a hymen. Crudely speaking, in the early days, the problem was not just what went into Mary, but what came out – and what happened to her body when it did.

And that, for ancient Christian authors, meant no end of trouble. Read the writings of the early Church Fathers and you can see them twist and turn, considering and reconsidering every aspect of the virgin birth, trying to solve this problem. If it was difficult to imagine how a woman could be impregnated by the Holy Spirit and retain her hymen, then it was harder still – and for many ancient writers entirely impossible – to see how she could have given birth without breaking it. This sort of discussion can make a modern reader feel uncomfortable; it was also – to judge by the writings of St Augustine, St Ambrose and others – the sort of discussion that made ancient Christians a touch uncomfortable too. You can sense the unease in their endless search for euphemism: these writers do not use anatomical terms, but opt instead for an oddly architectural approach, talking about Mary's 'closed doors' and the 'fence' of her chastity.[31]

To modern eyes, it is the virgin conception of Jesus that seems the far more marvellous feat – the virgin birth tends to be treated as a mere mechanical afterthought. But, in ancient times, a virgin conception was the easier of the two to imagine. Ancient authors had, in many ways, a sophisticated understanding of the human body – but this blended with a certain vagueness about reproduction: even an otherwise level-headed Roman medical author could write that, if a woman wanted to prevent conception, she should 'wear the liver of a cat in a tube on the left foot . . . This is very effective.'[32] So, it is perhaps unsurprising that Christian authors demonstrated a certain liberty with biology in explaining how Mary's virginity had been preserved while impregnation took place.

The moment of impregnation was generally agreed upon: this was understood to have taken place when the angel of the Lord appeared to Mary; the method, however, varied. Some early Christians suggested that impregnation had happened through her face, as the angel spoke to her, and this belief persisted: a twelfth-century enamel in the monastery of Klosterneuburg, in Austria, shows an angel pointing his right hand at Mary, while forks of lightning spring from his fingers and enter her eyes. Meanwhile, another anatomically ambitious ancient text explained that, 'Perfectly God / He entered the womb through her ear'.[33] The idea of aural impregnation remained popular and can be seen visualized in the remarkable frieze on the outside of the Marienkapelle, in Würzburg, Germany, in which a long trumpet-like tube comes from the mouth of God, with the foetal Jesus sliding along it, on his way to entering Mary's ear.[34]

It is clear, however, that many other ancient writers remained unconvinced by the virgin birth, whatever orifice was involved. And, in some ancient texts, one of those who expresses the bluntest scepticism is Joseph himself. In the gospels contained within the Bible, Joseph is understandably a little peevish when he finds that Mary is pregnant – but that is nothing compared to the reactions recounted in other gospels. In the *Infancy Gospel of James*, when Joseph returns from a long period away for work to find Mary six months pregnant, he is absolutely appalled, and 'struck his face, threw himself down on the ground on sackcloth and wept bitterly', before starting on a series of reproaches. 'Who has deceived me?' he asks. 'Who has done this evil in my house and defiled the virgin?'[35] Why, he asks Mary, have you done this? Mary, equally distraught, defends herself: 'I am pure,' she replies, 'and know not a man.'[36] Joseph, not unreasonably, is unconvinced. 'Whence then', he asks, 'is that which is in thy womb?'[37]

In one early Christian book, whose core text probably dates to the third century, Joseph is even more distraught. The *Liber Requiei Mariae* was another enormously popular text, read everywhere from Ireland to Ethiopia and Georgia – and is to this day a riveting read. In most ancient accounts of the birth, although Joseph is suspicious of Mary's pregnancy at first, he tends to warm to his wife and new son as the birth approaches. In this version, however, Joseph remains sourly sceptical of the paternity of his child long after Jesus has been born. As the Holy Family travels through Egypt after the birth, Joseph grumbles on, his foul mood only aggravated now that he has to flee to the Egyptian desert to escape Herod. When Mary asks Joseph what they have to eat, this is, for him, the final straw.

'What can I do for you?' he asks testily. 'Is it not enough for you that I became a stranger to my family on your account?' Angry, he starts to find fault with Mary: 'Why didn't you guard your virginity?' he asks, querulously. Sounding like a tourist who has found himself in a country where he doesn't like the food, he then complains that there is 'no fruit that you could eat in the trees.' Or, rather, there is, but it is useless, since, 'This date-palm is tall, and I cannot climb it . . . there is nothing that a person will find in this desert.'[38] St Joseph, who is in this account rather less saintly, hasn't finished yet. 'I have been afflicted from all sides because of you, because I have left my country. And I am afflicted because I did not know the child that you have; I only know that he is not from me.' As if that speech were not extraordinary enough, Joseph then delivers a final, lethal line. For, he says, 'I have thought in my heart, perhaps I had intercourse with you while drunk.'[39]

Eventually, one form of Christianity would dominate. It produced a Bible, and it claimed that this book was authoritative. Eventually, other texts and all other sects – those that said Mary was not a virgin, or that Joseph was Jesus' father – would start to fade away in the West. Eventually, each Christmas, the story of the virgin birth would be hymned across the world as one pure note: 'the Christian story' – in the singular. In the end, if not in the beginning, there would be 'the Word'. But it was not always so. Look in the right places – peer at the right painting by Giotto, or at a Christmas card that shows an ox and an ass, or a Nativity scene that pictures Mary in a cave – and you are seeing the descendants of these tales. To hear these notes, with their discordant ideas and ancient harmonies, is today an eerie experience. For they are the sound of a world that has been lost, and of a world that – had history tilted slightly differently – might have been.

Chapter Six

WHAT WOULD JESUS DO?

'Do not let him go outside the door, for all those who provoke him die.'

Joseph reflects on Jesus' troubling behaviour,
Infancy Gospel of Thomas, *c.* 2nd century AD

The Jesus who killed people was, later Christians agreed, more than a little embarrassing. However, if the *Infancy Gospel of Thomas* is to be believed, few were more embarrassed by him than Mary and Joseph themselves. On the eventful morning on which that gospel opens, not long after Jesus has 'withered' one boy and murdered another, he returns home to find trouble. The parents of the dead boy have turned up at his house to admonish Mary and Joseph. 'Since you have such a child,' they say, 'you cannot dwell with us in the village.' Or, they add, by way of compromise, if you do live here, 'teach him to bless and not to curse. For he is killing our children.'[1]

Joseph, chastened, calls the five-year-old Jesus aside and gives him what feels, under the circumstances, like a rather mild talking-to. Why 'do you do such things?' Joseph asks him. 'These people suffer and hate us and persecute us'. The sinister Jesus is unperturbed: 'these people shall bear their punishment', he replies.[2] And, sure enough, instantly, the parents of the boy 'were smitten with blindness.'[3] At which point, Joseph – who is generally represented as a forbearing sort of man – finally loses his temper. He goes over to Jesus and wrings his ear. Jesus becomes angry again. 'It is fitting for you to seek and not to find,' he says, gnomic and threatening, 'and you have acted most unwisely.'[4]

This ancient gospel (historians think it dates back to around the second century) continues with its account of Jesus' remarkable childhood. It tells how, when Jesus was eight, Joseph sent him to school. There, the teacher started to teach Jesus his Greek letters, beginning with the alpha and the beta. Jesus interrupts him. If you truly are a teacher, he says, cryptically, 'tell me the power of the Alpha, and I will tell you that of the Beta.'[5] The teacher, evidently an old hand at dealing with this sort of thing, 'was annoyed and struck him on the head.'[6] He was, however, not used to dealing with Jesus. The boy 'cursed him, and he immediately fainted and fell on his face to the ground.'[7]

It was not the first time Jesus' schooling had gone awry. A little earlier, he had been in another lesson and had unnerved his teacher so profoundly that the teacher had requested Joseph to remove him from his class. 'Take him away, therefore, I beseech you, brother Joseph,' he had begged. 'I cannot endure the severity of his gaze . . . This child is not earth-born; he can even subdue fire.'[8]

When Jesus had returned home, Joseph became anxious, and spoke to Mary. 'Do not let him go outside the door,' he told her. 'For all those who provoke him die.'[9]

In the last years of the nineteenth century, an American pastor named Charles Sheldon started telling stories. On Sunday evenings, instead of merely speaking about the Bible in the pulpit, he would share improving parables with the congregation of his Kansas church.[10] One of these, which later became known as 'In His Steps', opened with an account of a tramp who knocks on the door of a busy pastor and asks him for work. The reverend, irritated at the disturbance while he is writing his Sunday sermon, sends the man away – but afterwards feels a pang of guilt.

The pang is only strengthened when the man reappears in church, during the reverend's service, and turns to speak directly to the congregation. He begins by reassuring the congregation that he is neither drunk, nor mad. He is merely a man who has lost his job and then had to watch his wife die in a New York tenement, starving and gasping for breath. Having delivered this stirring address, the man asks the congregation what Jesus would do, if he were in their shoes, to help suffering men like him – before suddenly and dramatically collapsing in the aisle of the church.[11] A little later, with the briskness and lack of fuss commonly required of the poor in such tales, the hobo dies.

But not without causing the reverend to re-examine his morals. Chastened by what has happened, the reverend asks his flock, 'for an entire year, not to do anything without first asking the question, "What would Jesus do?" And after asking that question,' he says, they should each go on and follow Jesus exactly 'no matter what the result may be.'[12] The sermon became a book and the book became a bestseller – but the greatest success was the phrase, which became a sensation.[13] 'What Would Jesus Do?' lives on even today, an international evangelical meme, recognizable by its initials alone: W.W.J.D.

Sheldon's phrase worked – and still does work – because so many of us feel we know Jesus so intimately. We feel we know about his birth (in the bleak midwinter), about his childhood (mild, obedient, good), about his character (gentle, meek, mild). We feel we know about his morals and his morality, too: we know that he would turn the other cheek and not cast the first stone; that, if his tunic was taken, he would offer a man his cloak. We know his face, as we have seen it painted, pained and shadowed, by Velázquez. We know his almost naked body, for we have seen it sculpted in marble, soft as flesh and cold as death, by Michelangelo. We feel that what we are seeing in such representations is itself ancient and immovable.

We are wrong. We know a Jesus. But this was not always the only Jesus. In the early years and centuries of this religion, there were many Jesuses, many Christs – many of them unimaginably strange to us today. It was, in those early days, far from certain what Jesus would do or who he was. Jesus' appearance was one of the most obvious things that changed – and it changed so much that the Jesus of the earliest centuries has been nicknamed 'Christ chameleon'. Sometimes he appears as a bearded old man, at others as a beardless young one; in some images he is shown bare-chested and as macho as a Greek god, while at other times he is depicted as far more sexually ambiguous, with soft cheeks, long hair and (arguably) discernible breasts. In one ancient account Jesus is described as being small and ugly; in another, he is a giant who is (the figures are very precise) ninety-six miles tall and 'twenty-four miles wide.'[14]

Such superficial changes were, as modern scholars are increasingly ready to admit, the least of it. In the earliest centuries of this religion, almost any aspect of Jesus that could change, did change. There was the Jesus who abhorred sex and told people that they should 'refrain from this filthy intercourse' lest they produce children.[15] And then there was a Jesus who, it was said, used sex as a form of revelation that he gave to Mary Magdalene. In one short and extremely odd ancient fragment, Jesus is described as standing with Mary when suddenly he produces another woman, then starts having sex with her. Then he 'gathered his semen in his hand, and explained that "This is what we must do in order to live."' Mary falls to the ground in shock.[16] Those used to the Jesus of the Church of England might sympathize.

The differences go on. Some ancient strands of Christianity offered a Jesus who had a corporeal body; others offered one who was as insubstantial as air; there was a Jesus who was no more than an apparition; there was a Jesus who left no footprints. As one sacred text – which contradicts many an inspirational tea-towel – recorded, 'often when I was walking with him I wished to see whether the print of his foot appeared upon the earth . . . But I never saw it.'[17] Jesus' death, too, was contested. There were Jesuses who were crucified in agony; there was the Jesus who (or so it was said) swapped his body with another to avoid death; and then there were Jesuses who were crucified but who felt no pain at all, since Jesus was 'totally free from passions; unattainable to any sort of disturbance of feelings either pleasure or pain.'[18] And there were some people in these early years who claimed that the long-waited messiah was someone else entirely. There was a Jewish sect that, in the first century AD, was said to have become convinced that the messiah whom the scriptures predicted, the ruler who would come from Judah, had indeed been born in these years – it was just that they considered Christ to be King Herod, rather than Jesus. Herod, they believed, was the long-prophesied leader of the Jews.[19]

To modern eyes, such confusion can seem baffling: it is 'naturally' clear to modern readers that the 'true' stories about Jesus are those which are contained in the New Testament. But in the earliest days not only was there no authoritative Bible, but no one had written these stories down at all. The four gospels in modern Bibles were written down between AD 70 and AD 110, long after the death of Jesus. When, in the first century AD, some among the faithful started to put such stories on the page, others were suspicious of this innovation. As one first-century bishop called Papias explained, he preferred to hear stories from the mouths of living men since, 'I did not imagine that things out of books would help me as much as the utterances of a living and abiding voice.'[20]

The structure of the Christian Bible hints that, despite the later confident rhetoric, there was some doubt about what the true story was. As the biblical scholar Bruce Metzger has written, 'if it is necessary to have not one but several accounts of the one life of Jesus . . . this is as good as admitting that none of them is perfect.'[21] Consider the virgin birth: not only is it attested in just two of the four gospels, but it is flatly contradicted in numerous places within them, as Joseph is referred to repeatedly and explicitly as Jesus' 'father'. This was not always obvious: for centuries, pious scribes, evidently aware of how problematic this idea was, had substituted out the word 'father'. But, once upon a time, it had been there.[22]

Such disagreement was something that ancient critics of Christianity were quick to pounce upon. Porphyry observed that, 'The evangelists were inventors not historians of the events concerning Jesus. For each of them wrote an account, especially of the passion, which was not in harmony with the other respective accounts.'[23] As Porphyry would have known, these differences often occur at significant moments in the narrative – including not only Jesus' birth, but also his death.

Take the question of who arrives at Jesus' tomb first: the Gospel of Matthew states that it is two women – Mary Magdalene and 'the other' Mary; in Mark, it is three women – Mary Magdalene, Mary the mother of James, and Salome; in Luke, it is a group of unnamed women; while in John, it is only one: Mary Magdalene.[24] Who they see upon arrival is also different: in Matthew, it is an angel, 'his appearance was like lightning'; in Luke, it is two men in 'shining garments'; in John, it is two angels. In the Gospel of Mark, Jesus' resurrection is promised – but it does not happen within the text.[25]

Far more diversity once existed. A recent book published by Oxford University Press, called *The Other Gospels*, included, as its introduction explained, 'forty some Gospels' in its pages.*[26] It is known that there were once many more gospels, not to mention other sacred Christian texts. We will never know quite how many there once were – but lots, certainly. 'The church has four gospels,' as the early Christian author Origen put it. 'Heretics have very many.'[27] And each gospel contained dangerous and, at times, heretical ideas.

All of these tales would start to be called 'apocryphal' – though, it is worth being wary of that word. It traces its roots to a Greek word – *krupto*, which means 'to hide' – and 'apocryphal' thus means roughly 'things that are hidden'; though its meaning in modern English is far richer than that, for it manages both to combine a mild illicit thrill with a heavy dose of disapproval. Look up 'apocryphal' in the Oxford English Dictionary today and you will find that it is used to describe a story that is 'well known, but probably not true'. However, the term apocryphal is

---

* The number, as the authors explain, depends in part on how the word 'gospel' is defined: some scholars consider something a 'gospel' if ancient sources gave it that name; others argue that any source that tells the story of Jesus' life is arguably a gospel. Either way, it is clear that the number is large.

now not used, as it is profoundly misleading. Very little was secret about these books, some of which were among the most read and most influential in the Christian canon.*

Though it is worth remembering that even Christians who used the same texts frequently managed to disagree on their interpretation. One particularly fraught topic was the question of just how human Christ had (or hadn't) been. Ancient Christians lingered long over questions of whether or not Jesus ate, and what happened when he did. It was, wrote one ancient scholar, 'ludicrous' to suppose that Jesus needed to eat food. Instead, Jesus merely 'ate, not for the sake of the body, which was kept together by a holy energy, but in order that it might not enter into the minds of those who were with Him' to think that he was different.[28] Jesus, it was argued by some Christians, 'used to eat and to drink in a special way, without excreting his solids . . . So great was the power of his self-control, that the food in his body was not digested, because all form of corruption was alien to him.'[29] For centuries, a long, involved and theologically important debate rumbled over the question of whether or not Jesus had defecated. (The conclusion eventually reached was that he had, and many of those who suggested otherwise were later condemned as heretics.)

It is easy to forget, too, how even a single Bible can contain multitudes. Today, it is Jesus meek and mild who is remembered – so much so that the murderous Jesus of the *Infancy Gospel of Thomas* seems a shocking aberration. But that is not because modern Bibles offer an entirely meek and mild saviour. As the writer G. K. Chesterton observed, people 'never tire' of pointing out that, while Jesus is gentle and merciful, the Church – and particularly the Catholic Church – has often been a terror. This, Chesterton wrote, is 'very nearly the reverse of the truth. The truth is that it is the image of Christ in the churches that is

* Scholars prefer the term 'non-canonical', but it hasn't yet caught on outside academia.

almost entirely mild and merciful. It is the image of Christ in the Gospels that is a good many other things as well.'[30] There are, as Chesterton well knew, dark moments in the New Testament.

There is, for example, an odd and now little celebrated moment in the Gospel of Mark when Jesus is hungry; seeing a fig tree, he goes to eat from it – then finds it has no fruit. Jesus – who in this story has hints of the angry infant Jesus – curses the tree. 'May no one ever eat fruit from you again.'[31] Sure enough, when he and the disciples pass by a little later (this takes place after Jesus has, in another less-than-mild moment, walked into the temple and overturned the tables of the moneylenders), the disciples notice that the tree has withered up. They point this out to Jesus. His response is brief, and telling: 'Have faith in God,' he replies. It is an act that would later wholly baffle the philosopher Bertrand Russell: 'This is a very curious story, because it was not the right time of year for figs, and you really could not blame the tree.'[32]

The Jesus of the Bible – however he is remembered – makes no pretence at being solely a prince of peace: 'Do not think that I have come to bring peace to the earth,' he says. 'I have not come to bring peace, but a sword. For I have come to set a man against his father, and a daughter against her mother, and a daughter-in-law against her mother-in-law. And a person's enemies will be those of his own household.'[33] Jesus is famed for saying, 'Blessed are the poor' – but it is worth remembering that he did not end that speech there. 'But woe to you who are rich,' he continues, 'for you have received your consolation. Woe to you who are full now, for you shall be hungry. Woe to you who laugh now, for you shall mourn and weep.'[34] Those words have found their way into fewer happy hymns.

Chapter Seven

ON SARDINES AND RESURRECTIONS

'And he cast the sardine into the bath, and it lived and began to swim . . . And seeing this, many followed Peter and believed in the Lord.'

Acts of Peter, XIII, 2nd century AD

It was not one of the most moving resurrections of the era. Except, perhaps, for those who were particularly fond of sardines.

St Peter's patience had been exhausted. He had already defeated the wicked Simon once, casting him out of Judaea, where he had 'bewitched' the locals with his sorcery.[1] However, that was not the end of him. As a heavenly vision informed St Peter, Simon had now moved to the capital of the empire, where he was once again beguiling people with the craft of Satan.[2] St Peter, as the second-century *Acts of Peter* records, set out swiftly.

The scene that greeted Peter in Rome was a terrible one. Many of the Christians there had already forsaken the ways of Christ and become ardent followers of Simon instead – including some of the Christians' richest former donors. Pained by such theological, not to mention financial, irregularity, a distraught St Peter gave a lament about the 'divers arts and temptations of the devil', 'the contrivances and devices of the wicked', and a short exegesis on the 'ravening wolf, the devourer and scatterer of eternal life'.[3]

Those Christians who were still faithful promptly urged Peter to 'join battle with Simon and not suffer him any longer to vex the people.'[4] St Peter agreed. Word of the forthcoming contest spread rapidly and the people of Rome – who were showing very little sign of being vexed and every sign that they were enjoying themselves immensely – gathered round to watch.

Peter's first move against the wicked sorcerer was unexpected but nonetheless effective: he ordered a large dog to bound up to Simon, lift its forelegs up and insult him. The dog duly did so, growling such mouth-filling phrases as 'Thou exceeding wicked and shameless one' and 'most wicked one and deceiver of simple souls', as it balanced on two paws.[5] Simon was appalled; the assembled multitude was delighted; the dog, having done its duty, dropped down dead at Peter's feet.

The crowd immediately begged Peter to 'show us another sign, that we may believe in thee as the minister of the living God.' As they explained with honesty, if little constancy, Simon had done many miracles, 'and therefore did we follow him.'[6] St Peter must now do some too; then they would follow him instead.

St Peter turned and saw 'a sardine hung in a window.' He unhooked it and returned to the assembled group. 'If ye now see this swimming in the water like a fish, will ye be able to believe in him whom I preach?'[7] The crowd responded with one voice: 'Verily we will believe thee.'

St Peter took the fish, cast it into a nearby bath of water and ordered the sardine to come to life, 'In thy name, O Jesu Christ.' The sardine, which was having a better day than the dog, duly did so. The people of Rome were awed. 'Seeing this,' the text records, 'many followed Peter and believed in the Lord.'[8]

However remarkable the resurrections contained within the apocryphal tales might have been, perhaps the most remarkable resurrection of all has been that of the apocryphal texts themselves. To understand how that happened, it is necessary to travel to late Regency-era England, to the publishing house of a man named William Hone. Or rather, as furious Christians would later have it, the house of 'the arch blasphemer' of England.[9]

Hone was a man who had an almost infinite ability to irritate Christians. A journalist and satirist (he collaborated with the cartoonist George Cruikshank), his first clash with Christian morality had come just a few years before when he had written a piece of political satire modelled on the Lord's prayer. This, to modern eyes, looks benignly mild: 'OUR Lord who art in the

Treasury,' began its mockingly pious first line, 'Whatsoever be thy name . . .'[10] It was not considered mild at the time: it landed Hone in prison, and at the centre of what would prove to be the most important English libel trial of the century. Hone conducted his own defence and did so brilliantly, and so amusingly, that he won. It was a landmark moment in the fight for a free British press.*

Other writers might, after the experience of being jailed for a text, have chosen a more pacific topic for their next work. Not Hone. Instead, he returned almost immediately to Christianity and produced another work that would, in its own way, be almost as revolutionary. Hone's interest in Christianity had begun early. He had been born in 1780 into an oppressively religious household. One day, when he had done something wrong, his father had handed him the family Bible and 'enjoined upon me to learn by heart an entire chapter before he returned to dinner.' As Hone later recalled, 'I felt petrified. I knew it was utterly beyond my power'; so he simply closed the book in 'reckless despair'. When his father came back, he duly 'inflicted upon me the severest chastisement I had ever received; I believe the severest of which his arm was capable.' Later, Hone threw the Bible down the stairs, declaring, 'When I am my own master I will never open you.'[11]

Except he did. For, as well as being petrified by the Bible, Hone was fascinated by it. When he was about thirteen, he had stumbled on a text talking about Thomas Paine's *The Age of Reason*, a work which brusquely dismisses Christianity as a 'fable'. For the teenaged Hone, this was a moment of almost religious revelation. For the first time he realized 'that the Bible had been or could be doubted or disbelieved.'[12]

* It was arguably one of the funniest trials too: the autodidact Hone was so amusing that large crowds turned out to watch him speak. A few years ago, this was made the subject of a play by the *Private Eye* editor – and a man who is himself not unfamiliar with libel trials – Ian Hislop.

He would have another moment of biblical revelation many years later. By this time he was middle-aged, and a successful printer and satirist. As he was researching something in the British Museum, he happened to stumble across English translations of some ancient texts. These writings looked, in many ways, like texts from the Bible. They talked about miracles and the lives of Jesus and Mary and Joseph. They were clearly very old – they were rich in 'Verily I say unto thee's and 'Lo!'s and whatnot. But they were not like any biblical texts that Hone had ever seen. For these stories told of how a midwife had been present at the birth of Jesus; of how Jesus had turned up, in person, at the gates of hell and, most surprisingly of all, they told of how the infant Jesus had murdered people. Hone had, in short, found himself in the looking-glass world of the apocryphal gospels.

As Hone read through them on that day in the British Museum, he was spellbound. He would have instantly realized that the significance of what he had found lay less in the particular narratives – though it was undoubtedly interesting that one Christian gospel offered a Jesus who killed people – than in the mere fact that these texts existed at all. Hone had grown up being schooled, relentlessly, in *the* Christian story – but these books showed that very idea to be false. There had not been a single Christian story. The story that had survived had simply been one of many Christian stories. It could be doubted, or disbelieved. Hone – who was not only a satirist but a shrewd man of print – immediately understood not merely the power but the selling power of what he was looking at. In a fit of excitement, he read on eagerly then '*tore* out the Gospels for the printer'.[13]

In 1820, Hone published a compilation of the apocryphal tales. To understand the fascination and outrage that greeted its publication it is worth looking at the frontispiece of a slightly later edition of it, published in 1863. As its title explained, in breathless capitals, this book contained: 'THE SUPPRESSED GOSPELS AND EPISTLES OF THE ORIGINAL NEW TESTAMENT OF JESUS CHRIST, AND OTHER

PORTIONS OF THE ANCIENT HOLY SCRIPTURES, NOW EXTANT, ATTRIBUTED TO HIS APOSTLES AND THEIR DISCIPLES, AND VENERATED BY THE PRIMITIVE CHRISTIAN CHURCHES DURING THE FIRST FOUR CENTURIES; BUT SINCE, AFTER VIOLENT DISPUTATIONS, FORBIDDEN BY THE BISHOPS OF THE NICENE COUNCIL, IN THE REIGN OF THE EMPEROR CONSTANTINE; AND OMITTED FROM THE CATHOLIC AND PROTESTANT EDITIONS OF THE NEW TESTAMENT, BY ITS COMPILERS.'[14] The historical implications of this title were far from perfect (its dates were a bit out, and the early Christians hadn't sifted the gospels like newspaper editors – rather, certain groups simply favoured certain books). But the power of the headline was undeniable.

These apocryphal gospels had not been entirely unknown before Hone – he himself was drawing on translations done a century or so earlier – but they were more or less unknown to anyone but the few select scholars who could either access those translations or read the works in their original ancient languages. Hone brought them to widespread public attention and the result was fascination – and fury. His book was described as 'mischievous and malevolent', and 'the most dangerous' of 'various recent attacks on scripture', while Hone himself was called a man of 'a deep and desperate malignity', who had shown 'a systematic disregard for the truth'.[15] As one furious cleric reflected, in yet more energetic capitals, 'AN ENEMY HATH DONE THIS.'[16]

Anything about Hone that could be attacked, was: Christian reviewers insulted his person, his character, his low social status, his lack of academic qualifications – and even his typesetting. For Hone – who knew what he was up to – had laid out his alternative gospels in faux-biblical style, dividing each gospel into chapters and verses, with drop caps at the start of each section, and headings across the top of the pages. Open his book and it therefore looked just like a real Bible; except its page headings did not say things such as 'The Lord is my Shepherd' but instead 'Kills his schoolmasters', or 'Satan and the Prince of Hell quarrel'.[17] To devout Christians, this was not merely typesetting: it was mockery, in font form.

Hone was not insensitive to the criticism. As he later reflected, as soon as he had published the book he had been 'attacked with a malignity and fury that would have graced the age of Mary and Elizabeth, when Catholics put to death Protestants, and Protestants put to death Catholics.'[18] His book was still annoying Christians a century later. At the start of the twentieth century, when the medievalist and novelist M. R. James came to produce his own translation of the apocryphal gospels, he would write in an ungenerous preface that Hone's book was 'misleading' and 'unoriginal' and had 'enjoyed a popularity which is in truth far beyond its deserts'.* It was, James wrote, 'in fact, to speak frankly, a very bad book.'[19]

In their outrage, Christians had paid Hone the greatest compliment they could. Because what these Christians tacitly admitted with every insult, every piece of what Hone disdainfully called their 'craft of disingenuous criticism', was that his book mattered – it mattered a lot.[20] Hone was little more than the messenger. What was actually enraging the faithful was

---

* One of the (many) ways in which James and Hone differed was in their attitude to censorship. Whereas Hone fought against it, M. R. James was breezily in favour. In the 1920s, a scandal broke out in England over a book, *The Well of Loneliness*, by the author Radclyffe Hall. The novel has a gay female protagonist and thus, upon publication, was promptly seized as 'obscene'. Literary London rallied, and Hall's lawyer wrote to James to ask him if he would lend his name to support the book, as writers such as Virginia Woolf and Julian Huxley had. The draft of James' reply survives still – and even at the distance of a century makes for minty reading. 'I believe Miss Hall's book is about birth control or some kindred subject, isn't it,' James wrote. 'I find it difficult to believe either that it is a good novel or that its suppression causes any loss to literature. I am quite sure that if nine tenths of the novels, biographies, critical studies, poems that come out every week were buried nobody but publishers and authors would be the poorer. If I read this particular sex novel I should probably be bored and disgusted.'

not his book but the texts that it had revealed. For centuries, Christians had been taught that the Bible was the unchanging word of God. And now, apparently, here were all His other words.

And what fun they were. Since Hone's day, they have become even more fun, as more 'apocryphal' gospels and texts have been discovered, and their translations have become franker. We now know of apocryphal texts that tell of how dragons worshipped the young Jesus; texts in which Mary is fed by angels; texts that describe her youth and childhood; and one very engaging text in which Mary is capable of breathing fire. There are texts that explain how Herod's daughter was accidentally decapitated by her mother while worms poured out of Herod's mouth. There are texts that contain necrophilia and talking donkeys. There is one supremely pleasing text in which St John banishes bed bugs from a hotel, with full biblical bombast. Having spent half the night being bitten by the creatures, the holy John comes to the end of his tether and suddenly declares, 'I say unto you, O Bugs, behave yourselves, one and all, and leave your abode for this night and remain quiet in one place, and keep your distance from the servants of God.'[21] The bed bugs duly depart. And with them – and with all of these tales – went some of the unquestioned authority of the Bible.

There are certain themes within these apocryphal writings. Several of the later texts are clearly talking to stories within the Bible; some provide backstories to well-known characters in the gospels; others clear up biblical confusions or difficulties. Consider, for example, the tale of the camel and the needle's eye. In the tale in the Bible, Jesus states that it is 'easier for a camel to go through the eye of a needle, than for a rich man to enter into the kingdom of God'. It is a story that has distressed Christians (particularly the rich ones) for centuries.[22] This story pops up – and its more problematic aspects are dealt with – in the apocryphal book known as the *Acts of Peter and Andrew*. In this version, a rich man hears this biblical tale and, understandably, becomes angry.[23]

Happily, St Peter is ready to help (the apostles are often on hand to assist the affluent in these works). He calmly reassures the rich man that 'nothing is impossible with God'. Then he provides a vivid demonstration.

Seeing a camel coming, Peter demands a needle – just 'a needle with a small eye' – then sticks the needle in the ground and, in the name of Jesus Christ, commands the camel to go through its eye.[24] Sure enough, 'The eye opened like a gate and the camel passed through.' Peter repeats the trick twice more – once, for extra drama, with a 'defiled woman' sitting on top of the camel.[25] A few verses later, the rich man, amazed, promises to give all his wealth away. The story concludes with the apostles consecrating a church, and the rich man relieved of his anxiety about how a rich man like him is able to get to heaven. Perhaps not least because he now no longer is one.[26]

St Peter is a character who features heavily in the apocryphal writings, and in some of the most entertaining tales. The story of the sardine, for example, culminates with an even more dramatic resurrection competition between Peter and the sorcerer Simon. The son of an aristocratic woman has died, and she comes to Peter and begs for help. St Peter, ever the confident compère, turns to address the assembled crowd. 'Romans,' he says, 'let a righteous judgement now take place between me and Simon, and judge which of us believes in the living God, he or I.'[27] If Simon raises the dead man, then the crowd may 'believe in him as an angel of God.' But if Simon cannot and if, instead, Peter is able to 'restore the son alive to his mother . . . then you shall believe that [Simon] is a sorcerer and deceiver.'[28] The people of Rome agree – though, they also add that, if Simon wins and Peter fails, they will burn Peter alive. With such Christian feeling swelling in the breasts of the Romans, the contest begins. Needless to say, Peter wins.

As M. R. James pointed out, such stories are clearly implausible and many Christian historians have, for centuries, discounted them as absurd. Texts such as the *Infancy Gospel of James* or the

Infancy Gospel of Thomas were routinely dismissed and ignored by scholars, well into the second half of the twentieth century. One twentieth-century academic disparaged them as 'the schlock that is supposed to pass for "literature"' and added that it is 'mystifying, indeed, why serious scholars continue to talk about the pertinence of apocryphal material to the study of the New Testament.'[29] But this is to miss the point. Such texts matter not because they are believable – but because they were believed and read by Christians for centuries. It is understandable that some Christian historians may have wished to ignore them – but it is intellectually indefensible to do so. Do so and you are not writing history, but theology, with dates.

Moreover, when evaluating the apparent implausibility of apocryphal tales, it is worth remembering how implausible those tales that are contained within modern Bibles once seemed to many readers. Today, time and tradition and long handling have worn the tales of the Western Bible smooth; we do not notice their rough edges or inconsistencies. In the ancient world, these now familiar biblical tales had no such antique grandeur, no well-worn lustre. And classical critics duly attacked them mercilessly, in prose rich in synonyms of the word 'stupid'. 'Preposterous', snorts Porphyry when considering one biblical story; 'the absolute stupidity of it all', he scoffs at another. He accuses one revered Christian saying of being full of 'obscurity and stupidity' and another of being the sort of thing that 'no one is so uneducated or stupid' enough to believe. Celsus is blunter yet: he describes Christian stories as being the sort of thing that 'a drunken old woman would have been ashamed to sing . . . to lull a little child to sleep'.[30]

At times, these writers attacked particular stories in detail. In one of the lengthier surviving sections of Porphyry, he takes a shot at that miracle in which Jesus exorcises the demons from the possessed man, so causing them to enter that herd of pigs, which then runs down the hill and is drowned in the sea. Much to Porphyry's amusement.*

What 'a piece of unscrupulous nonsense', he writes. 'What a myth! What empty talk! What a clumsy, ridiculous story!'[31] Is this actually supposed to be true and not 'fiction'? Surely not, for in this tale there is so 'much to laugh at.'[32] Gathering himself, Porphyry then sets about a more systematic critique of the tale, attacking everything from its geography (there is no sea there, so how was it that 'all those swine came to be drowned, although it was a lake and not a great sea?') to the improbability of the story's agricultural setting (given the Jewish dietary laws on pork, he asks, 'How could there be so large a swineherd grazing in Judea?').

Porphyry also attacks its morals. What, he wonders, had the poor pigs done to deserve this? Why should Jesus drive the demons from one man, only to send them into helpless swine and, in the process, frighten the poor swineherds? It's all very well to free one man from demonic possession, but to release one man from invisible bondage only 'to place similar ties on others', and then 'to push fear into other men thereby' – that 'is unreasonable.'[33] Almost two thousand years later, the British philosopher Bertrand Russell, in his essay 'Why I Am Not a Christian', would find almost identical fault with the miracle. 'You must remember that He was omnipotent,' said Russell, 'and He could have made the devils simply go away; but He chose to send them into the pigs.'[34] Why?

Other critics took aim at other stories. Celsus, for example, vigorously attacked the Old Testament story of Creation – which he considered to be just as ludicrous. Some of his quibbles were practical – why, for example, did God request that light

---

* It is not absolutely certain that this ancient sceptic is Porphyry because, in the manuscript in which these criticisms are contained, he is not explicitly named as the author. However, there are good reasons for believing the fragments to represent his thought, and the current scholarly convention is to refer to these as being by him.

should appear right at the beginning of Creation? Surely an all-powerful, omniscient God 'did not use light from above, like people who borrow lamps from their neighbour'?[35] But his more powerful criticisms were philosophical.

Adam and Eve (or so some early Christians argued) had sinned in Eden when they ate from the tree of the knowledge of good and evil. In Christian interpretations, this moment would become known as 'the Fall' and would become one of profound intellectual importance in Western literature and philosophy, twining like a briar through the writings of Augustine, Aquinas, Milton, Malthus and many, many more. Classical authors, however, were deeply underwhelmed by this story. If an omnipotent God had made humans, Celsus argued, why did he not either make them flawless and without sin, or, if for some reason he chose to make them with sin (and, since he was omniscient, he must have known he was doing so), why did he then complain about their sinfulness afterwards?

'How can he repent when they become ungrateful and wicked and find fault with his own handiwork, and hate and threaten and destroy his own offspring?'[36] If this world and all that is in it 'are the Creator's works,' asked Celsus, 'how can it be that God should make what is evil?' Why do that? Why didn't this supposedly all-powerful god simply make mankind better? Or, having made them inadequately, why didn't he just force them to behave? If God was all-powerful, 'How can he be incapable of persuading and admonishing men?'[37] Later Christians might find their belief shaken by silly stories about bed bugs; for classical critics, the inconsistencies and absurdities within the Bible itself were a far more insurmountable barrier to belief. The Old Testament, wrote Celsus with scorn, was 'utter trash'.[38]

M. R. James would claim that the apocryphal stories were so silly that they would never have been included in any Bible: they had 'excluded . . . themselves' by their preposterousness. He was overconfident. That the apocryphal books were not contained within the Bible is true – though some had come close to being included. But that did not mean they were dismissed by Christians. Many had a far more profound influence, not merely on Christianity, but on Western morality, art and literature, than some of those contained within the Bible.

Consider, for example, the numerous apocryphal tales that relate to hell. To most people, the idea of a hell – a fiery place of everlasting punishment – feels integral to Christianity. It is nothing of the kind. For hell, in that sense, is more or less absent from the New Testament. This isn't clear if you read the Bible today, as the word 'hell' recurs repeatedly. '[I]f thy hand offend thee,' says Jesus in one translation, 'cut it off: it is better for thee to enter into life maimed, than having two hands to go into hell'.[39] But 'hell' is not actually what the original text says. The Greek word being translated, in this instance, is 'Gehenna', a valley outside Jerusalem. It was not a nice place – it was believed to have been a place of child sacrifice and, as Jesus says, 'Where their worm dieth not, and the fire is not quenched.'[40] But it was a very long way from hell in the complex sense that the modern mind imagines it. As one historian puts it: 'amazing as it may seem . . . it is quite evident that hell, as a place of individual, corporal and eternal torture . . . is absent from the New Testament.'[41]

It is not absent from the so-called apocrypha. Read these and, at last, you can see the hellfires starting to catch and kindle in Christianity. The *Apocalypse of Peter*, one of the earliest Christian descriptions of hell, dates to the second century and offers a symphony in sadism.[42] In its pages, the reader is taken on a brisk guided tour of hell, pausing as each torture is explained to the infernal tourist. The punishments are exquisitely apposite: blasphemers can be seen hanging by their tongues; women who 'adorned themselves for adultery' can be seen dangling by their hair over boiling mire; adulterers can be seen hanging by their 'feet' (a euphemism for genitalia).[43] This hideous imagery was, naturally, very popular: this text was considered for inclusion within the New Testament proper and, in fifth-century Palestine, pious Christians who went to church on Good Friday to meditate upon the Easter message would be read sections from its ghoulish verses.

The *Apocalypse of Peter* was followed by the similarly macabre *Apocalypse of Paul*, an invigorating read that offered another infernal tour, not to mention accounts of damned women being variously roasted in pits of fire (those were the 'whoremongers'), or having red-hot chains placed about their necks (the 'virgins which defiled their virginity'), or even suffering the baroque fate of being 'hung head downwards, torches burning before their faces, serpents girt about them, devouring them' (the women who had committed the similarly baroque, and very precise crime of having 'beautified themselves with paints and unguents [and then gone] to church to ensnare men').[44] The Church would eventually frown on such writings – the very titles of these books were, as one later decree put it, not merely to be abandoned by the Church, but actively eliminated by them. Rather ironically, this decree then added a line that would have been at home in those very hellscapes: these writings, and their authors, were to be 'damned in the unbreakable chains of anathema for eternity.'[45]

Such threats were to no avail. The Church might offer damnation, but the *Apocalypses* offered images of moneylenders standing for eternity in pus. There was no contest. From the moment of their creation, in the second century, such hellscapes were enormously popular, and they remained popular, despite later prohibitions, for centuries. They were read across the empire and beyond – in Rome, Syria and in Palestine; in Ethiopia and in North Africa and northern Europe.[46] They were translated into numerous languages – into Greek and Syriac and Coptic; into Arabic and Ethiopic and Latin.[47] They influenced Christian doctrine, morality, art and, above all, imagination. Later scholars might sniff at them, but they mattered. The cloths of European heavens were woven with the words of these apocrypha; the fires of its hells burned brighter with their images.[48]

Chapter Eight

FRUIT FROM A DUNGHILL

'Smart Gaulish professors are training the lawyers of Britain; even in Iceland there's talk of hiring rhetoricians'

Juvenal, Satire XV,
2nd century AD

Stand in ancient Alexandria in the summer, close your eyes and breathe in, and what you might have noticed, above all, was the smell. The smell was wonderful. Or, to be more precise, the smell of Alexandria was not wonderful; the smell was not appalling – and that, in itself, was wonderful.

Ancient cities stank. Rome might be famous today for the engineering brilliance of its sewers, for the magnificent architecture of the Cloaca Maxima, for drains so broad you could boat along them and sewers so wide you could drive a fully laden wagon of hay along them.[1] But even they were not enough to stop the stench of this city of a million bodies.* Rome's streets, as its satirists made clear, were a symphony of smells.

There was the smell of anxious men, sweating under their heavy woollen togas in the heat of the day; there was the stink of similarly sweaty animals, of horses and oxen, straining up streets, dragging carts of marble; there was the smell of food wafting from the pots – ancient takeaways – carried on the heads of slaves as they ran along, bringing hot meals to their masters; and there was the far less appealing smell of decomposing animals.[2] In the summer, things only got worse, as the air in cities filled with the heavy, dank smell of lakes and rivers as they dried out, their edges turning marshy in the heat, as everything, everywhere, started to rot.[3]

There was another kind of stale water to be smelt, too: that of the urine that swilled in massive jars at street corners. The jars

---

* As always, ancient estimates of number are just that – estimates. But a million is commonly agreed to be at least a reasonable figure for the population of Rome at its peak.

were kept for cleaning – nothing whitens a toga like urine – but, when they occasionally smashed, they merely added to the general filth, shattering and splashing entire streets (and unfortunate passers-by) in piss.[4] Richer citizens might try to smother such stenches with perfume, with cinnamon and lavender – but they filtered through nonetheless.[5]

But Alexandria was different. Admittedly, it still had bodies and filth and piss. But, despite its size – perhaps half a million inhabitants – and despite being constructed with its buildings so close together that they seemed to stand almost 'another on another', Alexandria didn't suffer from the stifling, stinking airs that made life in other cities so unbearable. Standing with its face to the Mediterranean and its back to a great lake topped up by the Nile, the air in Alexandria was always fresh, always moving. Sea breezes passed along its broad marble streets all summer long. As the geographer Strabo noted with admiration, 'the healthiness of the air is also worthy of remark', and, as a result of it, 'the Alexandrians pass the summer most pleasantly.'[6] Everyone considered the city to be a 'fount of health'.[7]

There were smells here, too – but pleasant ones. You could smell the world in this single city since, every day, by camelback and horseback, by boat and by barge, from India and Arabia, Somalia and China, a world of spice and scent was brought into Alexandria, filling its air with perfume.[8] Frankincense smouldered, constantly, on a thousand altars, and 'censers, filled with spices, breathed out a divine smell.'[9]

But, according to one fourth-century writer, there was yet another smell in Alexandria – the foetid stench of moral decay. Read the ferocious writings of a fourth-century Christian author and bishop named Epiphanius, and what you find is not an account of a city of handsome buildings and refreshing breezes, but of a place that is far darker, a place that demands such words as 'dirt', 'uncleanness', 'pollution' and 'defilement'.[10] Because, when he was a young man, Bishop Epiphanius had met a group of people in Alexandria whom he would remember for the rest of his life with horror. In his usual florid style, he described them as like 'fruit from a dunghill'; they were like scorpions; they were like a swarm of insects.[11] They were also sexually very attractive – and, given what happened next, that mattered.

Epiphanius' encounter with the dunghill had begun innocuously enough – even pleasantly. One day in Alexandria, he had been approached by some women who were, he writes, 'very lovely in their outward appearance'.[12] The attraction seems to have been mutual, for, as Epiphanius somewhat immodestly records, the women 'wanted me in my youth'.[13] However, their flirtation was – or so Epiphanius later said – far from innocent.

Precisely what happened next between Epiphanius and these women is difficult to say: we only have Epiphanius' record of it, and extracting information from the insults and the insect similes is not easy. One thing is clear: the sort of things the women got up to were things he considered to be so awful, so dangerous, that the outraged bishop felt he had to warn others about them. He would not, he writes, 'dare to utter the whole of this if I were not somehow compelled to.'[14] Still, having felt himself so compelled, the good bishop then braves the topic with detail, vigour and no lack of the word 'emission'.[15] And what slowly becomes clear is that, on that long-ago day in Alexandria, Epiphanius had stumbled on a secret sect.

In his breathless account, he explains what happens at a typical meeting. First, the women would lure young men in, with 'whichever is prettier flaunt[ing] herself as bait.'[16] As the gathering begins, the men and women – some of whom are married couples – first greet each other with a secret signal in which they 'clasp hands in supposed greeting', then 'men give women and women give men a tickling of the palm.'[17] Once everyone has been welcomed in, all the men and women would begin eating and drinking – the food at such events was always 'lavish', while the drinking (naturally) took the form of a 'bout'.[18] Such feasting was merely the start. The real action in this secretive ceremony only began once the 'overstuffed veins' of these worshippers had become warm with wine. That, Epiphanius wrote, was when these people would 'get hot for each other.'[19] At that moment, 'the husband will move away from his wife and tell her – speaking to his own wife –' to get up and 'perform The Love with the brother.'[20] This new 'wretched' couple then had to stand and, in front of the entire assembled group of worshippers, make love. According to Epiphanius, that was the very least of it. For these people then went on to do even worse things – some of which he reveals in revolting detail, and some of which he spares the reader. But then, the Bishop of Salamis – suddenly prudish – shuts down his narrative. There are, he says, some 'obscenities' that he will not go into.[21]

His disgust at the people performing this ceremony is not merely because their actions are, to him, repulsive. Almost more disturbing to him is the religion that they professed. For these perverted men and women considered themselves not to be part of any obscene unknown cult, nor any debauched Roman religion; nor were they members of any other pagan group.

Instead, they considered themselves to be Christian.

When Christians came to tell the story of how their tiny sect conquered the world, it would have two beginnings. There was the first beginning: the moment when Jesus was born in Bethlehem of a virgin. But then, almost as important, Christianity had a second, more bureaucratic, beginning, which came with the conversion of a Jewish tent-maker named Paul. At first, Paul was (famously) not entirely convinced by the Christian message. His initial reaction to this new sect was to persecute it, vigorously. Which was why, one day in around AD 40, Paul had set out to Damascus: he was hoping to find followers of Jesus, bind them and bring them back to Jerusalem. In the magnificent words of the King James Version, he was 'yet breathing out threatenings and slaughter against the disciples of the Lord'.[22]

But Paul never carried out this particular persecution. For, while he was on the road to Damascus, 'suddenly there shined round about him a light from heaven: And he fell to the earth, and heard a voice saying unto him, Saul, Saul, why persecutest thou me?'[23] God had spoken; Paul was converted; Christianity was changed forever. After this dramatic encounter, Paul went blind for three days, and was led into Damascus and taken to a house on Straight Street; when he recovered, he set out to spread the word with the zeal of the convert. To this day, Christians walk in his footsteps, marvel at his dedication, wonder at how far he travelled. And they are right to, for it has been calculated that Paul travelled 10,000 miles over land and sea to spread the Christian word.[24]

And yet, only to marvel at Paul's travels is also to miss the point. What was almost more remarkable than Paul's journeys was the breathtaking rise in infrastructure and transport that enabled him to make them: in other words, the roads, grain ships, seaways and highways of the Roman Empire. Read the accounts of Paul's travels one way, and they are a chronicle of awesome faith; read them another, and they are a chronicle of the even more awesome efficiency of Roman transport networks.

Paul might be famous for those 10,000 miles but, as the historian Wayne Meeks has pointed out, that distance is puny in comparison to the distances that others travelled in this period: the gravestone of a merchant found in Phrygia, in modern Turkey, records that he had travelled seventy-two times to Rome – a trip that is perhaps 2,000 km in either direction.[25] This is not to say that travel was wholly safe: it wasn't. People consulted interpreters of dreams about travel anxieties almost more than anything else, and not without cause: as the parable of the Good Samaritan clearly shows, being beaten up and left for dead while on the road was a well-known hazard.[26] But, nonetheless, in this period travel was being revolutionized. Within the empire, Meeks writes, people 'travelled more extensively and more easily than had anyone before them – or would again until the nineteenth century.'[27]

The Roman Empire was on the move, by land and river and sea. Not all of it: most people lived local, even parochial lives.* But those who did travel could go far. The white-flecked waters at the mouth of the harbour of Alexandria were passed, day and night, by the white sails of Roman ships. The boats might themselves be unglamorous but they were weighed down with the wealth of the world: with grain and linen, wine and oil, and, most precious of all, fragrance. Read a list of ancient trade tariffs and, through the dry legal prose, you can all but smell the empire's love of scent and exoticism: there you will find cinnamon and white pepper, myrrh and ginger, Indic spice and aloe, Barbary leaf and Babylonian furs; there is ivory and Indian iron, sardonyx and pearls, and emeralds and diamonds, as well as Indian lions ('and lionesses'), panthers ('male and female'), leopards, eunuchs and, finally, 'Indian hair'.[28] Bulky and big-bellied, these merchantmen were not as fast as the other ships, but they were more reliable. They were so stable that even emperors, with the entire imperial navy at their disposal, sometimes preferred to set to sea in them. 'Don't travel by galleys,' the emperor Caligula – in unusually helpful mood – had once warned a client king who was setting out to Palestine, 'but take one of our direct Italy–Alexandria merchant ships.'[29]

Roman writers tend to be surprisingly underwhelmed by all this. Feeling awed by those Roman roads that run across fields like, as Thomas Hardy had it, 'the pale parting-line in hair', tends to be a modern habit; Romans were not, in general, given to going into ecstasies over their transport infrastructure.[30] You are far more likely to find Roman authors expressing irritation with the shortcomings of this road, or the noise of that one, than

* One measure of this is dialect. In the twentieth century, travel became so expansive that accents – such as the mid-Atlantic – spread over oceans. In the Roman Empire, by contrast, for many people life was so local that if you look at inscriptions it is possible to see dialects changing as you walk. Leave a great city and, for every mile you travel, the style of inscriptions will become less 'correct'. (See MacMullen (1974), pp. 30–1.)

breathless admiration for the whole system. But even the Romans could, occasionally, be moved to praise their roads and not blame them. The construction of one new arterial road in Campania was, for example, so welcome that it moved one Roman author named Statius to poetry. He listed the builders' tasks: how they first dug furrows and trenches, then 'prepare[d] a basin . . . so that the foundations do not wobble.'[31] They are lines that have, admittedly, found their way into few ancient anthologies.

But there are far sillier things to eulogize than a nice firm road. Just as writers in the nineteenth and early twentieth century reveal a people marvelling at a world that is speeding up – at steamers that race across the oceans; at trains that can travel faster than fairies, faster than witches – so, just occasionally, do Roman writers express admiration for how their empire's infrastructure was changing the world. Statius sent the above poem to his friend with a note explaining that it should arrive more swiftly than usual. The marvellous new road meant that 'the very irksome delay' that used to affect all post, caused by the heavy sandy ground in that region, had now gone.[32] No longer did the hapless traveller have to drag along his cart as 'malignant Earth sucked in his wheels'; instead a route 'that used to wear out a solid day barely takes two hours.'[33]

Whether or not most Romans paused to think much about it, the scale of the trade that travelled through their empire by land and by sea was staggering. Archaeologists, who have used the number of shipwrecks found at the bottom of the Mediterranean as a guide to the number of ships that once sailed on its surface, suggest it was not until the nineteenth century that Mediterranean trade regained its Roman levels.[34] Greco-Roman traders gained such detailed knowledge of other lands that they could write authoritative guidebooks on the quality of the water in Indian ports and what sold well there (Italian wine was, apparently, considered a particularly exotic delicacy). International trade with the subcontinent grew so much that Roman writers fretted about the trade deficit that existed between it and Rome.

'At the very lowest computation, India, the Seres, and the Arabian Peninsula, withdraw from our empire one hundred millions of sesterces every year,' wrote Pliny, adding, primly, 'so dearly do we pay for our luxury and our women.'[35]

The number of coins in circulation increased in this period, as did the production of metal. Analysis of the ice caps of Greenland show that air pollution, caused by the smelting of such metals as lead, copper and silver, would not reach Roman levels again until the sixteenth or seventeenth century.[36] Another measure of the high levels of trade in this era is the amount of ancient packing material that remains – in other words, of Roman pots. Amphorae, which in Roman times were used to transport more or less everything, were produced on a colossal scale. To understand quite how colossal, travel to Rome, walk southwards down the Tiber from the Colosseum, and you will see a mound, patchily covered in grass. This fifty-metre-high hillock – which is known as Monte Testaccio – is made entirely from broken oil amphorae. Inside the mound lie the fragments of an estimated fifty-three million amphorae, in which an estimated six billion litres of oil were imported into Rome.[37]

Not only did people travel far; they also travelled fast. The speed of Roman travel, particularly for the wealthiest, was astonishing. Early in its imperial history, Rome's emperors had set up the Roman imperial post – probably in imitation of similar systems that had been read about – and envied – in ancient accounts about Persia. This was not a post system as modern minds might imagine it, to be used by everyone, but was for imperial messengers, and its infrastructure duly demonstrated imperial ambition and grandeur: every twenty-four miles or so was a rest station; at each station, forty of the finest, swiftest horses were stabled, along with a proportionate number of grooms. A courier could therefore arrive, switch horses and set off again, and travelling in this way might cover 'a ten days' journey in a single day' – in other words, it is now thought, 160 miles.[38]

As the historian Procopius explained, emperors had set such

a system up so that if there was a war, mutiny or any other disaster anywhere in the empire, the news could reach Rome fast – and it seems to have worked. The evidence for this is unusually good, because, while such disasters may have been unpleasant for the emperor experiencing them, they have been splendidly useful to later historians, since imperial deaths and assassinations tend to appear in histories with careful time stamps. They can thus be used to calculate how fast ancient travel could, in extremis, be. And the answer is: very fast indeed. After the death of Nero, for example, a messenger travelled from Rome to Northern Spain (a distance overland of around 1,800 km) in a breathless seven days. Probably that messenger did the bulk of the journey over the sea. Nonetheless, it is very, very fast.[39]

The results of all this travel could be seen everywhere. Stand in second-century Rome and – at least according to the rather xenophobic poet Juvenal – you would be hard-pressed to spot a native Roman there. Rome, he wrote, was a city full of foreigners. See that customs official over there? Egyptian. That slave over there, who's made millions? Another Egyptian. Remember that man who pipped you to the post when you applied for a job? He's a Greek. Then there were the Syrians, the Jews, and yet more Greeks who 'flock in from high Sicyon, or Macedonia's uplands, from Andros or Samos, from Tralles and Alabanda . . .'[40]

It wasn't just people who were on the move, either. Head to a fancy Roman dinner party and the supper on your plate could easily be as international as the guests reclining at your side, for, as one satirist put it, the 'bottomless gullet' and 'tireless gluttony' of Rome was perpetually on 'eager quest of dainties from all quarters'. A single gourmand might, for their dinner party, source 'a peacock from Samos, a woodcock from Phrygia, cranes of Media, a kid from Ambracia, a young tunny from Chalcedon, a lamprey from Tartessus, codfish from Pessinus, oysters from Tarentum, cockles from Sicily, a swordfish from Rhodes, pike from Cilicia, nuts from Thasos, dates from Egypt, acorns from Spain . . .'[41]

The plates such food was eaten off showed similarly international taste, and pottery made in Roman-era Tunisia has turned up in Iona, in Scotland.[42] Such volumes of trade could not take place without changing culture. And, looking at the writings of Romans from the first century BC onwards, there is clear evidence that it did. Diners from North Africa to Iona did not merely eat off the same plates as each other – increasingly, their conversation started to converge, too. The more affluent started to speak Latin – and to act Roman. Once, every place had been a world unto itself. Now, observed Juvenal, 'things are different: the whole world has its Greco-Roman culture. Smart Gaulish professors are training the lawyers of Britain; even in Iceland* there's talk of hiring rhetoricians.'[43] Later, diseases would show similar internationalism by moving along the same routes: one reason that the plague of Justinian spread so quickly in the sixth century is because it had Roman grain ships to board and Roman merchants to transport it.

Paul's divinely inspired journeys were immeasurably helped – and at many points entirely enabled – by this revolution in transport. When, in around AD 60, St Paul wished to set out on one of the longest legs of his journey, from Turkey to Rome, there is, as one historian has written, 'little doubt' that he travelled on a boat from a special fleet of Roman grain ships, 'designed and constructed by the Romans expressly to transport grain from the fertile land of the Nile to Italy, particularly to Rome'.[44] Similarly, as the Cambridge historian Tim Whitmarsh points out, when Paul headed into Galatia to convert the Galatians, his route – at least as recorded in the Bible – precisely

* The word in the Latin is *Thule*. It is a name that could be used to refer to specific places – though precisely where is not clear; Shetland, the Faroe Islands and even Iceland are possible – but it's probably more correct to think of it here as meaning simply 'somewhere very far north' – further north even than Britain.

followed the route of the Via Sebaste, built by the emperor Augustus.[45] God might be all-powerful, but his message has, historically, been considerably helped on its way by well-paved roads and fine merchant sailing fleets.

Christians tend to praise St Paul for spreading Christianity. Understandably: humans tend to look for human causes of things. If you were to ask one of those Gaulish professors what he was doing in Britain, doubtless he would have answered by explaining that he wished to bring Roman law to the benighted barbarians there; similarly, had you asked a Roman rhetorician why they were in Iceland, they would no doubt have offered their own personal reasons.

But such accounts would slightly miss the point. Laws, customs and diseases – all were transforming the world in this era. But they were only able to do so because Roman roads and Roman transport and Roman peace were opening the world up in a way never seen before. Globalization was underway. And one of the things that globalized fastest of all in this period was religion. Lighter than spice, more profitable than gold, gods were spreading along the arteries of empire.

Chapter Nine

GO INTO ALL THE WORLD

'I, Jesus, son of the carpenter Joseph, declare that I have sold my slave, Judas by name, to you.'

Jesus sells a man into slavery,
Acts of Thomas, 2, 3rd century AD

Sailing to India might have been common in the ancient world. That did not mean it was easy. Read a guidebook produced by one ancient merchant who made the journey and it is filled with horrors, with lurid tales of the 'rascally' locals who will menace you; the rough seas that will shake your ship; and the serpents with 'blood-red eyes' that will surge towards you from the shore.[1]

One of the most intriguing ancient travelogues was written by the navigator Cosmas 'Indicopleustes' – Cosmas 'India sailor' – who went from Alexandria to Sri Lanka in the sixth century. In his *Christian Topography*, Cosmas recounted the many marvels one might meet on this magnificent journey. He is impressed by rumours of the unicorn ('a terrible beast and quite invincible'), describes the pepper tree in detail (it is 'a deep green colour') and is repelled by the taste of dolphin meat ('rank').[2] He becomes particularly animated by the elephant trade in India. These animals, he observes, are priced by height, and they are highly valued, partly because Indian kings bought them to use in war – but also because the kings simply liked to watch them fight, as they 'thrash each other with their trunks till one of them gives in.'[3]

But while some things seem to catch Cosmas' attention, even to surprise him, others he regards with absolute complacency. When he finally reaches Sri Lanka, where the pepper plant grows and the sea gleams blue, he not only finds large numbers of Christians already living there, but he also comes across a long-established Christian church and 'moreover a bishop, who is appointed from Persia.'[4] Some might have been surprised at the presence of Christians at the southern tip of India – but not Cosmas. He greets the Christian presence there with absolute equanimity. As he writes, did the Lord not ordain that 'the Gospel shall be preached throughout the whole world'?[5] Well, here is merely proof of that command coming true. 'The whole earth has been filled with the doctrine of the Lord Christ,' he writes, 'and is still being filled.' He himself is able to vouch for this 'from what I have seen and heard in the many places which I have visited.'[6]

Had Cosmas been able to understand the texts that those Christians used, he might have been a little less satisfied. For almost certainly the Christians whom Cosmas saw in India were Thomas Christians, a group influenced by an ancient text known as the *Acts of Thomas*. In this text, Jesus sells a man into slavery, is described as having a twin brother and rants, at length, about the ghastliness of children.

'Go into all the world and proclaim the gospel to the whole creation.'[7] These, so the Bible said, were the words of Jesus to his disciples. The followers of Christ evidently listened, and obeyed, for Christianity spread far and it spread fast. By the third century, it had reached Egypt and Ethiopia and the Iranian plateau; and it kept going, onwards, eastwards, to Kyrgyzstan, Turkmenistan and to China.[8] By AD 650, the Church of the East had bishops as far east as Samarkand; envoys from Kyrgyzstan would later appear in Byzantium, much to the surprise of the locals, with crosses tattooed on their foreheads.[9] By the year 1000, there were churches in Nineveh, Isfahan and Herat. Eastern Christians were ministered to by priests with such names as Banus the Uigurian and helped by laymen called such things as Kiamata of Kashghar and Tatta the Mongol.[10] In the Middle Ages, the Eastern Christian church – not the Western – was the most widespread in the world.[11]

This can seem surprising to those raised in the West. Western Christianity, with its paintings of pale-faced saints and honey-haired Jesuses, has an almost unshakeable habit of thinking of

Christianity as Western. It was not. As historians have long pointed out, when Christ told his followers to spread the word to the ends of the earth, he was standing on a hill in western Asia and speaking Aramaic as he did so.[12] Many of Christianity's greatest early thinkers were from Egypt and North Africa, not Europe. Yet Western Christianity, which read most of its holy texts first in Greek, then later in Latin, long showed a resolute amnesia to such simple truths. In the nineteenth century, there was a 'rediscovery of the ancient Eastern Christians', as the scholar Aziz Atiya put it – but the 'rediscovery', it should be noted, was from the point of view of Western scholars: Egyptian Copts had not, on the whole, forgotten that they existed.[13]

It is easy to smile at the geographical misconceptions of ancient writers, but each age has its own geographical blindness. Considering 'the East' to be somewhere peculiarly remote and impossibly hard to reach has, perhaps, been a blindness of the West. The historian Philip Jenkins has offered a simple calculation that shows this beautifully. If you head east from Jerusalem, Jenkins wrote, you reach Baghdad in just 600 miles, Tehran in less than 1,000 and Samarkand in 1,850. Paris or London are, by contrast, over 2,000 miles away.[14] And, for much of the period of Roman imperium, these western areas were far more forbidding and foreign.

In those days, the unimaginable other was less to be found to the east of the empire than in its north-west, on that damp and dagger-shaped island known as Britain. This was widely considered to be an appalling and uncivilized place, used by the Roman poet Virgil as a byword for the ends of the earth.[15] In this ghastly land, as the geographer Strabo observed, 'the sun is to be seen for only three or four hours round about midday' and the inhabitants were alarmingly tall – 'half a foot above the tallest people' in Rome – and unattractive with it. Strabo had once seen some of them in Rome; they were, he recalls with disdain, 'bandy-legged and presented no fair lines anywhere else in their figure.' The only good thing one might say about the Britons was that they were better than the Irish, who Strabo can barely even be bothered to lift his pen to comment upon. 'Concerning this island,' he writes, 'I have nothing certain to tell, except that its inhabitants are more savage, since they are man-eaters as well as heavy eaters.' And, he adds, they have sex with their mothers. Or so they say.[16]

But, though Christianity spread, it did not stay the same. Were a traveller to walk east or south from Alexandria, they would have been hard pressed not to notice the religion changing, again and again. In Ethiopia, for example, Pontius Pilate was looked upon with favour – and is to this day revered as a saint.[17] The sacred books were different, too, for Christians there (as they did elsewhere in the ancient world) read a canon that included an extensive list of the wicked things in which angels inducted mankind, including the sinful habit of wearing bracelets and the 'beautifying of the eyelids'. It went on: 'Semjâzâ taught enchantments, and root-cuttings, Armârôs the resolving of enchantments, Barâqîjâl [taught] astrology, Kôkabêl the constellations, Ezêqêêl the knowledge of the clouds . . .'[18]

The ancient traveller might also have come across an engaging Christian sect known as the Ophites, who were said to believe that Christ had come – but that he was a snake. Thus, as one Christian reported, these people 'honour the serpent and regard him as Christ, and have an actual snake . . . in a basket of some sort.'[19] This group of Christians had developed a complex theology and various proofs for this claim: was not there a snake in the garden of Eden? Had it not shown mankind the route to knowledge? And are our intestines not shaped like a snake? The truth was clear: Christ is a snake.[20] During their worship, it was said that these Christians 'spread loaves around on a table, and call the snake to come; and when the den is opened it comes out. And then the snake – which comes up of its own accord and by its villainy . . . crawls onto the table and coils up on the loaves.' Once the bread has been 'consecrated by its coiling', these Christians 'offer a hymn to the father on high' and 'so conclude their mysteries.'[21]

Meanwhile, in other places, there were those who not only burned incense to Jesus, but who burned incense to the Greek philosopher Pythagoras and the poet Homer too, worshipping them alongside Christ. These people – or so it was said – claimed to have a portrait of Jesus painted by Pilate, and they put up portraits of 'certain philosophers besides – Pythagoras, Plato, Aristotle, and the rest', which they hung alongside their portraits of Jesus. 'And after setting them up they worship them and celebrate heathen mysteries.'[22] Elsewhere, the traveller might have come across yet other Christians, who – eschewing the male-only hierarchy that many Christian groups had already developed – recognized women as bishops. Or they might have come across a sect of ancient Christians who believed that Joseph had made Jesus, that angels had made the world and that Jewish customs should be preserved, and so insisted circumcision should still be practised on all adult male converts. That particular group did not spread very far.[23]

Almost everything that could vary among Christians did vary, from methods of worship, to beliefs, to personal conduct. The sexual habits of the Christians that Epiphanius wrote about so vividly, the Borborites, would become infamous.[24] They were accused of using their religion as a means to seduce women, by claiming that sex was an essential part of worship. 'Have sex with me,' these Christian men allegedly said, 'so that I may offer you'.[25] As it happened, this particular Christian sect also believed not in one divine being, but in 365 (called 'archons', in the jargon), and so the men had to have sex 365 times, to honour each one of those divine beings. For reasons that remain theologically obscure (but that can cynically be guessed at), for full enlightenment, the entire process then had to be repeated. Once this 730-stage worship had been performed, a man in this sect then considered himself able to say, 'I am Christ, for I have descended from on high through the names of the 365 archons!'[26]

The differences continued. Take, for example, the Origenists, Christians who rejected both marriage and resurrection, and whose sexual activity was (at least according to Epiphanius) 'incessant'. These Christians, he wrote, used to 'soil their bodies, minds and souls with unchastity'. They dressed themselves up as monks and nuns, and then, 'as Onan coupled with Tamar and satisfied his appetite but did not complete the act', so these Christians did the same with their 'nuns'.[27] Such stories, entertaining though they are, should be read with a certain suspicion: Epiphanius is a witness to treat with caution at the best of times, and sexual immorality was a staple criticism that was levelled at so-called heretics.[28] But, then, given the vast losses of texts that occurred, the historian is forced to use such sources: there is so little else left.

There were other slanders, too – darker ones. The Greeks and Romans, when they heard that Christians were told to 'love one another' and that they drank the blood of their saviour, were suspicious about what went on during Christian worship.[29] But, if Epiphanius is to be believed, some Christians deserved such censure. It was said that the Borborites used to abort then eat human foetuses: 'They extract the foetus at the stage which is appropriate for their enterprise, take this aborted infant, and cut it up in a trough with a pestle. And they mix honey, pepper, and certain other perfumes and spices with it to keep from getting sick, and then all the revellers in this [herd] of swine and dogs assemble, and each eats a piece of the child with his fingers.'[30]

Had our imaginary ancient traveller, on this tour of the ancient world, then turned towards Syria, he or she would have found a rich source of Christian differences – though, of course, Syrians would have baulked at the idea that it was their Christianity that was 'different'. In Syriac Christianity, for example, there were twelve magi, rather than the three of Western tradition. (The number and names of the magi varied widely from country to country – which is hardly surprising, since the Bible doesn't specify either how many there were or what they were called.)

So, while Christians in the West know the magi as Caspar, Melchior and Balthazar, in a Georgian manuscript they were called Wiscara, Melikona and Walastar, and in Persia they became Amad, Zud-Amad and Drust-Amad.[31] Other differences were greater still: one enormously popular version of Christianity that flourished in Syria rejected the idea of bodily resurrection, blended Christianity with astrology and followed a leader who, or so his critics muttered, 'did not read the prophets but the books of the Zodiac.'[32]

Other Syrian differences were theologically more profound. The Holy Spirit – which in many Western traditions is translated as 'he' – in the early Syriac tradition was at times rendered decisively as female. An Old Syriac translation of the gospels refers to the Holy Ghost with the word 'she': 'she shall teach you everything.'[33] In an ancient ode that dates back perhaps to the end of the first century, the Holy Spirit appears again as female: 'The Holy Spirit is she who . . .' reads one line.[34]

It is possible to argue that this was a mere grammatical glitch: there is no neuter in Syriac and so each word, even the word for something as abstract as a spirit, has to be one thing or the other, and the authors happened to plump for female. (On some occasions it is changed, in Old Syriac, to 'he'.) But Syrian Christians don't seem to have regarded it as a glitch. In one poem known as the Hymn of the Pearl, God is described as 'King of Kings' while the Holy Spirit is described as the 'Queen of the East' and 'Mother' of the soul.[35] One influential Syriac Christian author wrote lyrically about how a man 'loveth and honoureth God his Father, and the Holy Spirit his Mother.'[36] There is an ancient precedent for this: in the gospel known as the Gospel of the Hebrews (one of many gospels that was lost and is known today only from fragments), Jesus speaks of 'my mother, the Holy Spirit'.[37]

Nor was God always as overwhelmingly masculine in Syriac traditions as he was in Western ones. The *Odes of Solomon*, beautiful poetry used by Syriac Christians, contain lines that can feel, today, strikingly unorthodox – though they were unlikely to have been considered such when they were written, in the second century or so. In one ode, God is represented as having full breasts that are milked by his son and by the Holy Spirit: 'The Son is the cup, and He who was milked is the Father: and the Holy Spirit milked Him: because his breasts were full, and it was necessary for him that His milk should be sufficiently released; and the Holy Spirit opened His bosom and mingled the milk from the two breasts of the father.'[38]

The influence of some of these other Christianities seeped westwards over the centuries. What has been described as 'the earliest Christian hymnbook' was written in Asia, in Syriac, in around the first or second century; the ancient sounds of Syrian music, it is thought, echoed into the air for centuries.[39] It now seems possible, perhaps even probable, that Coptic monks travelled to the British Isles. Long before the so-called Apostle to the English, Augustine of Canterbury, arrived in England at the end of the sixth century, Coptic missionaries had arrived here from Egypt. The graves of seven Coptic monks have been found in Northern Ireland, and it is argued that hints of Coptic Christianity can be seen in Irish architecture and ceremonies. Scholars have speculated that the famous glittering swirls of Irish handicraft from this period 'and their unrivalled illuminations' might 'be traced to the influence of Egyptian missionaries.'[40] It is tantalizing to think how different the world of the West might have been if the Christianity of these Egyptian missionaries, rather than that of Roman Christianity, had taken hold in Britain, and the damp island at the west of Europe had become a stronghold of Coptic Christianity rather than Catholicism.

Difference flourished, everywhere. Even attitudes to difference itself varied. By the third century, the form of Christianity that would later gain supremacy within the Roman Empire had long been pouring odium on writings that it considered heretical, apocryphal, or pagan. But other Christians were far more liberal. In second- and third-century Alexandria, there flourished a group of so-called 'academic Christians', who acted exactly as that name implies. Far from arguing against the 'wicked' and 'extremely impious' doctrines of Greek philosophy, this appealing group welcomed all intellectual speculation.

These Christians openly blended Christianity with Platonism and, as the historian David Brakke has written, 'tolerated and even encouraged philosophical speculation and diversity of opinion on certain Christian teachings.' The academic Christians 'sought to discover Christian truth wherever it might manifest itself literarily, including pagan literature, Jewish writings of all kind, and Christian books that their fellow Christians may have considered suspect'.[41] They resisted the very idea of a closed canon of 'acceptable' books. The response to this liberal attitude was, naturally, ferocious: hostile Christians started to harden the idea that some books were unacceptable, and even argued that academic speculation itself was unnecessary. The very word 'teacher' started, in this anti-intellectual atmosphere, to become suspect.[42] The attitudes of the academic Christians were, eventually, suppressed.

And had our ancient traveller from Alexandria continued east and then east again, he or she might have come, eventually, to the same place as Cosmas Indicopleustes: to the Thomas Christians of India, whose Christianity was infused by the *Acts of Thomas*. It is, to this day, an interesting text. Near its opening, Jesus is seen giving the command to his followers that they should go forth into the world and spread his word. So far, its narrative feels familiar. But almost immediately it starts to surprise, for Thomas – who in this telling is surlier than apostles usually are (and who is also, somewhat alarmingly, referred to as Jesus' 'twin') – refuses.* 'Wherever you wish to send me, send me,' he says, 'but elsewhere. For I am not going to the Indians.'[43]

---

* It is, as a recent commentary on the *Acts of Thomas* mutedly put it, 'not clear in which way [Thomas] is supposed to be the twin of Christ.' Commentators resist the idea that the men are actual twins – understandably, for the theological

Jesus, however, is not to be put off. At that moment, he happens to notice a merchant walking about nearby; the merchant has, by good luck, come from an area near modern Afghanistan, to find a carpenter.[44] The resourceful Jesus approaches him. Need a carpenter? he asks. The merchant replies, 'Yes.' Well, says Jesus, 'I have a slave who is a carpenter, and I wish to sell him.' Jesus points out Thomas, who, blithely unaware, is visible in the distance. The Indian merchant buys him immediately and Jesus, with bureaucratic efficiency, writes the merchant a bill of sale, which reads: 'I, Jesus, son of the carpenter Joseph, declare that I have sold my slave . . . to you, Abban, a merchant.' Things move quickly: 'When the purchase was completed the Saviour took . . . Thomas, and led him to Abban, the merchant.' Thomas now accepts his fate, and boards a ship bound for India.[45]

The narrative continues in a similarly eventful manner, taking in numerous miracles and some surpassingly beautiful poetry. One of its most striking scenes takes place at a wedding. As the scene opens, a young royal couple are about to consummate their marriage. The groom, thinking that he is going to meet his wife, 'raised the curtain of the bridal chamber, that he might bring the bride to himself.'[46] He is, to say the least, surprised to find Jesus already in bower with his wife. Jesus, it transpires, has materialized there so that he can give the newly married couple a lecture on celibacy – and then promptly does so.

Settling himself down on their marriage bed, Jesus tells the now slightly less happy couple to sit on two nearby couches, then proceeds to explain, at length, why they should not have sex. His reasoning is forceful. Children are without exception awful, Jesus says: they 'become either lunatics or half-withered or crippled or deaf or dumb or paralytics or idiots', while their

problems that this would raise hardly bear thinking about. Instead, it is argued that the two merely look similar, and that this gospel simply reflects 'the idea that Jesus is able to appear in whatever body he likes'. It is a mark of how confusing the entire story has seemed to many readers that this feels like the least confusing option.

tedious parents become 'grasping'.[47] If you do have children, then there will be no rest for either party, for children inevitably do 'unprofitable and abominable works. For they will be detected either in adultery or in murder or in theft or in unchastity, and by all these you will be afflicted.' Therefore refrain, Jesus warns them, 'from this filthy intercourse.'[48]

Western Christians might have long disdained such stories, but Thomas Christians defend the antiquity of their religion. And theirs is, arguably, a claim that is supported by archaeology, for large numbers of ancient stone crosses have been found in numerous places on the south-west coast of India that have been dated to as early as the second century.[49] Which, if true, would make them older than any Western cross.[50]

Clockwise from top left: **1. Asclepius, Roman, 2nd century AD, but after a Greek original of the 5th century BC; 2. Wandering philosopher, probably representing Apollonius of Tyana, late 2nd century AD; 3. Detail of Christ, sarcophagus, Rome, *c.* AD 300**

As cynical classical authors didn't hesitate to point out, the ancient world offered numerous long-haired healers who claimed to be able to do miraculous deeds.

From top: 4. Dionysus is born from Zeus' thigh, Roman sarcophagus, *c.* AD 190; 5. Dionysus' first bath, mosaic, Cyprus, 4th century AD

The idea that a god might be born from a mortal woman was – as early Christian authors readily admitted – not a new one. When we say that Jesus 'was produced without sexual union,' wrote one Christian, 'we propound nothing different from what you believe regarding those whom you esteem sons of Jupiter.'

6. Votive relief to the hero Amynos, Greece, 4th century BC

No ailment, including varicose veins, was too minor to take to the gods in the hope of a cure. A set of 4th-century BC inscriptions gives a sense of the breadth of Asclepius' powers, as supplicants thank the god not only for curing blindness and lameness, but also for ridding them of lice, pus and worms.

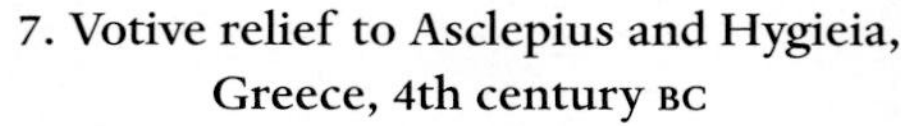

7. Votive relief to Asclepius and Hygieia, Greece, 4th century BC

Asclepius brought not only healing, but comfort. In one 3rd-century BC text, a supplicant praises Asclepius for the 'diseases that thou didst wipe away, Lord, by laying on us thy gentle hands'.

8. Plaque depicting a woman giving birth, Roman, 4th century BC–3rd century AD

Childbirth was perilous for mother and child – and doctors did not always improve matters. As one ancient gynaecological treatise recorded with disapproval, some advised that to assist the birthing mother, someone should 'put his hands under her armpits and lift and shake her vigorously'.

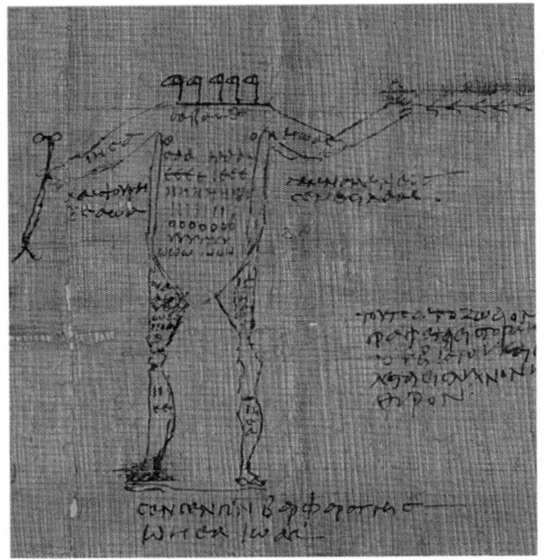

9. Illustration from a magical manual, Graeco-Roman Egypt, 4th century AD

The *Greek Magical Papyri* are strikingly atmospheric: some are stained with wax-drippings, perhaps from candles used in ancient ceremonies; others have fantastical drawings. This one is next to a spell advising that 'this figure is to be inscribed on a piece of clothing belonging to one who has died violently, and is to be cast into a pure lamp'.

10. Wall painting of a religious ceremony, Boscotrecase, Italy, 1st century BC

Roman religious ceremonies were recorded in beautiful and intricate frescoes, as depicted in this one, from Boscotrecase, near Pompeii.

11. Roman gemstones featuring Serapis, Anubis and a cock-headed anguipes, 2nd–3rd century AD

Gemstones may have been worn as rings or pendants to act as amulets. Many of them show a blending of Greek, Roman and Egyptian ideas.

Clockwise from top left:
12. The raising of Lazarus, ivory casket, Italy, 4th century AD; 13. Miracle of the loaves and the fishes, catacomb of Via Anapo, Rome, 3rd century AD; 14. The miracle of the loaves and the turning of water into wine, wooden panel, Basilica of Saint Sabina, Rome, 5th century AD

Jesus is frequently shown holding a wand when he is performing miracles in ancient Christian images.

15. The Annunciation, portal of the Marienkapelle, Würzburg, Germany, 15th century

Opinions on the mechanics of Mary's impregnation by the Holy Ghost differed: some thought that it had taken place through Mary's ear, an idea vividly depicted here. Look closely and it is possible to see the fetus of Jesus, halfway down the tube emanating from God's mouth.

16. The Annunciation, detail from an altarpiece by Nicolas of Verdun, 12th century

Another interpretation, depicted in this 12th-century enamel, was that the divine *logos* entered Mary through her eyes.

17. Salome, with hands severed, extends arms towards angel, miniature from a Book of Hours, France, 15th century

Many in the ancient world were sceptical about Mary's virginity. In one early Christian text, a woman named Salome declares that, 'unless I thrust in my finger, and search for the parts, I will not believe that a virgin has brought forth.' Her hand is promptly burned off.

18. The Flight into Egypt, detail from a fresco by Giotto, 14th century

Some ancient Christian texts expanded on the story of the flight into Egypt. In one such ancient text, Joseph grumbles at the food there, then casts doubt on Jesus' parentage. 'I have thought in my heart', he says to Mary, 'that perhaps I had intercourse with you while drunk.'

From top: **19. Simon Magus and the Devil, stone capital, France, 12th century; 20. The fall of Simon Magus, Italy, 13th century**

The duel that took place between the 'heretic' Simon Magus and St Peter involved a talking dog, a resurrected sardine and the gruesome death of Simon Magus – and provided rich pickings for medieval artists.

Clockwise from top left: 21. Helios driving his chariot, Troy, 3rd century BC; 22. 'Jesus-Helios', 3rd century AD, Rome; 23. Fresco of Jesus Christ, Rome, 4th century AD; 24. Apollo, Roman floor mosaic, 3rd century, Tunisia

Deified emperors such as Augustus, and gods such as Sol Invictus, were often shown wearing a 'radiate' crown with rays emanating from it. So much Christian imagery was so strikingly sun-related – they worshipped a 'God of Light' while facing towards the east, and did so especially on a Sun-day – that one early Christian was moved to deny that they were sun-worshippers.

25. The Nativity, detail from a gospel, Armenian, 15th century

The ox and ass images from the nativity come not from the Bible, but from another text called the *Infancy Gospel of James*.

26. Jesus quarrels with a teacher, illustration from a gospel, Austria, *c.* 1340

Early gospels feature Jesuses who differ markedly from the gentle Jesus, meek and mild, preached in Sunday schools today.

27. Jesus exorcises the Gerasene demon, 10th century

The miracle in which Jesus exorcises a demon and casts it into some nearby swine caused puzzlement among classical critics: why should the swine and the swine-herd suffer?

From top: 28. The Last Supper, miniature, Syria, 13th century; 29. Baptism of Christ, Biruni's *Chronology of Ancient Nations*, 14th century

The imagery of Christ and Christianity changed depending on where they were drawn and by whom, as these images show.

From top: 30. Hell, miniature from St Augustine _City of God_, French, 15th century; 31. Aeneas in the Underworld, miniature, Italian, 15th century

When Christians such as Augustine imagined the torments of the damned, they were following in a long tradition. As Virgil wrote in the 1st century BC, 'each of us undergoes his own purgatory.'

From top: 32. Pages from the Nag Hammadi texts, Egypt, 4th century AD; 33. Creation of Eve, Michelangelo, Sistine Chapel, Vatican, early 16th century

The Nag Hammadi gospels offered glimpses into versions of Christianity in which Eve was much less submissive than in better-known versions.

Clockwise from top left: 34. Isis and the infant Horus, Egypt, 4th century BC; 35. Isis and Horus, Hellenistic-Roman, 4th century AD; 36. Virgin and Child, miniature from the Book of Kells, Irish/Scottish, early 9th century

The goddess Isis was commonly shown feeding her son Horus. It is thought that images of Mary nursing Jesus, as seen here in the Book of Kells, were influenced by such images of Isis.

37. Constantine ordering the burning of Arian books, manuscript, 9th century AD

In a typically peppery letter, the emperor Constantine ordered that, 'If anyone is found guilty of concealing such books [by Arius] and of not having immediately denounced and burnt them, then death shall be his penalty and decapitation.'

38. Mosaic, Sant'Apollinare Nuovo, altered 6th century

At times, the books and images of heretics were destroyed and defaced. Here, heretical hands remained after the mosaic was altered.

39. The Three Magi worship the fire stone, miniature, Marco Polo, French, 15th century

Marco Polo recounts a Persian story that told how the three magi, after visiting Jesus, were given a stone by him. Unimpressed, they threw it into a well, whereupon a flame came down from heaven and struck the well. The magi collected some of the fire, carried it home and worshipped it evermore.

40. *The Nativity*, Follower of Fra Angelico, Italy, 15th century

Many medieval paintings contain images that may have been influenced by so-called 'apocryphal' works. The image of Jesus being born in a cave – a common image in art – is found in the *Infancy Gospel of James*.

Chapter Ten

IN EDEN

'They are possessed with a strange notion that they are the only true Christians in the world.'

Father Jerome Lobo considers Ethiopian Christians,
Voyage to Abyssinia, 17th century AD

In the autumn of 1950, the explorer Wilfred Thesiger arrived in the southern marshlands of Iraq. These marshes, which are washed by the Euphrates and Tigris rivers, are believed by some to be the location of the biblical Eden. And, for the forty-year-old (and rather grouchy) Thesiger, this was an Eden of sorts. As he later wrote, here, 'thank God, was no sign of that drab modernity which, in its uniform of secondhand European clothes, was spreading like a blight across the rest of Iraq.'[1] What Thesiger found instead was a way of life that had barely changed for centuries. It was a place that would leave him with memories of 'firelight on a half-turned face, the crying of geese, duck flighting in to feed, a boy's voice singing somewhere in the dark, canoes moving in procession down a waterway, the setting sun seen crimson through the smoke of burning reedbeds . . .'[2]

And he saw something else, too. There, in the marshes, where men moved about on boats waterproofed with bitumen that bubbled out of the ground to form molten pools, he had met people he called the Sabaeans.[3] They were the boatbuilders of the area, and instantly recognizable because of their large beards and red-and-white checked headcloths. Their religion, too, was distinctive. Unlike the other people who lived in the area, they were not Muslim; instead, they 'practised baptism by immersion every Sunday' and baptized themselves again if they felt that they had incurred any other kind of pollution.[4] They also talked about John the Baptist, knew who Jesus was and worshipped a 'Supreme Being'. For all of these reasons, as Thesiger tartly observed, 'ill-informed Europeans' assumed that they were a kind of Christian. They were not, he concluded. They were, instead, 'pagan'.

It is hardly surprising that those ill-informed Europeans were confused. The religion these people followed is called Mandaeism and it is in some ways similar to Christianity – but also profoundly different from it. Dating it is difficult: some say it is as old as Christianity; others that it is later; others that it is far older. Certainly its stories are ancient: Mandaeans believe in Adam and in Noah, and in John the Baptist, and their texts mention Jesus. But in this religion while John the Baptist is revered, Jesus is not. Indeed, far from being considered God on earth, Jesus is instead considered to be a fraud, a sorcerer and worthy of contempt: the 'false messiah'.[5] One Mandaean text refers to him as 'the wizard Messiah, son of the spirit of Lie who has given himself out to be [a] god.'[6]

There are echoes of Christian tales in Mandaean ones – but these tales are subtly, at times dramatically, different. In the Bible, for example, John baptizes Jesus in the Jordan. He does so in the Mandaean tradition too, but here the scene is considerably less serene. In it, John is instructed to 'Baptize the Liar in the Jordan', then 'take him up the bank and let him stand there.'[7] In another Mandaean text, John even has a set-to with Jesus: 'Thou hast lied to the Jews,' he tells Jesus, 'and hast deceived men and priests!'[8]

To find such religions is, as the diplomat Gerard Russell, who studied Mandeanism, once put it, like finding 'that the worship of the goddess Aphrodite was still continuing on a remote Greek island . . . or that followers of the god Mithras were still exchanging ceremonial handshakes in subterranean Roman chapels.'[9] It is, in other words, like finding a living relic.

History, it is often said, is one damn thing after another. In truth, it is not: it is far more often one damn thing before another. Things happen forwards; but history is then written backwards. Historians begin in the present, and trace the roots of the present in the past. This is not a new habit. One of the first histories ever written, by Herodotus of Halicarnassus, did this explicitly: as its enormously lengthy first sentence explained, its aim was to look at the conflicts between the Greeks and 'barbarians', and 'especially to show why the two peoples fought with each other.'[10] The historian begins with something in the present, then hunts for its origins in the past.

This has tended to happen with Christianity. The historian has, for centuries, seen the magnificent, monolithic Catholic Church that in the end came to dominate Europe, hunted for it at the beginning of the story, found it – and then written about it at length, often to the expense of the alternatives. The historian David Brakke has likened writing about early Christianity to writing about a race whose result is known: it is so hard to pay serious attention to any of the other contenders; they seem so clearly preordained to lose.

But, as is now realized, this is not true. Heretics were not preordained to fail and as sects they were not manifestly lesser. The scholarly mood towards heretics and heresy has changed. The writings of the heretics – once derided as 'shit' in every sense – are now studied seriously. Scholars now talk about 'early Christianities' rather than 'early Christianity'. And, where once Christian writers used to describe heresies as 'weeds' and 'tares' attacking the 'true crop' of orthodox Christianity, today more equitable agricultural metaphors are offered. As one historian recently put it, 'The overall picture of Christianity in the second century resembles a field of competing saplings more than a central tree (orthodoxy) surrounded by deviant offshoots (heresies).'[11] And some of these variants flourished for well over a millennium – in places, they still do today.

Consider the Ethiopian *Book of the Cock*. This sacred text explains how Jesus, not long before he was crucified, had resurrected a cockerel from a stew that had been placed before him on the table at dinner.[12] Merely by touching his meal, Jesus caused the bird to stand up, once again whole, once again alive.[13] Having escaped from the dinner table, the resurrected bird is then charged with setting off to spy on Judas. A little later, the cock returns to Jesus and explains to him what Judas has planned for him; whereupon the disciples weep and Jesus sends the bird to the sky for a thousand years. The Western tradition might disdain this story, but a Victorian traveller to Ethiopia found that it was still being read in Ethiopia, on Maundy Thursday; to this day, the book has a 'privileged place in the liturgy of the Ethiopian church.'[14]

Similarly, the *Acts of Thomas*, the book that tells of how the apostle Thomas travelled to India to spread the word of Jesus, was disdained as drivel – and worse – by Western Christians. But it is worth remembering Thomas Christians still exist to this day in India. And far from considering themselves in error, they pride themselves on being some of the first people to be converted to Christianity. Thomas Christians have a tart response to other Christians' boasts about their own antiquity: 'Show me the evidence for Peter going to Rome,' they can be heard to say, 'and I shall show you the evidence for Thomas coming to India.'[15]

Peer into other ancient texts, and other shapes, other religions, can be seen to be evolving, and rapidly, in that era of travel and trade in the early years of the first millennium. It was not merely that there were different Christianities; in places Christianity can be seen to be evolving into something else again. In a text called *Jesus Messiah Sutra*, buddhas found themselves conscripted into the world of the Christian God: 'All the buddhas as well as kinnaras and the superintending-devas,' explained this seventh-century text, 'can see the Lord of Heaven.'[16] It went on to explain that, if there were any people who tried to understand the precepts of Buddha, but did so without fearing 'the Lord of Heaven', then these people had failed: 'they cannot be counted among those who have "received the precepts" in spite of professing that they rely on the teachings of Buddha. They are, in reality, traitors!'[17]

In the medieval era, distorted forms of ancient Eastern Christianities could, at times, arrive in the West.[18] In the twelfth century, a strange letter started to spread across Europe that had been written, or so it was claimed, by a king called 'John the Priest' – 'Prester John'.[19] It was a modest appellation, implying a man of Christian humility – though little else in the letter did. Instead, in a tone that veered from pride to overweening arrogance, Prester John explained that he was 'lord of lords' and 'exceed[ed] all kings of the entire earth in virtue, power, and all the riches which are under heaven.'[20] His kingdom, like so many of the lands of this era, was located somewhere on the beguiling border between geography and fantasy. In the east it stretched to the sunrise, while in the west it ran 'down into the Babylonian desert, next to the Tower of Babel.'[21] Its geography was remarkable: one of its greatest streams gurgled charmingly – and no doubt for Greeks, unexpectedly – from the foot of Mount Olympus.[22]

But who would quibble with geography when the fantasy was so perfect? That spring didn't flow with mere water; instead, its clear liquid 'changes every hour of the day and night'. The rivers in his land were equally remarkable, and glittered with emeralds and sapphires, with beryls and amethysts, with topaz and onyx. The natural resources of his land were, John explains, breath-taking. The entire place 'abounds in gold and silver and precious stones, elephants, dromedaries, camels, and', John concludes, apparently losing steam, 'dogs.'[23] There are hints, to the modern eye, that Prester John was not the most reliable of correspondents. When he describes the animals in his land, that list begins plausibly enough, with 'camels, hippopotami, crocodiles . . .' But he goes on to add 'centaurs, savage men, horned men, fauns, satyrs and women of the same race, pygmies, dog-headed men, giants whose height is forty cubits, one-eyed men, cyclopes and a bird which is called "phoenix".'[24]

Prester John was fictional – but the idea that there were other kinds of Christianity out there was real. Somewhat to the distress of the Western Christians who encountered them. When a Jesuit priest called Father Lobo travelled to Ethiopia in the seventeenth century, he was horrified to find that the members of the

Ethiopian church 'are possessed with a strange notion that they are the only true Christians in the world; as for us, they shunned us as heretics.'[25] Similarly, when envoys were sent from the Vatican to India in the sixteenth century, they were distinctly put out to find that the Indian Christians considered 'the Patriarch of Babylon' to be 'the universal pastor and head of the Catholic Church' – which, as all Catholics knew, was a title that 'was due only to the most holy father, the Bishop of Rome'. A synod was promptly convened, and the Roman Christians forced the Indian Christians into line. From now on, to use their old title for the Patriarch of Babylon was declared a 'heresy', punishable with excommunication.[26] Each was orthodox unto themselves, and looked upon other iterations of religion with suspicion, puzzlement, and often frank contempt.

In the year 1292, the Venetian traveller Marco Polo arrived in the city of Zayton, on the eastern coast of China, and was impressed by what he saw. 'All the ships from India arrive laden with costly wares,' he wrote, bringing pearls and precious stones and spices into this bustling port.[27] And, along with their goods, the merchants, as always, brought their faiths. He found a thriving Christian population in the area, who had been there for centuries – and he also found a conundrum.[28] In a nearby city, he was approached by 'a learned Saracen' who asked him to help solve a puzzle. There was a certain type of person in that area, the Saracen explained, 'whose religion is a mystery to everyone.' These people were not idolaters, since they had no idols; and 'they do not worship fire; they do not profess the faith of Muhammad; and neither do they seem to follow the Christian rule.' Could Marco Polo come and speak to them, the Saracen asked. 'Perhaps you will be able to make out something about their way of life?'[29]

And so Marco Polo went and spoke to the group – who were terrified of him, thinking that he had been sent by the Great Khan to persecute them. Nonetheless, he went back again and again and calmed them – 'tamed' is the word used. Finally, these not-quite-Christian Christians allowed him to look at their wall decorations, and at a sacred book of theirs which, he concluded, was a Christian psalter. He asked them how they had come by the Christian way of life, and they replied simply, 'From our ancestors.'[30] These people, Marco Polo concluded, were Christians.

He was almost certainly wrong, though his mistake was understandable. The people he spoke to believed in a God of light, and followed Christ – but very probably they also worshipped the Buddha, Zoroaster and a prophet called Mani. For it is now thought that, as the historian Sam Lieu has put it, 'the Polos had stumbled across a secretive group of Manichaeans.'[31]

To read the writings of the now-extinct Manichaean religion today is an odd experience: like putting a shoe on the wrong foot, its texts feel both familiar and strange. Their leader, a third-century Iranian prophet called Mani, had styled himself an 'Apostle of Jesus Christ' – and Jesus pops up frequently in these texts: he is described, familiarly enough for Christians, as 'Jesus the Splendour' and as a saviour who will appear at the end of days as a judge.[32]

Manichaean texts also offer commandments, and, as in Christianity and Judaism, there are ten of them. They begin in a familiar fashion too, ruling that one shall not kill. But then differences appear, for that commandment doesn't stop there: it goes on to explain that one shall not kill beasts 'as infidels do', but instead 'take pity on the animals that are [their] food.'[33] Another text warns sternly that, 'the man who breaks faith with the Buddha and Apostle and leaves the Church and violates the commandments will be led, in great shame and fear, before the Last Judge.'[34] While another warns, unarguably, that, 'He [who drinks wine] becomes stupid.'[35] And, unlike other religions, which tended to argue that they had been divinely and uniquely conceived, this religion prided itself on its mixed heritage. It was, as one text put it, to be like 'the world-ocean' into which 'all roaring and thundering waters' flow.[36]

Eventually, this mingled religion would be utterly wiped out. Its followers would be persecuted, tortured and killed, and its sacred writings destroyed. This happened slowly – very slowly – in some places: it is entirely possible that the last surviving Manichaean in China might have died in the twentieth century. But now it is gone. Today this religion survives for most people in a single linguistic fossil: the word 'Manichaean', used to mean that someone has an overly binary view of things. It is ironic, in a way, that binary division should be remembered as this religion's legacy. For if its existence teaches anything, it is that the world it was born into was not a world of binary division but of perpetual religious blending, of cults that mixed and mingled, joined and separated, rejoined and blended again.

Chapter Eleven

THE BIRTH OF HERESY

'In the name of the God of peace and love . . . Attack the followers of heresy more fearlessly even than the Saracens.'

Pope Innocent III, Letter, 1208

His Holiness Pope Innocent III was clear. On 10 March, in the year 1208 of the incarnation of our Lord, Innocent wrote an infamously uncompromising letter. One of his men – a papal legate named Pierre de Castelnau – had just been killed in the south of France. However, as Innocent made clear, that murder paled in comparison with the other evils taking place there. For, in those lands, he wrote, 'We are told that faith has vanished, peace has perished, that the plague of heresy and the madness of our enemies have gone from strength to strength.'[1] His words made it clear that such a terrible evil would require a terrible response; and Innocent duly demanded it.

'We therefore advise and urge you all most strongly,' his letter went on, 'do not delay in opposing these great evils. In the name of the God of peace and love, apply yourselves vigorously to pacifying those nations. Work to root out perfidious heresy in whatever way God reveals to you. Attack the followers of heresy more fearlessly even than the Saracens – since they are more evil – with a strong hand and a stretched out arm.'[2]

And, Innocent added, almost as an aside, those who did attack and kill heretics would then have the right to the lands of those whom they killed. In other words, murder French heretics and you would enjoy not merely papal approval and heavenly reward, but a little extra earthly property too. It was an irresistible combination. The troops started to gather. The Albigensian Crusade – a crusade launched not against a foreign enemy but against fellow Christians – had begun.

Many of the bitter and bloody events that followed would become notorious but, even in a notably savage crusade, what happened in the small French city of Béziers stood out. It had been a little over a year since Innocent's letter – and it had done its job. Enough men – enough 'crusaders' – had responded to the Pope's demand, and now they turned their attention to that handsome honey-coloured city, which sits in a bend of the river Orb in southern France. They had come because it was well known in the local area that numerous Cathars lived in Béziers – or, rather, as one chronicler put it, the city was 'entirely infected with the poison of heresy'.[3]

By late July, a mass of crusaders had gathered outside the city walls. They ordered the townspeople to hand over the heretics to them – or warned that they too would die when the crusaders attacked. The townspeople refused. The next morning, a few defiant locals even headed out to jeer and shout at the besieging crusaders, hoping 'to scare the enemy thus, as one might scare birds in a wheatfield.'[4]

A scuffle broke out, one of the troops was killed – and immediately the army massed and attacked. According to one text, 15,000 of them rushed up the hill and captured the city within an hour.[5] The priests inside the city, realizing the direness of their situation, put on their vestments and 'had the bells tolled, as though they would sing a Requiem Mass at the burial of the dead.'[6] Meanwhile, the citizens of Béziers ran for the churches, thinking that they might gain sanctuary. Thousands, it is said – men, women, children, babies – took refuge in the cathedral.[7]

It was a terrible mistake. The crusaders didn't stop at the cathedral doors, but burst in. The 'refuge' had become a trap. Once inside, the men started to kill everyone they found. Or rather, as one chronicler put it: 'up to seven thousand' of the 'shameless dogs' of that heretical city 'were killed on the day of the city's capture.'[8] Nor was it only men of fighting age who were killed. The Pope's crusaders 'killed almost all the inhabitants from the youngest to the oldest, and set fire to the city.'[9] And, as the chronicler notes with satisfaction, all this did not take place on just any day, but 'on the feast day of the Blessed Mary

Magdalene. What a splendid example of divine Justice and Providence!'[10]

That particular chronicler does not imply that there was any doubt felt by the troops as they cut down and killed the inhabitants, old and young, of Béziers. But, in a slightly later – and probably spurious but nonetheless telling – account given by a German chronicler, it is observed that some of the attackers did suffer a moment of hesitation. It was no simple matter for a soldier to tell the difference between a Catholic and a heretic merely by sight. How, the soldiers had allegedly asked, would they know who to kill? It is worth noting precisely why they were anxious about this: as this chronicler makes clear, it was not because they feared they might kill some innocents, but instead lest they might leave some heretics unslaughtered.

Their abbot's reply became legendary: 'Kill them all,' he replied. 'For the Lord knoweth them that are his.' And so, the chronicler concludes, 'Countless numbers in that town were slain.'[11]

It is hard to imagine European history without heresy. It was heresy that set those troops to their slaughter in Béziers. It was heresy that, a few decades later, would lead to the issuing of the papal bull *Ad Extirpanda* – 'For Rooting Out' – which laid down, in calm legal language, what violence might be permitted 'for the rooting-up of the plague of heresy.' Legs and arms, this papal decree stipulated, were not to be broken. But otherwise, a ruler 'is bound to compel all heretics whom they have arrested . . . to explicitly confess their errors.'[12]

Heresy changed European history in ways large and small. It led to the founding of the Inquisition – and to its extensive bureaucracy. For this organization, which came to be seen as almost supernaturally sinister, had strikingly humdrum habits: it met on Tuesdays, Thursdays and Saturdays (a habit it kept to for half a millennium); its inquisitors wrote handbooks on effective interrogation techniques; and they kept detailed expenses.[13] To this day, there survives a list of the costs for the burning of four heretics in Carcassonne in 1323. It reads:

> For large wood: 55 sols 6 deniers.
> For vine-branches: 21 sols 3 deniers.
> For straw: 2 sols 6 deniers.
> For four stakes: 10 sols 9 deniers.
> For ropes to tie the convicts: 4 sols 7 deniers.[14]

Heresy would tilt European history for centuries: it would kindle the fires beneath Thomas Cranmer; lead to the excommunication of Martin Luther; and the mere 'vehement suspicion' of it would keep Galileo Galilei under house arrest for years for 'having believed and held the doctrine (which is false and contrary to the Holy and Divine Scriptures) that the sun is the centre of the world'.[15] The charge of heresy retained its power for a surprisingly long time: in 1947, a group of British bishops attempted to pass a vote of censure for heresy against a fellow bishop from Birmingham because he had written a book that rejected the virgin birth. The bishops failed – but that they even tried is instructive.[16]

Heresy is so central to European history, it is hard to remember that it could so easily have been otherwise. Religious heresy did not exist before Christianity. The word 'heresy' – *haeresis* – had existed for centuries. But its meaning and tone had been very different indeed. In Greek, it meant 'choice', and choice in the Greek world was not seen as a dangerous thing.[17] Ancient literature has been scanned to see if, prior to Christianity, the word *haeresis* has any negative connotations – but none have been found; on the contrary, if 'heresy' has any connotations at all, they seem to be positive.[18] As the historian Marcel Simon has put it, 'for the Greeks . . . choice was praiseworthy, a legitimate decision to embrace a certain way of thinking by the use of human reason.'[19] Look at the ancient world and you frequently find places where intellectual choice was not merely not suppressed but actively encouraged. When the second-century emperor Marcus Aurelius wished to promote philosophy in Athens, it is said that he founded not one chair of philosophy but four, one for each of the main philosophical sects: Platonism, Aristotelianism, Epicureanism and Stoicism. For who really knew what was the right way to knowledge?[20]

The speed with which Christian writers turned against heresy was striking. Within a century of Jesus' death, Christian writers had begun inveighing against choice – against 'heresy'. In Christian hands, this Greek word gained a new and freighted meaning. Abstain from these 'strange plants' of heresy, wrote Ignatius of Antioch, a Christian bishop, at the turn of the first century. For in heresy you will find that Jesus has been mingled with impure other beliefs, thus 'providing something like a deadly drug with honeyed wine, which the ignorant man gladly takes with pleasure; and therein is death.'[21] No longer is choice praiseworthy; it is poison. The Christian attacks on heresy had begun – and they would never cease.

From the very beginning, heretics cease to be merely people in Christian texts. They become instead a 'poison', a 'polluted contagion'; they are 'criminals' and a 'contaminating presence'; their church is the great 'whore'; they themselves are 'frauds', 'tramps', 'wretches'; a 'disease' to be 'cured', a gangrene to be 'cut out', a pollution to be eliminated. And, above all, they are animals.[22] Peer into Christian texts (and, later, laws) on heresy and they often read less like works of theology than zoology: they writhe with snakes, buzz with wasps, swarm with insects. In their pages, heretics metamorphose into a vast and grotesque menagerie: they are 'dung-beetles' that 'roll in foulness'; they are 'swine' and 'wolves' and 'wild beasts'.[23]

Above all, heretics are, like Satan himself, snakes: they are vipers and asps; they are the 'basilisk that is in the pit' and, on one occasion, they are the pleasingly precise 'snake-like filth of the aborted issue which is hatched from the infertile eggs of asps and other vipers.'[24] At other times, Christian authorities were blunter in their metaphors: as Augustine so memorably put it, heretics were 'shit'.[25] Not all Christian writings were so vicious, to be sure. In the words of one more generous bishop, those who split from the church were 'without doubt brothers' – though, he added, they were 'not good brothers.'[26]

But, generally, the tone was relentless. A new genre of literature sprang up, called 'heresiologies', in which, with the care of Victorian naturalists, Christian authors classified heretics, recording their different species, subspecies, distinguishing marks and (reliably repellent) habits. One of the most famous of these works is by a second-century bishop named Irenaeus. Its chapter headings were added later, but, as always, they offer a taste not merely of this volume, but of the entire genre. Chapter 10 of Bishop Irenaeus' work, for example, bears the title 'The Heretics Interpret Scripture Perversely'. That is followed by the similarly stout, 'Chapter 11: The Heretics Have Fallen into a Profundity of Error', as well as the bracing 'Chapter 24: The Gnostic Arguments, Letters, and Syllables are Absurd', before the whole book concludes with the vague, but final, 'Chapter 35: Various Gnostic Notions Are Rejected.'[27] Heresiologies were rarely works of even-handed neutrality.

Modern readers know that heresy steps onto the stage with Christianity and are not surprised by its arrival. But we should be: this is a radical change. This is not to argue that the pre-Christian world was a religious utopia – it wasn't. Romans could, and at times did, attack other religions when they broke certain social boundaries. The Christians themselves would famously suffer from this – though they were not the only ones. Roman law might step in to attack any religions considered to threaten peace on earth, or in heaven. Thus the infamously orgiastic Bacchic rites were suppressed in Rome in 186 BC; self-castration, performed by some religious sects, was also proscribed; while human sacrifice was banned in 97 BC. Magicians – who were considered able to cause harm whether or not you believed in their spells – could be treated with horrifying brutality.[28] Later, in the vicious atmosphere of Diocletian's reign, Manichaeans would also suffer appalling penalties: as one law put it, they, 'together with their abominable writings [should be] burnt in the flames.'[29]

Moreover, Romans were not exactly 'tolerant' of other religions in the way that modern minds might wish. Ancient toleration often lacks the pious and earnest air that modern toleration demands. It is absolutely not the case that Rome allowed a great profusion of religions to flourish because ancient Romans, with expansive ecumenical hearts, 'tolerated' them.[30] It was simply that religious homogeneity was on the whole neither expected nor desired by classical minds. As the historian Herodotus observed in the fifth century BC, there were lots of gods – and people always preferred their own. 'For if anyone, no matter who, were given the opportunity of choosing from amongst all the nations in the world the beliefs which he thought best, he would inevitably, after careful consideration of their relative merits, choose those of his own country.' And it would be unlikely, added Herodotus, that 'anyone but a madman would mock at such things.'[31]

Centuries later, this view was still held – even by the cynical Celsus. Every nation, he wrote with typical bluntness, always considers its own religion 'by far the best.'[32] But the most beautiful ancient plea for toleration was the one offered by the Roman senator Symmachus. 'We see the same stars, the sky is shared by all, the same world surrounds us,' Symmachus wrote. 'What does it matter what wisdom a person uses to seek for the truth?'[33] For Christians, nothing mattered more: 'I am the way, and the truth, and the life,' Jesus had said. He had not said, 'I am one of the ways, one of the truths, one of the lives.'[34] And so to the fervent Christian, other religions and other forms of Christianity were no longer – as Symmachus and Herodotus had seen them – iterations on the same idea; they were wrong. More than wrong: they were a dangerous evil.

It was an attitude that irritated the classical world intensely.

Why, classical authors argued, did Christianity consider itself so exceptional? Where was the proof that Christianity was indeed the single way to salvation? Where was the proof that Christian stories alone were true, while Greek and Roman religious traditions were, as one irked ancient writer put it, merely 'a figment and a misplaced attempt to convince'?[35] What was the evidence that Christians were any more moral than anyone else? Christians might claim that they were, but, as classical critics pointed out, those ten commandments that they followed and made so much of were hardly novel. Thou shalt not kill? Thou shalt not steal? 'What nation is there,' wrote the exasperated emperor and Christian critic Julian, 'which does not think that it ought to keep [such] commandments?'[36]

Christians disagreed. And, in the relentless, hectoring tracts that they produced in these early centuries, they started to turn their rhetorical fire on those old, pluralistic, doubtful ways. In such Christian tracts, not only choice – 'heresy' – but even those things that might prompt a person to attempt to make their own choices started to be attacked. Christians warned that mere curiosity was to be mistrusted. As the fiery author John Chrysostom argued, for the true Christian, there was no need for curiosity: 'where there is faith, there is no need for investigation . . . Investigation is the destruction of faith. For he that investigates has not yet found. He who investigates cannot believe.'[37]

Philosophy also started to come under attack. Not by all Christian authors – some continued to steep themselves in it – but many others were far less keen. With good reason: ancient philosophy had frequently instilled doubt in its practitioners. Socrates, who had offered doubt in dialogue form, had said that he was a little wiser than another man not because he knew more than him – but because 'I, as I do not know anything, do not think I do either.'[38] Such doubt was anathema to Christianity. The names of philosophers such as Plato, Pythagoras and Zeno start to appear in Christian writings, not to be praised but instead to be castigated for their 'science of idolatry, impiety and godlessness', among other crimes.[39] The Christian author Tertullian accused philosophy of being not merely a heresy, but also the parent of heresies. Away with philosophical schools, he wrote. Didn't Epicureanism teach that the world was made of atoms and that the soul dies? What rubbish! Away with them![40]

The tone could be savage. The Christian poet Prudentius wrote a poem jeering at the 'bearded Plato's ravings' and the 'illusion' of Cynic philosophy and the dizzying contrivances of Aristotle. These philosophers, wrote Prudentius, 'are all lost in the uncertainties of a maze in which they wander round and round.'[41] A later author named Gregory warned that philosophers were 'those who strayed, who worshipped the creature' – as in Satan – 'rather than the creator'. But, as Gregory contentedly observed, in his day – Gregory was writing when Christianity had gained political power, and had started to exert it – many philosophers had given up their 'error' from fear of coercion.[42]

Christians did not do away with ancient philosophy entirely: far from it. Much of this fulmination was merely rhetorical; the Christian attitude to ancient philosophy was more complicated than such thunderous words would make it seem. Christian writers did insult and disdain much ancient philosophy, but some also used it, appropriated it and indeed (a chronologically bold claim) claimed that they had invented much of it.* Nonetheless, rhetoric mattered.

Greek and Roman authors looked at such Christian attacks on philosophy with bafflement. It would be one thing to reject the literature and philosophy of all other cultures if your own were superior. But, ancient critics argued, Christian writings were manifestly no such thing. Has God, asked the emperor Julian with his usual asperity, 'granted to you to originate any science or any philosophical study?' If so, then 'what is it?' It certainly wasn't astronomy – for that was 'perfected among the [Greeks], after the first observations had been made among the

* See Chapter Sixteen for a fuller explanation of this.

barbarians in Babylon.' Nor was it geometry, for that 'took its rise in the measurement of the land in Egypt, and from this grew to its present importance.' And it wasn't arithmetic – that began 'with the Phoenician merchants, and among the [Greeks] in course of time acquired the aspect of a regular science.'[43] So then, Julian asked, tell me: precisely what branch of knowledge can the Christians claim? Precious little, he argued. So how perplexing it was that the Christians obsessively read their own writings – and ignored everyone else's. 'You are so misguided and foolish that you regard those chronicles of yours as divinely inspired, though by their help no man could ever become wiser or braver or better,' he wrote. While philosophy, 'by whose aid men can acquire courage, wisdom and justice, these you ascribe to Satan and to those who serve Satan!'[44]

Almost everything about the Christian obsession with heresy struck classical observers as strange. Not least of all its ironic consequences. For, as Greek and Roman authors did not hesitate to point out, the followers of this God of love were prone to tearing themselves apart with startling viciousness over bafflingly small disputes. Christians, Celsus wryly observed, are all 'divided and rent asunder; and each wants to have his own party'.[45] Indeed, pretty much the only thing on which Christians seemed to agree, he noted, was the name 'Christian' itself.[46] In truth, they rarely agreed on that. Even Christians admitted the truth of Julian's point: as Augustine dolefully wrote, while pagans worshipped numerous gods and Christians worshipped one, nonetheless, 'they, under their plurality, have no division yet we, under our one, have no unity.'[47] And, no peace – for theological disputes could quickly become physical ones. As the non-Christian historian Ammianus Marcellinus disdainfully saw it, 'no wild beasts are such dangerous enemies to man as Christians are to one another.'[48]

But, soon, Christians wouldn't only be dangerous to each other. As the fourth century opened, the balance of power in the Roman Empire was changing. Christian emperors would soon hold power in Rome, and start to pass Christian laws. And before the century was out, new messages began to travel along those efficient Roman roads, and on those Roman merchant ships. These messages came from the imperial court and they stated – in words as vivid as any heresiology – that the 'feral mysteries', the 'insanity' and the 'contagion' of the heretics were now to be stopped.[49]

Chapter Twelve

ON LAWS

'I like sex that is easy and obtainable.'

Horace, Satire 1.2

When people want to know about Rome, they tend to turn to the writings of its great men – with good reason. Read Rome's poets and historians and politicians and you can learn things, big and small. You can learn that the Roman Empire was to be an *imperium sine fine* – an 'empire without limit' – or so Virgil said.[1] You can learn, too, that conscientious Roman workers might find themselves sick of fretting about politics and dream – as Horace did – of lying instead under the shade of a spreading plane tree, while a slave dipped cups of fine Falernian wine in a nearby stream, to cool them.[2]

Read the letters of the empire and you get another view again: the personal thoughts of one educated gentleman to another. These thoughts are captured in letters that feel so intimate, so detailed, you can almost hear the scratch of the stylus as you read. Take the letter that Pliny the Younger, the lawyer, wrote to his friend Tacitus, the historian, about his new way of working. That particular day, Pliny writes, excitedly, instead of working in his study, he had decided to combine writing with exercise and so had gone out on a boar hunt instead. So it was that, as 'I was sitting by the nets . . . I had by my side not a hunting spear and a dart, but my pen and writing tablets.' While Pliny waited for the boars, he worked and he wrote. 'It is really surprising how the mind is stimulated by bodily movement and exercise.' So, concludes Pliny, 'when next you go hunting, take my advice and carry your writing tablets with you as well as your luncheon basket and your flask.'[3]

Such writing can feel immensely intimate – at times, too intimate. Take Horace's Satire 1.2. Unlike some of the more famous lines of this great phrasemaker (*carpe diem* was his; so too was *nil desperandum* and, less gloriously, *dulce et decorum est*), the words of this particular satire are less likely to be immortalized on a fridge magnet. For in it Horace discusses passion, and what limits a civilized man should set on it. Horace thinks one should limit one's feelings – but his methods for doing so are rather unexpected. 'When your throat is parched with thirst, you don't ask for golden goblets, do you?' he writes. 'When you're hungry, you don't turn your nose up at everything but peacock and turbot, do you?' Well then, continues Horace: 'When your crotch is throbbing and there is a slave-girl or home-grown slave boy ready at hand, whom you could jump right away, you don't prefer to burst with your hard-on, do you? I certainly don't. I like sex that is easy and obtainable.'[4]

Read the works of St Augustine, written four centuries later, and you find yourself in a world so vivid you can almost smell it. Here, in his home town of Thagaste in North Africa, the thirst this sun brings upon young bodies is so severe, it is almost a weapon: young children in his town are denied water by their nursemaids as a lesson, to teach them self-denying strength.[5] In his writings, the sea is a distant dream; the boys in his village have to peer into a bowl of water to imagine what it might look like. Augustine would be entirely unable to imagine the flavour of strawberries and cherries until he travelled to Italy and tasted them.[6]

The moral atmosphere of this world is – under the pressure of Christianity – starting to feel increasingly arid too. This was a world in which sex had suddenly become complicated; a world in which a boy might go on a trip to the baths with his father and be embarrassed when his father noticed, as Augustine's did, 'the turbulent signs of adolescence' on his body. And perhaps be even more embarrassed by his mother's reaction: as Augustine records, when she heard about these signs (whatever they may have been; despite academic musing, no one is sure), she was 'stricken with a holy fear' and warned him 'not to commit fornication; but especially never to defile another man's wife'.[7] This was a world of fruits that tempted, but which were forbidden; it was a world in which a man might pray to God to make him chaste – but not yet.[8]

But if you really want to know an empire, don't read the whispers of its poets or the confessions of its great men.[9] If you really want to understand what is happening, pass over the fancy odes and epodes and epics and epistles – and look instead at its laws. They are not fine literature, these. They are not eloquent, or poetic, or finely worded. They are humdrum and quotidian and repetitive and blunt, and their topics are practical to the point of dull. They speak about tax assessment and tax exemptions, about tax collectors and tax collections. They speak about the price of fish, the price of bread in Ostia, the grain supply in Carthage. They speak about swine and wine and cattle, about boatmen and breadmen and ragmen and bad men. And they are absolutely riveting.

These ancient laws, in their clumsy, legal way, tell a story as eloquent as any epic – and, in many ways, more honest. They deal not with people as they want to be seen; instead, they address the tiresome, vexatious, quarrelsome Roman world as it actually was – or as the law felt it should be. To examine Roman laws is to peep behind the curtain, to see past the carefully constructed scenes of its poets, past the staged set pieces of its orators, into the rougher workings of the grand imperial theatre behind. Pick up either of the two books of imperial law that the Roman Empire produced – the fifth-century Theodosian Code and the sixth-century Justinian – and another Rome, a rougher Rome, a poorer, harder, more brutal Rome springs into life beneath your fingers.

These massive collections of laws (to carry them to a table in a library, even today, requires both hands and a little concentration) are arranged into books, then sections, then subsections – each bearing a title, each of which speaks volumes. These headings contain novels written with curt legal clarity. Law 9.9, for example, deals with 'Women who have united themselves to their own slaves'; while law 5.10 deals with 'Those persons who purchase newborn children and those who take such children to rear' and law 9.8 explains what should happen 'If any person should corrupt a girl whose tutor he has been' (in short: extremely unpleasant things). Law 8.14 is simply (and pleasingly) on 'Ungrateful Children'.

These laws speak of a far more violent world than the one captured by the privileged men of Roman literature. This is a world of cut-throats and infant killings, a place that endures homicides and parricides, rapes and beatings, thefts and robberies. It is a world that frets not over which wine is better to drink under the shade of a tree, but instead muses over how much violence should be involved in 'the disciplinary correction of slaves' (in summary: as much as you like, up to and including death, provided that death is 'accidental').[10] This is not a world of bored poets on riverbanks; it is a harder place, in which parents sell and kill their own children frequently enough for the law to have views on such matters. It is a world of pains and passions and sorrows far beyond the pens of cultured men, and it would, were it not for Rome's legal fastidiousness, have been all but swept from the pages of history.

And, while it has moments of leniency, this is a bitterly vengeful world, too. Whatever violence the brigands and bandits and cut-throats might have inflicted, that surely paled before the punishments that lay in wait for them in Roman laws. The patricide – that cursed individual who has killed their own father – shall not, as law 9.15.1 explains, 'be subjected to the sword or to fire or to any other customary penalty'. The fathers of the senate desired nothing so simple for the father-killer. Instead, as the ancient law had it, a man who has committed such a crime 'shall be sewed in a leather sack and, confined within its deadly closeness, he shall share the companionship of serpents. As the nature of the region shall determine, he shall be thrown into the neighbouring sea or into a river, so that while still alive he may begin to lose the enjoyment of all the elements, that the heavens may be taken away from him while he is living and the earth, when he is dead.'[11]

This is a world that thrills to the thought of retribution, in which wronged men itch to take the law into their own hands. Law 9.14.2 explains that, if 'a nocturnal ravager attacks either a traveller or someone's home for the purpose of committing robbery' and, the law explains, is resisted by his victim with arms, or even 'killed for his rash lawlessness', then that is the brigand's bad luck. He has merely received 'the death which he threatened' and undergone 'that danger which he intended for another.'* Laws designed to defend the purity of women are numerous and arrestingly violent. As law 9.9 went on to explain, those women who 'unite themselves' to their slaves in a clandestine affair 'shall be subject to the capital sentence', while the 'rascally slave shall be delivered to the flames.' Elsewhere, the law warns that any slave who commits rape or assists in it is 'to be burned without any distinction of sex.'[12] If a young woman's nurse should lead her charge astray into an affair, then the nurse 'shall receive molten lead in the mouth and throat, so that that part of the body may be deservedly closed from which incitement to crime is known to have been afforded.'[13] Other punishments add some astute emotional torment: if a woman has an affair with a slave and then the slave reports her himself, he shall be released, while she shall instead lose her home and 'shall mourn the absence of her exiled lover.'[14]

As the laws make clear, the world of fourth-century Rome was one of rigid social hierarchies. These legal codes speak of firm class distinctions, of snobbery distilled into subclauses. There are edicts on who may ride horses (former soldiers may; shepherds absolutely may not); on what colours one may wear

* Anyone who listened to BBC Radio 4's *Today* programme in 2004 will feel a familiarity with such sentiments. The programme allowed its listeners to vote on what law they would most like to be introduced. After a poll which saw a little over 26,000 listeners vote, the most popular law (somewhat, one sensed, to the distress of the BBC) was a proposal 'to authorise homeowners to use any means to defend their home from intruders'.

(never imperial purple or gold); on who can wear jewels (definitely not actresses); on what fabrics one may dress in and on how foreign one is allowed to look (not very).[15] 'We command', snaps one brusque law, 'that no person shall be allowed to wear very long hair' within the city of Rome – and not even a slave can wear animal skins. 'Within the City of Rome,' adds another, 'no person shall wear either trousers or boots'.[16] If looking like a hairy northern barbarian (for that was what those laws were aimed at stopping) was unacceptable, then looking above oneself was worse. No person, states one faintly prissy law, 'shall have woven gold borders, either on tunics or on linen garments.'[17] Other matters of dress were also sternly legislated upon. As the intriguing law 15.7.12 states, curtly, actresses, and all those immodest women 'who acquire gain by the wantonness of their bodies', are not, absolutely not, allowed to dress up as nuns.[18]

Naturally, as when reading any story, the reader of the Code should be careful. The law – like any other piece of writing – can strike a pose. It, too, can be guilty of preening self-presentation, or obfuscation, or of being a braggart. Moreover, its relationship to real life is not clear: simply because a law appears does not mean that it was enacted, for the laws in the Theodosian Code were less orders to act than local licences to do so. (They were produced in a rather piecemeal fashion, too: some were issued as edicts, but many were merely issued to clarify queries from local officials.) They have been likened to modern gun licences, and no doubt they were a little like gun licences in their take-up, with some officials deploying them with militant enthusiasm and others not interested in the slightest.[19] So laws do not tell you everything. But they do tell you something. And the final section of the Theodosian Code tells you a great deal about how the Roman Empire was starting to see religion.

Because the Roman religious world was changing. In AD 312, before a battle, an emperor named Constantine had looked into the sky and seen 'a cross-shaped trophy formed from light', and beneath it the message 'CONQUER BY THIS.'[20] Not perhaps the most pacific of Christian sentiments, and later Christians (though notably not earlier ones) would be a touch embarrassed by it. The so-called 'triumph of Christianity' had begun. Christians would – not surprisingly – celebrate this moment for centuries. A few years prior to it, some Christians had experienced ferocious brutality and martyrdom at the hands of Roman officials. The vision of the flaming cross in the sky, and an emperor's conversion to their cause, marked an almost unbelievable transformation in their fortunes.

However, the vision itself was less remarkable than some later Christians might have implied. For one thing, this was not the first heavenly revelation that Constantine had been offered. Because Constantine – Constantine 'Equal-to-the-Apostles', as he would later be known – had enjoyed another heavenly vision a little earlier. This other vision had also come upon Constantine while he was on the road – this time in Gaul – and once again it had promised Constantine military success.

The main difference was that, on this earlier occasion, the deity had not been the Christian God, but the very 'pagan' sun god Apollo. One day, as Constantine turned to visit a shrine, he had been greeted by a remarkable sight and had seen, as one writer put it, 'Your Apollo, accompanied by Victory, offering you laurel wreaths'.[21] A little later, in AD 313 – after the vision of the Christian God – coins were issued showing representations of the sun, and one even showing Constantine in profile, cheek-to-cheek with 'his' god Apollo.[22] That vision was rather less lauded by later Christian chroniclers.

Look at the vision of Constantine not within Christian history but instead within Roman history and it starts to look even less remarkable. In a religiously malleable empire, religions rose and fell, gained imperial support and lost it, and visions appeared and faded before one emperor after another. Even the emperor Augustus – that most level-headed and wily of politicians – had received one. Much like Constantine, Augustus had experienced his heavenly halo at a militarily convenient moment. For, while still a young man, not long after the death of Julius Caesar in 44 BC, Augustus had been travelling back to the capital and, 'When he returned to Rome . . . the sky was clear of clouds, but a rainbow-like halo formed around the sun.'[23]

In the late third century, less than half a century before Constantine, the emperor Aurelian had also had a marvellous vision, again conveniently around the time of a battle, from yet another god. In this case, it was Aurelian's foot soldiers who had been reassured by a 'divine form' in the battle; afterwards, Aurelian himself visited a temple and 'beheld that same divine form which he had seen supporting his cause in the battle.'[24] When Aurelian returned to Rome, he built a temple to the sun there. The birthday of Sol Invictus would later be celebrated on 25 December.[25]

Sun gods and gods of light were popular among Roman emperors. When Christianity turned up, classical critics saw it as an unremarkable continuation of this; indeed there was so much sun imagery in early Christianity that one Christian author would feel the need to defend Christians from accusations that they were merely sun worshippers, what with their Sunday (in Latin, *dies solis* – the 'day of the sun') worship and their tendency to pray towards the east.[26] Sometimes even Christians themselves seemed a trifle confused. A remarkable third-century mosaic discovered in the Vatican Necropolis shows Jesus represented as the sun god Helios, with that god's typical rays coming from his head, riding on his chariot.[27]

For an emperor to embrace a god of light was hardly new. Half a century before Aurelian, the inventively debauched emperor Elagabalus, who was said to serve peas garnished with gold and to have had himself drawn about in a cart pulled by four naked women, had introduced the worship of a Syrian sun god to the capital. He had then (or so the stories said) circumcised himself and started to abstain from swine's flesh as part of his worship. Elagabalus' desire, or so one later historian said, was 'that no god might be worshipped at Rome save only

Elagabalus.'[28] Other emperors might promote entire pantheons: in AD 361, after Constantine died, his nephew Julian came to the imperial throne and attempted to revive the worship of the old 'pagan' gods that his uncle had so slighted.

Julian failed where Constantine succeeded. The reason is to be found less, as ancient texts might argue, in heaven than on earth. For, while divinities might be immortal, the emperors who patronized them tended to be less fortunate. For all the pomp and luxury that emperors enjoyed, they were marked men: 62 per cent of Roman emperors died violent deaths. A Roman gladiator had better odds of surviving a fight than an emperor did of enjoying a peaceful conclusion to his reign.[29] The briefest look at the emperors mentioned above would tend to confirm this pattern: Aurelian was assassinated after five years; Elagabalus (entirely unsurprisingly, and to widespread relief) was assassinated within four, while Julian – who one Christian bishop had dismissed as 'but a cloud which will speedily be dispersed' – was killed on campaign after less than two years in power. Julian's attempted reforms went unfinished; the empire reverted to Christianity and Julian is, to this day, known by the insulting Christian epithet of 'the apostate' – 'the deserter' – or perhaps even, given the viciousness of the insult, 'the traitor'.

His uncle Constantine, by contrast, lived on and on. By the time Constantine died, he had enjoyed a rule of three decades. What was so very different about Constantine was not, then, that he had a religious vision, nor that he introduced a new god, nor that he plumped for an eccentric Eastern deity – all these things were profoundly unremarkable. What was different about Constantine was that he lived for such a very, very long time. And by doing so he changed the fate of Rome, and of the empire – and therefore of Europe – for ever.

Despite the drama of Constantine's conversion, if you comb through the Theodosian Code chronologically, the evidence that anything might be starting to change in the Roman Empire is, at first, small. In the years after Constantine comes to power there are, it is true, a few benefits for Christians scattered here, a few nudges against 'heretical' Christians or against 'pagans' there. But there is not much. Then, suddenly, in AD 326, a terse new law appears.[30] 'The privileges that have been granted in consideration of religion', reads this law, 'must benefit only the adherents of the Catholic faith. It is Our will, moreover, that heretics' – it is notable that the word is already being used as a legal category – 'and schismatics shall not only be alien from these privileges but shall also be bound and subjected to various compulsory public services.'[31]

It is not really dramatic, this law. It offers mild rewards for Catholic priests, mild pain for everyone else. It is very far from compulsion: it offers no violence, no vivid punishments, no sewing into sacks, no molten metal poured into mouths. It is muted and it is small. And it is no less than the start of a religious revolution.

Chapter Thirteen

THE BREEDS OF HERETICAL MONSTERS

'All heresies are forbidden by both divine and imperial laws and shall forever cease.'

Theodosian Code, August AD 379

The dawn of this new Christian era would dazzle historians for centuries. When Constantine came to power, 'a day bright and radiant,' wrote the Christian historian Eusebius, 'with no cloud overshadowing it, shone down with shafts of heavenly light on the churches of Christ throughout the world.'[1] The literature of this era is luminous with delight. The moment when an emperor who favoured Christianity sat, for the first time, on the throne of Rome was a time of 'dazzling festival; light was everywhere'.[2] Men 'who once dared not look up greeted each other with smiling faces and shining eyes. They danced and sang in city and country alike.' Men 'had now lost all fear of their former oppressors.'[3] According to Eusebius, even laws softened in this new era. In 'every city the victorious emperor published decrees full of humanity and laws that gave proof of munificence and true piety. Thus all tyranny had been purged away.'[4]

Eusebius told one story. The Theodosian Code tells another. Read it carefully and another world appears before your eyes. Not the jubilant world of Eusebius, but an oppressive world in which first this liberty and then that one are slowly pared away. There may, initially, have been 'decrees full of humanity' and laws that gave evidence of 'true piety' in this newly Christianizing world. But within fifty years the legal mood of Rome can be seen, clearly, to have darkened. And among those for whom this period would become the darkest were the so-called heretics.

At first, as with that law of AD 326, the signs that anything was changing were few; a nudge here; a confiscation there. And then suddenly, in August AD 379, after just a little over fifty years of Christian rule, the tone changes. 'All heresies', states a law, 'are forbidden by both divine and imperial laws and shall forever cease.'[5]

Soon, heretics were forbidden from building churches, forbidden from making wills and were 'to be afflicted with the supreme penalty and with inexpiable punishment.'[6] Fines were levied – small sums to begin with, but then they started to get higher. Heretics were to be fined twenty pounds of gold – thirty, forty, fifty – staggering sums.[7] Violence started to appear in the laws. Those who enabled heretical meetings to take place on private land would, as one law of AD 405 explained, 'be flogged with leaden whips' then exiled.[8] Those who let heretical clerics preach on their land would lose their land and have to pay ten pounds of gold. If such a person failed to come up with the money, then 'he shall be beaten with clubs and condemned to deportation.'[9]

The rulings go on: there should be 'frequent floggings' to recall people from their errors; one heretic was to be 'arrested and beaten with leaden whips'; while if anyone should 'seduce' a freeborn person or slave into any 'impious sect or ritual, he shall suffer capital punishment.'[10] Then the law hardened further: from now on, heretics were to be actively hunted out. This new Christian regime encouraged people to spy on their neighbours, report them, denounce them: 'Your Sublimity, therefore, shall appoint investigators, shall open court, and shall receive informers and denouncers.'[11] The most loathed heretics 'shall be driven from all the hiding places of this City . . . [their] hiding places shall be spied out with a diligent search.'[12] Those 'insane' heretics who still dared to worship 'shall pay the severest penalty both to God and to the laws'.[13]

Not merely the heretics but even their books became liable to punishment. 'We command that the books containing the doctrine and matter of all their crimes', ordered one law of 398, 'shall immediately be sought out and produced, with the greatest astuteness and with the exercise of due authority, and they shall be consumed with fire immediately under the supervision of the judges.'[14] More frightening still, 'any person should be convicted of having hidden any of these books . . . shall suffer capital punishment, as a retainer of noxious books and writings and as guilty of the crime of magic.'[15]

Some of the laws in the Code closely target particular religious groups – the 'malicious subtlety' and the 'madness' of the heretics, or the 'insane' pagans, or the Jews and their 'feral' and 'nefarious' religion.[16] Others are more sweeping. Take law 16.4.4, which is: 'On those persons who contend about religion.' As it explains, 'There shall be no opportunity for any man to go out to the public and to argue about religion or to discuss it or to give any counsel.' If anyone dared to do so, then, as the law made clear, they would regret it. For, 'If any person hereafter, with flagrant and damnable audacity', broke this law, 'he shall be restrained with a due penalty and proper punishment.' Another law ruled that those who persisted in 'contending' about religion in public 'shall pay the penalty of high treason with their lives and blood.'[17]

Though perhaps the most unnerving law in this period is a simple but sinister one, stating that now: 'The name of the One and Supreme God shall be celebrated everywhere.'[18] It is telling that such a law had to be passed. Eusebius, and other Christian historians after him, implied that the joy at Constantine's conversion was all but universal: all fear had gone, all tyranny had been purged. They, like Milton and Gibbon after them, would imply that the world had been waiting for this moment.

The idea is simply incorrect. It was true that the joy felt among many Christians at their new emperor must have been immense – their numbers, however, were not. As always, caution is needed: reliable numbers are hard to come by in the ancient world – there are, famously, no ancient statistics. Even if there were, it would not be entirely obvious what was being counted as it is not wholly clear what being 'Christian' meant in this period. Opening windows on men's souls is hard in the moment; let alone at a distance of two thousand years. But estimates have been made of how many Christians there were at the start of that century when Constantine converted, and they are small: by the opening of the fourth century, it is likely that only six million people in the empire were Christian – around 10 per cent.[19] 90 per cent were not. And it is hard to imagine that the remaining 90 per cent would have been as delighted as Eusebius describes.

This matters. What happened when Constantine came to power was therefore not, as Eusebius and countless others after him would represent it, the liberation of the majority from the tyranny of a pagan minority. It was closer to the reverse. When Constantine came to power, most people were not Christian – or not the right kind of Christian. What happened over the course of the next century was that the law would attempt to make them so. Because, as one simple law had it, the 'insatiable honour' of the Catholic Church must be upheld.[20]

Despite the angry rhetoric, not all will have been converted by force; on the contrary, many will have converted voluntarily, persuaded by the kindness of much of Christian teaching – or of Christian deeds. In this period, as now, many Christians promised not merely the bread of heaven but bread on earth, too. From the earliest times, Christians were well known for their acts of charity; for their support of widows and orphans and for distributing food to the hungry.

Though such largesse didn't impress everyone: as the emperor Julian somewhat ungenerously observed, Christians were like those slavers who 'entice children with a cake, and by throwing it to them two or three times induce them to follow them.' As with slavers, Julian argued, the Christians had ulterior motives: for as soon as the children are 'far away from their friends [they] cast them on board a ship and sell them as slaves, and that which for the moment seemed sweet, proves to be bitter for all the rest of their lives.'[21]

These laws are undoubtedly vicious, and aggressive. Yet

historians, both ancient and modern, have tended to touch only lightly on them.[22] As G. E. M. de Ste. Croix wrote, 'For Christians, naturally, all the emphasis tends to be placed upon the persecutions of Christianity; the much more extensive, longlasting, and often successful persecutions by Christians, of pagans, Jews, Manichaeans, and Christian sects other than their own, are easily overlooked.'[23] To this day, it is the Romans who are known as the infamous persecutors, while the Christians are known as the persecuted. But, for all their eventual infamy, the Roman attacks on Christianity were late, sporadic – and frankly ineffectual. Christianity grew and grew and grew under Roman rule – a fact that led de Ste. Croix to archly say that the Romans' so-called 'persecution' of Christians had been 'Too little, too late'.* Christianity persecuted too – but it was far, far more effective.

But perhaps the different religious attitudes of this era are not best illuminated by quibbling over abstract nouns such as 'toleration', but instead by planting the question firmly on the ground. In other words, perhaps they are best understood by going for an imaginative walk across Rome. Or, rather, two walks – one some decades after the other.

The first Rome to be crossed is that of the pre-Christian era, in about AD 280. The walker is the emperor Constantine, who would have been at that time just a boy. If the young Constantine had walked from the Forum across the city, as the historian A. D. Lee (who suggested this stroll) has pointed out, he would have passed one religious building after another. On his hypothetical walk, the young Constantine might have walked past the great Temple of Jupiter – 'the most magnificent building in the whole

---

* De Ste. Croix's point being less that Rome should have persecuted the Christians more and earlier; more that their methods were ineffectual and they merely inflamed the situation. 'Persecution' deserves to be in inverted commas, because what happened is more accurately described as 'prosecution'. See Candida Moss's excellent *The Myth of Persecution: How Early Christians Invented a Story of Martyrdom* for a superb and readable account of this period.

world', as the Roman historian Ammianus Marcellinus called it; or seen a temple to the deified Vespasian – that emperor who had healed the blind and cured the lame.

If he had left the Forum and gone up the nearby Palatine Hill, he would have walked past temples dedicated to Apollo (another healer). Had he turned southwards, he might have noted a temple dedicated to the god Mithras, the shady interior of which contained a mysterious inscription that referred to salvation through shed blood.[24] If he had gone further still, he might have passed a temple to Isis – another whose Eastern cult also promised salvation, and whose mother goddess was commonly shown as holding and breastfeeding the infant Horus. (Such images are thought to have influenced representations of the Virgin Mary with Jesus, including the famous image of Jesus and Mary in the Book of Kells – the earliest extant manuscript image showing mother and child in this particular pose.[25])

Continuing on past that temple, the young Constantine might also have seen a temple to Sol Invictus, whose candlelit midwinter festival would cause a later Christian scribe to suggest that its date had been appropriated by the Christians for their own midwinter festival celebrating their own saviour of light. As well as all of these, Constantine would almost certainly have passed the less wealthy and less dramatic house churches belonging to Christians of all kinds.

Constantine, on that first imaginary walk, would have passed temple after temple, to god after god: to male gods and female gods; Eastern gods and Egyptian gods; healing gods and saviour gods and gods-born-of-mortal-women and man-gods and back-from-the-dead gods. A clamorous pantheon testifying to a millennium and more of religious expansion, assimilation and immigration.

Now, for a moment, imagine another young boy or girl attempting to make that same walk across the capital, but this time a hundred or so years later; perhaps in AD 390. There had, by that time, been just a little under a century of Christian rule – and yet this child would have walked through a city that was profoundly different. In those first hundred years, laws had not only been passed against heretics and Jews, but also against the old religions of Rome and their temples. For, in the AD 380s and 390s, the laws of Rome had become what has been described as a 'legislative juggernaut', a body of legislation, as the academic Brent D. Shaw put it, 'specifically aimed at the repression of non-Christian rituals, ceremonial venues and priestly personnel.'[26] Choice – heresy – was starting to be eliminated.

So our imaginary traveller would still have passed temple after temple – but those temples would have seemed very different indeed. Most obviously, they would have looked different. In the 340s and 350s, mere decades into Christian rule, laws had been passed ordering that the doors of temples should be closed 'in all cities, and access to them forbidden, so as to deny to all abandoned men the opportunity to commit sin.'[27] Some of their grandeur may have gone, too: Constantine had ordered that many temples should have their doors removed, their roof cladding taken off, their gleaming sacred statues taken away and their gilding smelted down and added to the treasury, to confute 'the superstitious error of the heathen' (and, critics wryly noted, to fill Constantine's coffers).[28] The temples would also have carried a very different imaginative charge, because the law had not merely ordered them all to be closed, but stated that anyone who dared to enter them and perform a sacrifice would be struck down by an 'avenging sword.'[29]

The debate over who was and was not tolerant in the ancient world is a difficult one. 'Pagan' Rome had not, it is true, shown genuine 'toleration' in the many-layered modern sense of the term; at times, it had not shown much toleration at all. And yet so much had been tolerated. Broadly speaking, the pre-Christian attitude to religion had been 'anything but'. The Christian attitude, by contrast, was closer to 'nothing except'. On that second walk, and after a century of Christian rule, almost every single religion except for Catholic Christianity had been outlawed. This is not to say that these other religions were not practised – but, if they were, it was in many cases under the threat of punishment, possibly even execution. Religious choice – 'heresy' – had become criminalized.

Naturally, laws were easier to make than enforce – and clearly many of those laws were heartily ignored, for decades – in places, for centuries. As one peevish later ruling complained, 'A thousand terrors of the laws that have been promulgated [and] the penalty of exile . . . has been threatened' and still people kept worshipping their old deities. But, the law warned, they would pay for their intransigence, bitterly. Because, the law stated, if any person kept committing such crimes, then, 'Our wrath shall rise up against his fortunes, against his life.'[30] Whether or not the laws were adhered to, they were there. And that in itself is significant.

The world was changing – and even Christians marvelled at the speed at which this change was taking place. As the historian Peter Brown has observed, the first century of Christian rule would see thousands converted, often in mass baptisms.[31] Riding at dawn outside Constantinople at Easter, AD 404, 'the emperor Arcadius saw the crowds of newly baptized in their white robes, looking like a field of flowers.'[32]

The Theodosian Code provides some clues as to what prompted these conversions – but it is also misleading. Look through the Code today and what catches the eye of the modern reader are those violent penalties: the floggings with lead weights; the brandings; the hunting-outs; the ominously opaque 'supreme penalties'. And, without a doubt, these punishments will have had their effect – both on those who suffered them and on those witnessing them. But such punishments would almost certainly have affected only a minority of people. Inertia and the sheer bureaucratic impossibility of enforcing such laws meant the numbers directly affected would have been small.

In truth, the most effective laws may have been the far more humdrum ones. In AD 395, for example, a tedious-sounding law was passed explaining that particular heretics were now forbidden from working in imperial government service, and from making a will.[33] Another law, from the same year, goes further. Heretics were now not merely forbidden from working in the imperial service – they were to be tracked down and dismissed. 'We direct Your Sublimity,' this law ran, 'to investigate whether any of the heretics dare to have membership in the imperial service, in violation of Our laws.'[34] Any heretics who were found in the government – as well as those with whom they had 'connived' to get their job – should not only be removed from the service, 'but even be kept outside the walls of this City.'[35]

Such laws are in a way underwhelming – but they are likely to have been supremely effective. To suppress a heresy the sharp goads of the torturer are rarely necessary: the sharp goads of public opinion, combined with the equally sharp goad of financial necessity, can change behaviours just as effectively, and with less drama. In 1922, the philosopher Bertrand Russell – an avowed agnostic – gave a lecture titled, 'Free Thought and Official Propaganda'. In it, he considered what barriers there were to free thought in the modern world. He was not living in a time of scourges or the rack, but Russell argued that thought was, nonetheless, far from free; and one of the things that he believed restrained it was 'economic pressure'.

The example he gave was from his own life. A few years before, Russell had been invited to become a lecturer by Trinity College, at the University of Cambridge. This was a desirable position and an honour – but the position he was offered was not quite as honourable or desirable as it should have been. For the college didn't invite Russell to become a fellow: its religiously minded hierarchy had no desire for an agnostic to be granted that much voting power. As Russell made clear, the difference between fellow and lecturer 'is not pecuniary; it is that a Fellow has a voice in the government of the College, and cannot be dispossessed during the term of his Fellowship except for grave immorality.' In other words, it would be easier for the college to sack a troublesome agnostic lecturer than a troublesome agnostic fellow.

And, sure enough, a little later, the college duly did so. For, 'in 1916, when they disliked my views on the War' (Russell had a talent for espousing unpopular causes), he promptly found himself out of a job. This was hardly a problem for Russell – who also happened to be an earl. But, as he well knew, he had been lucky: 'If I had been dependent on my lectureship, I should have starved.' Or, more likely – as he well knew – he should not have spoken out at all. 'The habit of considering a man's religious, moral, and political opinions before appointing him to a post or giving him a job,' Russell wrote, 'is the modern form of persecution, and it is likely to become quite as efficient as the Inquisition ever was.'[36] Russell's point was correct, but his chronology was out: the Catholic Church had been using moral and political opinions to withhold jobs and control public opinion for centuries.

As the fourth and then the fifth centuries wore on, the rhetoric and the laws proliferated. Heretics must be berated, hunted out, deported, exiled. Heretics who appeared to repent and then 'stealthily revert' would, one law of AD 415 warned, 'incur the penalty both of proscription and of their life, on account of their rash lawlessness in practising their crime, so that the true and divine worship may in no way be desecrated by such contagion.'[37] Heretics, another law stated, should be cast out of civilized life: 'Manichaeans, heretics, schismatics, and every sect inimical to the Catholics shall be banished from the very sight of the various cities, in order that such cities may not be contaminated by the contagious presence of the criminals.'[38]

But perhaps the most telling law is one issued in AD 407 – just five years short of the first century of Christian influence. It starts in the usual manner: it notes that the emperor is going to pursue certain heretics. More unusual, however, is what comes next. For it goes on to observe that these heretics 'have nothing in common with the human race, so far as either customs or laws are concerned.'[39] Even by the standards of the laws of this period, it is remarkable. Heretics are no longer merely not Christians; they are not even humans. And from now on they are to be pursued with 'exemplary severity'.[40]

Chapter Fourteen

LIKE GRAINS OF SAND

'These are the hidden sayings that the living Jesus spoke and Judas Thomas the Twin recorded'

Prologue, *Gospel of Thomas*,
c. 1st to 2nd century AD

The cliffs around the village of Daba, in Egypt, are a strange and otherworldly place. Here, just a little north of Luxor, the Nile sweeps in a slow curve below the plateau of the Western Desert, then flows on towards Cairo. Demons, or so the old stories say, lurk in the cliffs that loom above. Spirits haunt the plains below. Nonsense, of course. But nonetheless it is true that there are ghosts in this land.

These stones have swallowed up the dead of Upper Egypt for centuries. The cliffs are peppered with graves and dotted by tombs: some of them grand and showy affairs, cut four-square into the face of the rock; others little more than cracks in the stone into which corpses in their shrouds have been pushed.[1] The names of most of the dead, if they were ever engraved on the stones in the first place, have been eroded by time and sand. Today, Ozymandias-like, all are monuments to forgetfulness rather than remembrance. And yet the people of the past feel close enough to touch, here – at times, quite literally. When tourists came here at the start of the twentieth century, they noticed little fragments of bone and scraps of cloth lying in the dust.[2]

Around two millennia ago, this bend in the Nile was an ancient necropolis, a city for the dead. But, from the start of the fourth century AD, these tombs and caves and cliffs also started to swallow up the living. For it was in these years that a holy young Christian named Pachomius – St Pachomius, as he was later known – first came here. Pachomius had already distinguished himself as a follower of Christ: pure in body and in mind, it had long been his habit to eat only bread and salt, and to shun such fripperies as fine clothes, fancy food and even olive oil. Pachomius preferred to season his bread instead with ashes and his own tears.

And then, one day, he came to this bend in the river to collect firewood. The area had a twofold appeal: not only did the land here contain wood, but it was also rich in thorn bushes, and it was Pachomius' particular pleasure to gather wood without shoes on, and 'if thorns happened to pierce his feet he endured them without removing them, remembering the nails that pierced our Lord on the cross.'[3] As he was engaged in this holy work of collecting wood and making his feet bleed, Pachomius was surprised by a voice from heaven. 'Pachomius, Pachomius,' the angelic voice said, 'dwell in this place and build a monastery.' The angel, with a certain bureaucratic briskness, then promptly handed over a tablet of iron to Pachomius, on which, the angel explained, were written down all the rules which Pachomius' future followers would have to obey.

One of the first Christian monasteries had been born – and started to fill, rapidly. Year after year, more and more Christian men (and, later, women) gathered around Pachomius to devote their lives to work and prayer.[4] Their life was one of regimented religious rigour. As the angel's rather stark rules had ordered, each man would 'each day pray twelve times, at evening twelve times, and in the night twelve times, and at the ninth hour, three times,' a total of thirty-nine prayers a day.[5] So little? the pious Pachomius had asked. It is necessary, the angel explained, to make allowances for the weak.

Those who joined Pachomius – and, perhaps surprisingly, many did – took on a life of striking austerity. Rest, conversation and individual liberty were all curtailed. At meals, the monks ate in silence; while they toiled – hoeing and chiselling and weaving baskets – they chanted Bible verses, lest their minds wander; when they slept, they slept on upright chairs made of brick, lest they become too comfortable. All were athletes of austerity, torturing themselves in this life so they might taste glory in the next.[6] And yet, despite their divine intentions, it is clear that, at times, an all too human discord threatened the peace. The first draft of Pachomius' monastic laws, handed over by that angel, paints an idealistic picture of the monks' lives. Pachomius' men would, the angelic document explained, perform their duties openly, and with 'shining countenance'.[7] It is a beautiful image.

However, it seems that over the years the countenances of the good monks occasionally clouded a little. For, appended onto angelically idealistic *Rules of Pachomius: Part I* are the slightly less serene *Rules of Pachomius: Part II*, and the even crabbier *Rules of Pachomius: Part III*. These testy codicils testify less to heavenly harmony than to the very earthly irritation that comes from living too close to one's companions for too long, with nothing but basket-weaving for distraction. Crossness codified, they give vent to years of accumulated irritation, as action after action is outlawed and increasingly furious punishments are instituted.

So, while *Rules of Pachomius: Part I* merely states that talking at dinner is not allowed, *Part II* confirms this – but adds that looking around at dinner is also not allowed; that putting one's hands on the table before one's elders is not allowed; that missing prayers at table is not allowed; and that, if any monk should laugh at table, 'he shall be judged.'[8] Like an oppressive partner, the laws go on, codifying in minute detail what is acceptable and what is unacceptable at all times of the day and night. Every aspect of life is circumscribed. Washing oneself is not allowed, nor is anointing oneself, nor talking in the dark, nor taking someone else's hand, nor – as one cross, but frankly not unreasonable, law added – 'any part of his body'.[9]

Laundry, as so often with communal living, irked everyone. Another irascible law notes that, if anyone leaves their garment hanging up so that 'the sun rises over it three times, the owner of the garment shall be judged on account of it, and he shall prostrate himself in the church, and shall stand while the brethren eat.'[10] Other things were also frowned upon. Accumulating your own possessions 'even to a needle' was considered a loathsome crime, punished by 'fifty days threefold with fasting with water and bread', while the forced prostration of the guilty monk before the altar was to be 'increased to two hundred times.'[11] In other places, the laws show evident irritation with behaviour that, after years of desert isolation, seems to have wandered a little from social norms. 'No one', one law rules, 'shall cut the hair of anyone unless he has been commanded'.[12] No one, added another intriguing yet unarguable law, 'shall ride on an ass alone, or without garments, with another.'[13]

Yet, despite all the rules and the privations, soon over a thousand men had gathered here, following Pachomius' rules, tilling the land – and brewing quiet resentments against their holy brethren.[14] Though not all Christians round about obeyed the holy Pachomius. Not long after the monastery was founded, someone – perhaps, some think, someone from the monastery, though that is far from certain – arrived at this area of the Nile carrying some manuscripts, probably contained within a sealed pottery jar. And then they hid them.[15] Time and forgetfulness and the sands of the Egyptian desert closed over them. This is a good place to hide a secret.

And here this secret lay until, in 1945, it was rediscovered. The story of precisely how these particular manuscripts came to light is vexed, to say the least. According to the most well-known telling, they were found by a group of local farmers who were digging nearby. As these men were working, they came across a jar, made of red pottery, covered at the top with a bowl which had probably been sealed on with bitumen. The leader of this group of men was – so this story goes – unsure what to do with his find. His initial reaction was one of fear. Thinking that the jar might contain an evil spirit, a jinn, within its stoppered darkness, he hesitated to open it. Then another thought occurred: it might contain treasure. He therefore took his mattock and smashed it. At that moment he saw a strange material, 'like grains of sand perhaps capable of turning into gold, swirling up and disappearing into the air.' Or so it was said.[16]

Much of that story has since been vigorously questioned.

However, while the details of where and how the find was made are contested, what the farmers found is much clearer: they found books, about twelve of them.[17] The antiquity of these volumes was, at first, hard to judge. One of the books was so old and delicate it may have dissolved on opening, perhaps leading to those swirling motes of golden dust – probably papyrus fragments. Others looked so fresh, they might have been just a few years old. Wrapped in leather, and bound by thin leather straps, their covers were still supple to the touch. In photographs, they look exactly like the kind of bijou leather-bound notebooks one might buy in the more expensive tourist shops.[18]

Eventually, these manuscripts found their way into the antiquities trade. News about them started to spread among antiquarians – first slowly, and then with increasing excitement. In 1955, word of this discovery reached a professor of religious history in the Netherlands. He flew to Cairo, went to a museum that had photographs of the text, borrowed these pictures, then went back to his hotel.[19] Peering at the first words, the professor read: 'These are the hidden sayings that the living Jesus spoke and Judas Thomas the Twin recorded.'[20] The Nag Hammadi scriptures had been found. The world's understanding of early Christianity was about to be transformed.

Chapter Fifteen

ON THE OTHER ORIGIN OF THE WORLD

'He has certainly shown himself to be a malicious grudger.'

The *Testimony of Truth* considers the character of God,
late 2nd to early 3rd century AD

Here is one beginning:

In the beginning, God created the heavens and the earth. Now the earth was formless and empty, darkness was over the surface of the deep, and the Spirit of God was hovering over the waters.

And God said, 'Let there be light,' and there was light.[1]

This God was great. Indeed, as he later declared, he was the greatest. He said, 'I am the LORD, and there is no other, besides me there is no God.'[2] He said, 'You shall have no other gods before Me.'[3] He said, 'I the LORD your God am a jealous God.'[4] And the seraphim arrayed themselves about the throne of this God and glorified him. And one called to another and said, 'Holy, holy, holy is the LORD of hosts; the whole earth is full of his glory!'[5]

This God continued in his act of creation. He made night, and day, and water, and land, and he made cattle and creeping things, and beasts of the earth, and fish, and fowl. And then he looked at what he had made, this God, and he saw that it was good.[6]

That, at any rate, was one ancient telling. But there were others. Many others.

Here is another:

In the beginning, there was darkness, and chaos. Here, too, there was a divine being. In fact, this time, there was more than one. There was a divine mother, and she gave birth to a son. He moved in the depths of the waters. This immortal son, like many a child, barely noticed his mother or what she had done for him. He believed that he had come into this world alone, all by his own power. He looked around him. He saw darkness, and water, and he became confused – and conceited.

The god, as this ancient text explains, 'saw only himself and nothing else except water and darkness. He thought that only he existed.'[7] He therefore started to boast: he 'exalted himself, and he was glorified by the whole army of angels.'[8] The creator god 'was delighted. He boasted over and over again, and said to them, "I don't need anything." He said, "I am God, and there is no other but me." '[9]

This time, however, such boasts go down less well. The other immortals – for there are many other immortals in this story – were angered by this ignorant, boastful god. And so, when the creator declared, 'I am God, and there is no other but me', in this text, his mother interrupts.

Hearing her foolish son brag, 'she became angry'. And, without being seen by him, she said, 'You are wrong, Samael' – which means 'blind god'.[10] And the creator god was shocked and embarrassed. For, as this text concludes a little later, this creator god 'was a fool.'[11]

That, at any rate, was another telling.

That jar in Nag Hammadi did not contain any demons. It instead contained something that, for Christianity, has long been more unsettling: it contained books. And not just any books, but a series of texts that, until that moment, had been believed entirely lost to history: books about heretics, written by the hands of the so-called heretics themselves. And they were dazzling.

Some things about these books became clear immediately: they were written in Coptic (the written form of a late stage of ancient Egyptian) and they had almost certainly originally been composed in Greek. It was also clear that they were ancient – the manuscripts themselves seem to have been written down in the first half of the fourth century and perhaps buried in the second half of the same. It soon became obvious that many of the texts they contained were even older. The dating of these texts from Nag Hammadi is deeply fraught. Many are clearly later than, and are talking about, or referencing, the texts that make up the New Testament. But one text, or so some argue, might be as old as those contained within the New Testament itself. Perhaps even older. Needless to say – for in the world of the gospels older is often assumed to equal more reliable – that claim is heartily contested.[12]

Interpreting what these texts meant was rather more complex. Many were clearly Christian – though they were unlike any form of Christianity that has survived into the modern world. Their titles alone were striking. Modern Bibles offer only the four gospels of Matthew, Mark, Luke and John. The books found in Nag Hammadi added such titles as the *Gospel of Truth* and the *Gospel of Thomas* and the *Gospel of Philip*. Similarly, where the Bible offers merely the Apocalypse of John, these manuscripts (depending on how they are translated) contain the *Apocalypse of Paul*, the *Apocalypse of Adam*, and the *First* and *Second Apocalypse of James*.

Some of their titles had a drily philosophical air: one was titled the *Authoritative Discourse*; another *Excerpt from the Perfect Discourse*. Others of the texts had stronger Jewish influences. Many were tinged with Greek philosophy and peppered with Greek philosophical terms. Still others offered a thrilling hint of the clandestine, with such titles as the *Secret Book of John* and the *Secret Book of James*. To this day, some remain hard to categorize at all; one text is titled, with magnificent impenetrability, *The Thunder, Perfect Mind*.

To peer into them is a bewildering experience. In these rediscovered texts, belief after cherished Christian belief is picked up, tilted and set down at a different angle. Sometimes these manuscripts tell the same stories as the more well-known form of Christianity, but tell them in a different way; sometimes they tell entirely different stories; at other times, they tell the same stories in more or less the same way, but lean on certain points, pressing on a word here, or a phrase there, and so changing the way in which the reader must interpret the entire tale. Often they frankly laugh at the revered gospels. Though what they say – their precise criticism – is less important than the mere fact that they are saying it. For what is being glimpsed in their pages are forms of early Christianity that are far more experimental and radical than the one that survived; forms of Christianity that criticized, critiqued, played with, changed and openly attacked both sacred texts and even God himself.

Consider the story of Creation, which is told and told and told again in their pages. Creation, in many of these texts, has an entirely different atmosphere from the Creation in the Bible. It is not a moment of surpassing mystery and beauty, but a hideous divine mistake. In these texts, the god who creates the world is not there in the beginning: he has been created in his turn by a divine mother (who is herself the offspring of yet another higher power). And whereas in the Bible the creator God is the object of near-universal adoration, in these texts he is far less revered: indeed, as soon as his mother has created him, she makes it clear that she is appalled by him. He is repulsive to her.

In a similarly revolutionary vein, while God in the Bible insists that everyone worships him, and causes seraphim to array themselves about him, chanting 'Holy, holy, holy', in these texts his requirements for perpetual worship are resisted and he is instead described as 'an arrogant beast'.[13] His boasts that he alone is God are repeatedly challenged. Not that that stops him making them. Having been slapped down by his mother, the creator god, undeterred, then creates some offspring and tells them, 'I am God of all.'[14] Whereupon his mother's daughter, with the sort of public scorn that only a sister can muster, promptly 'called out and said to him, "You are wrong."'[15]

In the Nag Hammadi texts, the inconsistencies and loose narrative threads of Christian stories are picked at, unravelled and woven into new stories. Consider the idea that there is only one God. The Christianity that survived was insistent on this point. But as some of these texts argue, the Bible itself offers hints – and more – that other gods exist. There is, most obviously, the well-known moment when God declares himself in the Bible to be a 'jealous God'. As the *Secret Book of John* tartly points out, 'by announcing this, he suggested . . . that there is another god. For if there were no other god, of whom would he be jealous?'[16]

One story they return to repeatedly is that of the expulsion from Eden. In the traditional telling known to most Christians today, Adam and Eve are invited to eat of every tree, but they are told, 'of the tree of the knowledge of good and evil, thou shalt not eat of it: for in the day that thou eatest thereof thou shalt surely die.'[17] But then the crafty serpent, with its serpent tongue, tempts Eve. Did God say to you that you may not eat of it? the serpent asks Eve. She assents: God said not just that she and Adam should not eat, but he said, 'Ye shall not eat of it, neither shall ye touch it, lest ye die.'[18]

Many of the Nag Hammadi texts treat this tale with frank contempt. 'What kind of a god is this?' asks one of the manuscripts, known as the *Testimony of Truth*, which has been dated to the late second or early third century.[19] What sort of a god is it who 'begrudged Adam's eating from the tree of knowledge'? Moreover, the text points out, the supposedly 'omniscient' god of this story doesn't seem all that omniscient. For, in Genesis, God realizes Adam has done wrong only when he is walking in the cool of the day and calls out to him to ask him where he is. The *Testimony of Truth* is unimpressed: 'he said, "Adam, where are you?"' This, the text argues, is a silly idea: an omniscient god would have known where Adam was.

Furthermore, God would have known this not only before he asked the question, but before Adam had even eaten the fruit. So, the text concludes, 'God does not have foreknowledge; otherwise, wouldn't he have known from the beginning?' Besides, it goes on, impatiently, why did this odd god make such a ruling in the first place? Why would he not have wanted his creation to eat from the tree of knowledge of good and evil? What could possibly be bad about knowledge? God, this text concludes, has 'certainly shown himself to be a malicious grudger.'[20]

In another manuscript, called *The Nature of the Rulers*, the serpent is represented not – as it would come to be in the West and in Milton – as fork-tongued and mazy-minded, but instead as 'wiser' than all the other animals.* Here, the serpent does not lead Eve astray, but instead comes, in a far more positive guise, as 'a female spiritual presence' and 'an instructor'.[21] As in Genesis, it is the serpent who teaches Adam and Eve that, contrary to God's threat, they could eat of the fruit without dying – but, here, the female serpent adds a little slur on God. She says to Eve, 'You will not surely die, for he said this to you out of jealousy. Rather, your eyes will open and you will be like gods, knowing good and evil.'[22] In another text, the moment when Adam and Eve eat from the tree and then realize that they are naked is not cast, as it is in Christian interpretations, as a 'fall', but as the moment when, 'Insight appeared to them as light and awakened their minds.'[23]

Other Nag Hammadi texts feel even more unfamiliar to modern readers. One manuscript explains that the creation of man was performed not by God, but by a throng of angelic creatures, who assembled mortals bit by bit: 'Abron created the skull . . . Yeronumos the right ear, Bissoum the left ear . . .' On and on and on runs this account of Creation, like a gnostic kneebone song, through the teeth (Amen made them), molars (Ibikan did those), fingernails (Krima), right elbow, left elbow, testicles (Eilo), right leg, left leg . . . all the way down to the toenails (Miamai).[24]

At other times, the differences offered by these texts are minor, but profound. Take the gender of God. Christian theologians have long argued that their God is sexless; however, as the historian Elaine Pagels has pointed out, someone sitting in church, hearing God referred to as He, Him, Lord and Master, might be forgiven for thinking otherwise.[25] Christians in Syria

* Which is also the sense in the Hebrew; though accumulated years of disdain make it hard to see.

had taken a different approach to the Holy Ghost – and some of the texts found in Nag Hammadi have echoes of that more androgynous deity. One text hymns not the Father, Son and Holy Ghost, but instead 'Father, Mother, Child, / perfect power', and celebrates 'the Holy Spirit, who is called the Mother of the Living.'[26] Another second-century text talks of a 'firmament of the female' and of how it was a female who 'had produced the first creation.'[27]

Several texts acknowledge the existence of the boastful male Creator known from the Old Testament, but they scorn him and instead celebrate 'the perfect glory', the 'universal womb, for she precedes everything.' One text goes on to worship,

> the Mother-Father,
> the first Human,
> the Holy Spirit,
> the triple male,
> the triple power,
> the androgynous one with three names.[28]

Women were not always secondary in these writings. The mother of the creator god is, in many of these texts, infinitely wiser than her foolish, bragging son. In another text, we learn that Eve, far from being castigated as the source of man's evil, instead is perfectly able to get along without men altogether, for she 'gave birth to her first child without a man'.[29] That text also offers the 'Song of Eve', which declares:

> I am the wife, I am the virgin.
> I am pregnant, I am the physician.
> I am the comforter of birth pains.[30]

To those who are raised in the relentlessly male Christian divine tradition, texts that give such power to women – making them not only independent of men but critical, and even scornful of them – can feel almost shocking. But, as Pagels has argued, our shock is, in a way, misplaced. Consider the matter in the broad sweep of history and it suddenly seems less surprising that some Christian sects had powerful female characters and deities, than that any religion ever arose without them. The anomaly is Christianity, for the 'absence of feminine symbolism for God marks Judaism, Christianity, and Islam in striking contrast to the world's other religious traditions, whether in Egypt, Babylonia, Greece, or Rome', for all of these 'abound in feminine symbolism.'[31]

And, in these writings unearthed from the sands of Egypt, there is text after text that rejects the authority of the nascent Church. In many of these manuscripts, bishops are not men to abase yourself before, nor to celebrate, but are instead slightly ludicrous creations; they are men who 'call themselves bishops and deacons, as if they had received their authority from God', but who are, in truth, no such thing. The clergy of the Church, one text observes with bitterness, 'oppress their brothers and say to them . . . "salvation comes to us alone".' But, this text argues, the idea is absurd. These bishops pretend to be conduits for the divine spirit, but no spirit runs through them: 'those people are dry canals.'[32]

Such arguments were a profound ideological threat to the increasingly powerful Christian Church. By the time the texts buried in Nag Hammadi were being written, the Church's bishops had been consolidating their power for centuries. As one less than self-effacing bishop wrote, 'It is manifest . . . that we should look upon the bishop even as we would upon the Lord Himself.'[33] Bishops started to command that everything in a church must go through them: baptism without a bishop did not, or so bishops argued, count; Eucharist without a bishop did not count either.[34] Prayers, bishops argued, worked better with a bishop present. As the historian Peter Brown has put it, 'We are dealing with the claims of an austere, transcendent monotheism, put forward by the clergy in the name of their own monopoly of access to the divine.'[35] Heaven, which once had been open to all, was being closed: gates were being erected at its entrance, and it was the bishop who would hold the keys.

When examined in the light of the Nag Hammadi texts, the contours of ancient Christianity, which had been drawn so simplistically by ancient anti-heretical writers, suddenly started to look different. Areas that had been in shadow were illuminated; things that had seemed simple started to look more complex. The face of ancient Christianity started to change. One of the most influential academics to work on these texts was a philosopher named Hans Jonas, and he suggested a metaphor to understand how radically different the ancient form of Christianity that these texts revealed was. Picture the ceiling of the Sistine Chapel, he wrote, with its well-known images in their bubble-gum-bright robes. There is Eve beside the tree; there is David, slaying Goliath; and over there is Judith with Holofernes' head on a platter. And of course there, in the centre, is the most significant moment of all, the moment when Michelangelo's God reaches out the most famous finger in art: the moment of Creation.

But, said Jonas, had another form of Christianity won through, Michelangelo would have had to paint something very different indeed. Imagine, Jonas wrote, the Sistine ceiling once again. But this time the picture is different. To look at it feels strange; like looking at a reflection in a distorting mirror, it is at once familiar and disconcerting. The scenes are like those we know – but each has been changed a little, rearranged a little. There is a creator god, but there are other divine beings around him too – for, 'how much more numerous [is] the cast'.[36]

And, at times, how much less appealing. God is here still, in this other Sistine Chapel – but he has changed. Here, in this form of Christianity, the Creator is no muscle-bound beauty, but an ugly, misshapen creature – like, as that text put it, 'an aborted foetus'.[37] The moment of Creation is also present – but now it is just one creation among many. For there would have to be the moment when the Creator himself was created from his mother; and another panel for her creation, too; and yet another to show the creation of her daughter, that divine being who so disliked her boastful brother who called himself God of all. On and on this would go, branching, proliferating layers of beings, seven of them, thirty more, hundreds more again . . . Here, in this Christianity, there is doubt, disagreement, argument – above all, there is variety.

What is startling about the texts that were pulled from the sands of Nag Hammadi is less the particular narrative difference that this manuscript, or that one, offered. What is startling is that such differences are there at all. One form of Christianity survived, and suffused the art and literature of the West for centuries. It would acquire power, and money – the kind of power and money that could afford to build the Sistine Chapel, and commission artists such as Michelangelo to decorate it. But it had not, in the beginning, been the only form.

However, these other kinds of Christianity, as Hans Jonas pointed out, 'found no Michelangelo to retell [them], no Dante and no Milton.' Instead, the 'sterner discipline of biblical creed' won out, and so the other teachings which 'challenged, tempted, tried to twist the new faith are forgotten, their written record buried in the tomes of the refuters or the sands of ancient lands. Our art and literature and much else would be different, had [this other] message prevailed.'[38] It did not.

Chapter Sixteen

TO UNWEAVE THE RAINBOW

'His life . . . is related in so fabulous a manner by his disciples, that we are at a loss to discover whether he was a sage, an impostor, or a fanatic.'

Edward Gibbon, *The Decline and Fall of the Roman Empire*, 1776

Father Arnall's descriptions were detailed and they were revolting. In James Joyce's *A Portrait of the Artist as a Young Man*, the Catholic priest outlines to a group of terrified schoolboys what lies in wait for them in the next life if they are not good in this one. The sermon is Victorian in its tone and baroque in its tortures. In splendidly sadistic detail, Father Arnall explains to the children – 'my dear little brothers in Christ' – that what awaits them is hell. Hell, he explains, is 'a strait and dark and foul-smelling prison, an abode of demons and lost souls, filled with fire and smoke', in which there is a 'never ending storm of darkness, dark flames and dark smoke of burning brimstone.'

Warming magnificently to his theme, the good Father explains that brimstone doesn't merely scorch, it also stinks, and 'fills all hell with its intolerable stench' – as indeed do the smouldering bodies of the damned themselves, which 'exhale such a pestilential odour' that 'one of them alone would suffice to infect the whole world'. Father Arnall's description continues for several paragraphs, and does not stint on phrases about 'nauseous loathsome decomposition' and 'fetid carcasses'. The sermon has its desired effect. As he listens, the young hero of the story, Stephen Dedalus, is horrified; his flesh 'shrank together as it felt the approach of the ravenous tongues of flames.'[1]

At about the same time as Joyce's fictional Victorian schoolboys were being disturbed by Father Arnall's hell, a wholly different afterlife was disturbing the quietude of another late Victorian preacher, this time in America. Andrew Preston Peabody was brilliant: he had gone to Harvard in his early teens and had become a tutor in mathematics – and, almost in his spare time, he had translated classical works.[2] But this man of many talents was also devoted to the church and eventually became a professor of 'Christian Morals' at the university.[3] And it was while translating a work by Plutarch – a Greek 'pagan' writer who had died in around AD 120 or so – that he noticed something which perturbed him – or at least which demanded an explanation. For this particular work of Plutarch appeared to precisely describe Christian hell – but it had been written by a man who could not possibly have read about hell in any Christian text.

It is easy to see why Peabody was disturbed. The work he was translating is called *On the Delay of the Divine Justice* and it contains some profoundly Christian-sounding passages on the afterlife. The Greek story told by Plutarch is a simple one: a debauched young man named Thespesius* is the despair of his family until, one day, he falls from a precipice and strikes his neck on the ground. He is not bleeding, but he falls into a faint and lies there for three days 'as one dead'. By the third day, he is being carried out to his funeral when – in a twist that is by now familiar – he is 'suddenly aroused from his swoon'.

It soon becomes clear that it is not the old, debauched Thespesius who has returned from near death to his family. Instead, now the young man has revived, he is found to have 'made an incredible change in his manner of life.'[4] His period of unconsciousness appears to have entirely changed his personality. What had happened? Plutarch's interlocutor explains that, while the man had been lying unconscious and still in his body, his soul had embarked upon a remarkable journey, as he was taken to see the various afterlives that lie in wait for the dead of this world.

First, Thespesius had been carried up to heaven, where he saw the souls of the dying rise like bubbles through the air and fly into 'the zenith of the circumambient heavens', glowing and goodly.[5] But, as well as these happy spirits, Thespesius had also seen those souls that, after death, sink down. He peered into the

* He is also called Aridaeus (a nod to Plato), but for simplicity here I stick with Thespesius.

netherworld below and saw a shadowy line of souls, some of which had bodies 'streaked with what looked like scales and flabby scourge-marks'; others were 'very much discolored, and disgusting to the sight, like snakes branded all over with black spots.' He had not merely seen them; he had also heard them, for some 'gave utterance to inarticulate sounds like battle-cries mingled with strains of lamentation and terror.'[6]

These, Thespesius' infernal tour guide had explained, were disembodied souls, and the marks visible on their bodies were the result of the posthumous punishments with which they were being tortured for their wickedness in this life. For, as the pitiless guide explained, Zeus ordains 'punishment for wrong-doings of every kind' – and no one can escape this. Precisely what sort of punishment you would receive depended on which deity in the underworld dealt with you. But, as the guide made clear, all were unpleasant.

Some of these souls had their clothes stripped off, then were beaten, even as they 'beg[ged] with tears that the scourge may be laid aside.' Others experienced something a little more like a smithy. Thespesius himself saw three 'lakes lying side by side, one of boiling gold, one of lead intensely cold, another of rough iron', and around the lakes sat 'certain daemons, like metal-workers, with their instruments', who forked up accursed souls, then plunged them alternately into the molten gold, the frozen lead, and the iron. This left them 'so fractured and bruised by the hardness of the iron, as to look like different beings'.[7] The truly wicked needed a lot of work to reshape them: Nero, naturally, was still down there when Thespesius dropped by, being 'pierced with red-hot nails.'[8]

Plutarch's story was splendid fun – and, like all stories in Plutarch, beautifully told – but it was not his own invention. The idea of proportional punishment in the afterlife was, by the end of the first century AD, a well-worn one. Well over a century before, the Latin poet Virgil had described a similarly unpleasant underworld, filled with 'groans, the sound of the savage lash, the clank of iron and the dragging of chains', as the dead were tortured to purify their souls.[9] (Not for nothing would Dante choose the 'pagan' Virgil to be the guide to his Inferno.)

Even in Virgil's day, such stories were old news: three-odd centuries before, the philosopher Plato had created a particularly vivid hell. Situated in 'the deepest pit beneath earth', Plato's afterlife had all the usual accessories, including 'a huge region all ablaze with fire', a lake that boiled with mud, and an infernal triage system in which humans were first judged, then taken away for treatment.[10] (Although, as Plato's somewhat smug dialogue explained, those who had been 'purified by philosophy' didn't have to bother with any of that: instead, they would spring free into the 'pure dwelling above', where they lived 'bodiless for the whole of time to come.'[11])

By the second century AD, when Plutarch was writing, such hellish visions had become so commonplace in ancient literature that they had drawn the attention of satirists. In his *True History* (which naturally is anything but), the reliably sceptical Lucian offered his readers an underworld that stank of 'pitch and brimstone burning', the smell of which was 'intolerable', as if – a detail of which Father Arnall would surely approve – 'men were broiling upon burning coals'. Lucian's underworld was an engaging place, which offered the vision of one particularly unfortunate soul who had been 'tied by private members, and [was] hanging up in the smoke'. The whole place resounded, Lucian wrote, to the 'lash of the whips, and the roarings of the tormented'.[12]

Plutarch's hell has a happy ending, of sorts. The young Thespesius was so appalled by what he had seen that, when he woke, he resolved to change his life entirely. The man who was once dissipated became a model of virtue. To this day, Plutarch's narrator explains, the man's neighbours know 'of no other person in his time more honest than he in keeping his engagements, more religiously devout'.[13]

Andrew Peabody was a brilliant man, and a well-read one. He could not avoid seeing the many similarities between

Plutarch's hell and the Christian one. As he himself admits in his introduction, much of what Plutarch writes, is 'decidedly Christian in spirit'. Indeed, 'in many passages' of Plutarch one can see 'an almost manifest transcript of the thought of the Divine Founder of our religion.' But he is not able to believe – as others had argued – that Plutarch had read any Christian literature. No, the very idea, Peabody writes, must be considered 'utterly false'. Plutarch had been writing far too early, and too far away from Jerusalem, for it to have been possible for him to lay his hands on any Christian writings. Besides, Peabody points out, there was no evidence of any Christian church in Plutarch's area in that period. Moreover, Plutarch never mentions Christianity by name. For all of these reasons, Peabody concludes, it is impossible that Plutarch has been influenced by Christian works through reading them.[14]

But then Peabody's introduction takes what seems to modern eyes a strange turn, because he nonetheless will not give up the idea that it was Plutarch who was influenced by Christianity. 'I cannot doubt . . . that an infusion of Christianity had somehow infiltrated itself into Plutarch's ethical opinions and sentiments'.[15] For, just as the sun lights up 'sheltered groves and grottos that are completely dark', creeping into every corner, so too, Peabody argues in rich Victorian style, the 'Sun of Righteousness' must have shone into Plutarch's mind, even though he did not know it. Christian thought had crept 'into regions where its source was wholly unknown', probably, he suggests, through the chatter of slaves, bringing with it the 'loftiness, precision, delicacy, tenderness, [and] breadth of human sympathy' of true holiness.

So it was that, even though Plutarch may not have knowingly heard the name of Christ, or read a single work of Christian literature, he and his writings were suffused with Christianity nonetheless.[16] The idea that the influence might have run in the other direction – that classical works might have influenced Christian hells – is not even mentioned.

*

In 1901, the pioneering psychologist William James gave a series of lectures in Edinburgh titled 'The Varieties of Religious Experience'. But it was their daring, almost sacrilegious, subtitle that hinted at how radical these talks were going to be, for they were, 'A study in human nature'. In other words, in his lectures James was going to look at religion not as a divine creation, but a mortal one. He was going to go further: he would look at different 'religious' experiences – and consider them not merely in the light of theology, but also of psychology and pathology. In other words, he would look at religious experience not purely as a gift of the gods, but as a very mortal malfunction of the mind.

Few knew better than James that many might object to such a matter-of-fact approach to the divine. As he himself admitted, this was a difficult topic to broach. Religious experiences feel, to the person experiencing them, incomparable in every sense. People 'recoil', as James put it, from any comparison of religious experiences, since 'any object that is infinitely important to us and awakens our devotion feels to us also as if it must be sui generis and unique. Probably a crab would be filled with a sense of personal outrage if it could hear us class it without ado or apology as a crustacean, and thus dispose of it. "I am no such thing," it would say; "I am MYSELF, MYSELF alone."'[17]

Comparison is rarely comfortable for religions – and Christianity, like the crab, long resisted it. For a long time, books on the history of Christianity rarely used to offer extensive chapters on other healers or saviours or raisings from the dead. On the contrary, a discreet veil was often drawn over such echoes. Books on Christianity also tended not to offer extensive chapters recording the scorn of Porphyry, or the scathing criticism of Celsus. Many barely even mentioned 'pagans' at all. One of the most influential Victorian histories on Christianity contained, as a later historian pointed out, 'no reference to a pagan source and hardly a line indicating the least attempt to find out what non-Christians thought and believed.'[18] The idea that other cultures and religions might have influenced Christianity was not merely ignored by many Christian historians, it was often heartily denied. As late as 1975, an academic might write that the Christian gospels were 'unique with respect to their literary character, and they do not have any predecessors or any successors.'[19] The message was clear: Christianity was ITSELF, ITSELF alone.

Such authors were following in a venerable tradition. From its earliest days, Christianity had a habit of denying that it owed anything to the classical world from which it had sprung, in either ritual or thought. In fact, many Christians vehemently argued that the reverse was true: the classical world had stolen its ideas from them. The second-century Christian writer Clement of Alexandria claimed that Greek authors (those 'pilferers') had 'imitated and copied the marvels recorded in our books' and, moreover, have 'plagiarized and falsified' Christian ideas.'[20] Greek philosophy, Clement wrote, was 'like the torch of wick which men kindle, artificially stealing the light from the sun.'[21] Pythagoras and Plato had, whatever the Greeks might claim, not been original at all: they had stolen their ideas from Moses. Elaborate travel plans were invented by ancient Christians to argue that Plato had picked up Moses' writings while on a tour of Egypt.

Even Virgil, that most classical of Latin poets, was not immune to being captured for Christian ends. Virgil had died in 19 BC, almost two decades before Jesus was born. And yet he had written in his *Eclogues* that, 'Now the Virgin returns . . . now a new generation descends from heaven'. These lines would alternately puzzle and delight Christians for centuries.[22] How could Virgil possibly have foreseen Jesus' birth? For many fervent Christians, from Augustine to the emperor Constantine, the answer was obvious: Virgil, the poet who had hymned the imperium of Rome, was in fact a Christian prophet. The idea would almost certainly have rather surprised Virgil himself – and even some Christians baulked at it (the reliably crabby St Jerome dismissed the idea as 'infantile').[23] But many others were convinced. As late as the nineteenth century, a fervent English cleric could write that it was 'God himself' who uttered those lines, while the scholar John Keble, in Oxford, wrote, 'in fact I believe' that something prophetic clung to them.[24]

Christians believed their religion to be both unique and uniquely true. And yet, as the Victorian era wore on, a steady stream of discoveries started to shake such certainties. Consider the cuneiform tablets of the British Museum. They are covered in a script made up of small triangles (*cuneus* is the Latin word for 'wedge'); the once malleable clay swells plumply around the words and, like anything covered in a script that one can't read, they look intriguing, almost secretive. Often such thrilling appearances belie disappointingly dull content: all too often, when ancient scripts are finally deciphered, they turn out to contain little more than information on taxes, grain, beer or goats. But not in this case.

In the second half of the nineteenth century, a young man named George Smith started to translate some of these tablets. His reaction to one in particular was, to say the least, remarkable: as Smith began to work through it, he suddenly cried out, 'I am the first man to read that after two thousand years of oblivion.' He then set the tablet on the table, 'jumped up and rushed about the room in a great state of excitement, and, to the astonishment of those present, began to undress himself!'[25]

To read what Smith had just translated is, even now, to understand his excitement. For what he saw in that tablet was an account of a flood – but not the flood of the Bible. It was yet another, Mesopotamian version of it. Smith was looking at the story known as the *Epic of Gilgamesh*, which contains a flood story within it – though, it was later realized, the flood Smith was looking at was related to an even older Akkadian epic called *Atrahasis*, which has been found on tablets dating to 1700 BC – far, far older than any written record of the biblical flood.[26]

The similarities between these two versions and that of Genesis have long since become well known, but are so striking that they still bear retelling. In Genesis, God creates man 'of dust from the ground and breathed into his nostrils the breath of life, and the man became a living creature.'[27] In *Atrahasis*, the birth of man happens when one god is killed and the birth goddess 'shall mix clay with his flesh and his blood. Then a god and a man will be mixed together in clay.'[28] Mud is mingled with divinity.

The presence of more than one god in *Atrahasis* would seem, initially, to be a difference to the Christian version – which is usually remembered as being performed by a single deity. However, that is not, in fact, what the biblical text says. Look again at the precise words in the Bible and many modern readers might feel a moment of surprise. For what the Bible actually says in Genesis 1:26 is, 'Let us make man in our image, after our likeness'.[29] Not 'my own image', but 'our'. Not 'my likeness', but 'our likeness'. The conclusion that there is, in Genesis – as there is in every other version of this story – more than one god, here, seems inescapable.*

The echoes become more pronounced as the stories continue. In both, it is not long before things go wrong. Mankind, having been created, goes on and multiplies. It multiplies so successfully that, in the *Atrahasis* version, it is not mankind's sin but their general noisy babble that annoys the gods above. 'The noise of mankind has become too much,' declares one. 'I am losing sleep over their racket.'[30] In *Gilgamesh*, the gods merely 'decided

---

* And so naturally, this conclusion was resisted, vigorously, for centuries. Some scholars created a grammatical category, a plural of 'majesty', to solve the problem. God was so great, he had become plural; a sort of divine equivalent of the royal 'we'. Later Christian apologists offered a different solution: the plural was a true plural, but this merely reflected the fact that God was a trinity – three in one. So, here, when God said 'us', he was simply talking to Christ. Another Christian scholar suggested that it wasn't just Christ to whom he was speaking: all three members of the Trinity – Father, Son and Holy Spirit – were here discussing the creation of man, all together. A Council of Sirmium supported the Father–Son hypothesis, and offered yet another argument to convince doubters, namely excommunication. The Council might have been persuasive, but it was wrong. Scholars now recognize that the reason for the plural is, quite simply, that those who composed the version in Genesis believed there was more than one god in heaven.

that the great gods should make a flood.'[31] In Genesis, meanwhile, it is not long before 'God saw that the wickedness of man was great in the earth' and 'the Lord said, I will destroy man whom I have created from the face of the earth.'[32] In each tale, punishment comes in the form of a flood, while salvation comes in the form of a moment of divine pity, and a boat.

In *Atrahasis*, one god takes pity on a single man and tells him to 'Dismantle the house, build a boat / Reject possessions, and save living things.' The boat, he is told, should have a roof, and he must use strong bitumen, 'to give strength.' He then 'put his family on board', as well as cattle and birds and wild animals too, before the storm clouds gathered and the winds started raging.[33] In *Gilgamesh*, one man builds a vast boat of wood – an acre in circumference – and coats it in pitch. He then 'loaded her with all the gold, loaded her with the seed of living things, all of them. I put on board the boat all my kith and kin. Put on board cattle from open country, wild beasts from open country.'[34] In the Bible, Noah, 'a righteous man, blameless in his generation,' is instructed to build a boat, and 'the length of the ark' is to be '300 cubits, its breadth 50 cubits, and its height 30 cubits'; he is told to make a roof for the ark and 'cover it inside and out with pitch'; then he is told by God that, 'of every living thing of all flesh, you shall bring two of every sort into the ark to keep them alive with you.'[35]

In each story, the rains then begin to fall: for six days and seven nights, in *Gilgamesh*; in Genesis, it takes seven days before they begin to fall, but then they do so for forty days and forty nights; in *Atrahasis*, the days and nights are unnumbered, but we are told that the deluge 'roared like a bull'.[36] Birds are sent by the surviving man to see whether the flood has abated: in *Gilgamesh*, it is a dove, a swallow and a raven that fly and return; in the Bible, it is a raven and then a dove, which returns with an olive leaf (olive trees, as has been pointed out, grow in Palestine but not in Mesopotamia).[37] In each story, the flood begins to recede, and the population of mankind – chastened, for a time – starts to recover. What would never fully recover was the status of Genesis. The decipherment of the tablet created a sensation.

The discovery of such similarities was a dramatic revelation for Victorian Christians who had been so long assured of the uniqueness of their religion. However, ancient Greek and Roman writers had, almost two millennia earlier, frequently pointed out the clear similarities of biblical stories to those in other cultures. Such ancient authors had argued, forcefully, that the Bible's flood myth was simply one more retelling of the classical story of a man named Deucalion.

The similarities between the two tales are, once again, notable: in the story of Deucalion, there is an angry god and a good man, who is once again saved by building a boat and then endures a devastating flood which he, together with his virtuous wife, survives . . . * The stories are far from identical, of course: in that Latin version, after the flood retreats, the surviving couple lands on Mount Parnassus; while, in the Bible, the boat comes to rest on Mount Ararat.[38] But the stories were similar enough – so similar that numerous ancient writers had remarked upon them: one Greco-Jewish author simply referred to Noah as the man 'the Greeks call Deucalion'. Early Christian writers initially made the same point, referring to the man 'who is by us called Noah, and by you Deucalion.'[39] The Greek writer Celsus also spotted the similarities – but was, typically, irritated by them, and jeered at the 'prodigious ark' of Noah, criticizing the Christians for telling 'a debased and unscrupulous version of the story of Deucalion.'[40]

The Latin story wasn't the only iteration. In the erudite world of Hellenistic Babylon, yet another version of this story had existed and was recorded by a writer named Alexander Polyhistor. This story too began with 'a time in which there existed nothing but darkness and an abyss of waters'.[41] This time, it was the Greek god Kronos who warned that a flood was coming and

* I cover the similarities in more detail in my first book, *The Darkening Age*.

that mankind would be destroyed. Once again, one virtuous man was warned and saved. Though, in true literary Hellenistic style, Kronos did not immediately tell this particular man to build a boat, but instead ordered him 'to write a history of the beginning, procedure, and conclusion of all things', and to bury it. Only once the writing had been done was the man told to move on to the rather more practical (but, for the Greeks, evidently more minor) matter of the boat, onto which he should 'convey on board everything necessary to sustain life, together with all the different animals; both birds and quadrupeds, and trust himself fearlessly to the deep.'[42]

It was perfectly clear to numerous ancient observers that religions were less separate entities, virgin-born and pristine, than variations on a theme. Travel in any direction from Rome and, as Greek and Roman authors pointed out, the same gods could be spotted appearing in one form here and another there. The names were different perhaps, but the deities were fundamentally the same. Zeus and Jupiter; Juno and Hera; Athena and Minerva; Artemis and Diana – on and on . . . When Julius Caesar invaded Gaul, he briskly categorized Gaulish gods with Roman names: here, he wrote, was the Gaulish equivalent of Mercury; here too you could see their 'Apollo, Mars, Jupiter, and Minerva.' As Caesar – not a man to be troubled by cultural appropriation (or indeed any other kind of appropriation) – concluded: 'Of these deities they have almost the same idea as all other nations.'[43] Caesar possibly went too far, but underlying his suppositions was a sentiment shared by many ancient writers – that these things were all related. Symmachus' plea for toleration had been prefaced by a declaration that all religions, more or less, were the same thing in different guises: 'Whatever each person worships it is reasonable to think of them as one.'[44]

Even the language of religious worship could be seen to spread between sects, moving from one to another through imitation and assimilation. Today, terms such as 'gospel' and 'saviour' are unavoidably associated in modern minds with

Christianity – but to ancient ears they would almost certainly have been more readily associated with the cult of the emperor Augustus – yet another (allegedly) divine man with a miraculous backstory. In Augustus' own lifetime – he died in AD 14 – inscriptions had been put up that praised him as a 'saviour' and a bringer of peace. Coins proclaimed him the 'divine' Augustus; the son of a god – the 'divine Caesar' – he was a god himself. The 'gospel' of his coming was praised. The day of his birth, gushed one inscription, 'was the beginning of his gospel'.[45] When we think of the new religions that appeared in this period, we usually concentrate on Christianity. But history deceives us. The fastest growing and most important new form of worship in the first century AD was not Christianity, nor the worship of Apollonius; it was the imperial cult. And as this cult spread, a new religious language, of saviours and gospels and all the rest, spread with it.[46]

Classical authors had observed and readily admitted similarities between their own religions and other people's. But Christianity, which tended to insist that it was unique, was much less able to do this. Instead, many Christian writers turned to a novel explanation for how such manifest similarities had arisen: Satan. Christianity looked similar to other religions? Well, Christians argued, that is what the Evil One wants you to think. Satan had put these religions on earth to deceive people into following the wrong gods. Asclepius looked like Jesus? Again, that was Satan's doing: he had created Asclepius deliberately to mislead people. The Devil had brought forward 'Asclepius as the raiser of the dead and healer of the other diseases.'[47] Asclepius might heal bodies – that much Christians admitted – but in doing so he damned spirits: 'when it came to souls he was a destroyer'. Asclepius, Christian authors warned, was 'the demon', that 'beast, so dangerous to the world'.[48] He was a fraud, deceiving mankind and 'drawing the gullible away from the true Saviour and attracting them to godless error.'[49]

The worship of the popular Eastern god Mithras was even

more distressing to many ancient Christians. Quite what happened in Mithraic worship is now shrouded in mystery – not entirely surprisingly, as it was a so-called 'mystery' cult and initiates were not supposed to broadcast their experiences. But some things are clear. It is known, for example, that Mithraic worship involved some sort of ritual meal with bread (and great mystical significance). As the Christian writer Justin explained, in Mithraism, 'bread and a cup of water are placed with certain incantations in the mystic rites'.[50] It is known, too, that the religion promised some sort of salvation and redemption effected through the shedding of blood – in its case, that of a bull.[51]

However, one thing about Mithraism is very, very clear indeed: it enraged early Christian authors. It is easy to see why: it was far too similar for comfort. Christianity had sacred rituals that involved eating bread; Christianity promised redemption; Christians promised salvation through the shedding of blood. Ancient authors hurried to explain how such similarities existed. Once again, they argued, this was not because of borrowing or influence. Instead, these similarities were yet more evidence of the craftiness of Satan and his minions: 'wicked devils have imitated [the Christian ceremonies] in the mysteries of Mithras, commanding the same thing to be done.'[52]

Such deceptions were everywhere. The Christian author Tertullian fulminated against those 'wiles which pervert the truth', arguing that it was the Devil who, 'by the mystic rites of his idols, vies even with the essential portions of the sacraments of God.' The Devil, according to Tertullian, had other tricks. He even 'baptizes some – that is, his own believers and faithful followers; he promises the putting away of sins . . . [and] celebrates also the oblation of bread, and introduces an image of a resurrection.'[53] Seeing Satan in similar religions was a habit that lasted a long time. Two and a half centuries later, Augustine observed that 'evil spirits counterfeit certain shadows of honour to themselves, that they may deceive those who follow Christ.'[54]

Was Mithraism – or any other religion – actually all that

similar to Christianity? Today, it is dispiritingly hard to know. So much information on other religions was lost in the ensuing centuries of Christian domination as the 'insatiable' Catholic Church suppressed almost all rites but its own. What is left of Mithraism seems to show that this loathed cult was in many ways less like Christianity than the outrage of ancient Christian writers might imply. True, it had echoes – that sacred meal, some sort of redemption through bullish blood – but it also involved much that was less similar: it was (probably) an all-male religion; it performed bizarre ritual tortures (or the threat of tortures) on its initiates. But to try to know more is practically futile. To try to understand Mithraism from the few scraps of (largely hostile) writings and archaeology that remain is, as the theologian and classicist A. D. Nock put it, like attempting to understand Christianity by reading a single atheist magazine and looking at the ground plans of a church. In other words, it is more or less impossible.[55] There is almost nothing left.

Asclepius would suffer too: Constantine would dramatically tear down a shrine to this god – or, as the historian Eusebius called him, this divine 'destroyer' who had 'practised fraud for many long years'. As Eusebius wrote with satisfaction, Constantine did the 'proper thing, and protected by the jealous God as his veritable Saviour, he ordered this shrine to be demolished. At one command the vaunted wonder of the noble philosophers was razed to the ground, pulled down by a military force.' Thus, Eusebius contentedly observed, it 'was utterly destroyed, so that no trace remained there of the former madness.'[56]

But if Asclepius and Mithras were bad, Apollonius was far worse. He had so many similarities to Jesus: not merely the healing hands, but the miraculous birth, the divine backstory, the charisma, the preaching, the raising from the dead, the public trial, the ascension into heaven . . . For centuries, Christian authors were emphatic: Apollonius was not merely evil. He was an antichrist. Modern readers are sometimes surprised to learn about Apollonius – why, they wonder, have they not heard of him? In part it is because of what happened in the centuries after Christianity gained power.

Apollonius had once been popular – enormously so, it seems. Quite possibly, for a time, he was more popular than Christ. Yet, as the centuries of Christian rule rolled on, the 'pagan Christ', as he came to be called, underwent a terrible metamorphosis. The gentle Apollonius started to be known as a baby-murderer, a leader of evil spirits, a scoundrel, and a man of 'devilish power'.[57] At the end of the seventeenth century, a French historian named Godeau wrote, perfectly seriously, that the Church had never had a more threatening enemy than this 'magician'.[58] Not because Apollonius was vicious, but for precisely the opposite reason. That deviously blameless life, and those so-called miracles – they were manifestly all a ploy. The Devil, wrote another eighteenth-century historian, 'seems to have sent him into the world'. He had done this, as the English translation of the work explained, 'about the same time as Jesus Christ was pleased to appear in it . . . to rival his Authority in the Judgement of those, who might take the delusions of this magician for true miracles.'[59]

It might be tempting to smile at such excess now, but it was not always so droll. When, at the turn of the nineteenth century, a French writer started to look at Apollonius with a slightly calmer eye, this author explained why so few had written about him before. It was because until very recently it had been 'neither prudent, nor without danger, to speak out about Apollonius', since, if one did so, one risked being 'pursued by the religious inquisition' and also risked 'Church censorship and the Bastille dungeons'.[60] Satan was no laughing matter. When, in the late seventeenth century, the first section of Apollonius' life was published in English, the outcry was so strong that the rest was never published. Sixteen centuries after Apollonius had died, he was still, as one modern historian has put it, 'considered a threat to the Christian religion.'[61] The first complete translation of the biography of Apollonius was not published in England until the nineteenth century.

So sensitive were Christians about Apollonius that it was not even necessary to name him to incur the wrath of the most fervent. It has been said that one never writes of Apollonius, but only of Christ – as the historian Edward Gibbon would discover to his cost. In his book, *The Decline and Fall of the Roman Empire*, Gibbon briefly recounted the story of Apollonius, then added a short footnote. The life of Apollonius had, he wrote, been narrated in such a 'fabulous' manner by his disciples 'that we are at a loss to discover whether he was a sage, an impostor, or a fanatic.'[62] Gibbon, when he wrote that footnote, must have known as well as anyone how it could be read. And indeed that is precisely how it was read, as the reactions of generations of enraged clergymen proved. Gibbon's book – for a multiplicity of reasons – was placed on the Catholic Church's Index of Prohibited Books before it was even published.

Apollonius remains the trickiest figure for modern minds to know what to do with. Was he as similar as enraged Christian polemics imply? Again, it is hard to know. So many of the writings about him have been lost. Once, several biographies of Apollonius existed, but only one remains today. Once, there had been other evidence too: temples and talismans, statues and inscriptions.[63] Yet almost all of these have gone. It has been suggested that Christian hostility was in part responsible for such losses. 'The idea arises', the historian Maria Dzielska wrote, 'that the lack of literary works on Apollonius and of his effigies is due to the fight carried on by Christianity against paganism.' The sole biography that remains 'is the only one which managed to survive the fight.'[64]

Even if all the ancient sources still existed, Apollonius would be hard for modern readers to understand. According to some legends, this man-god had been the incarnation of the shape-shifting sea-god Proteus – and there remains something slippery and hard to grasp, something a little protean about him. Read his (very odd) remaining biography and he changes from chapter to chapter, and even page to page: now divine, now human; now a healer, now a holy man; now a rebel, now a sage; now a seer, now a lunatic.

Proof of just how pliant his image could be lies in the poem 'Lamia', by the Romantic poet John Keats. In this poem, Keats attacks Apollonius not for being too mystical and irrational, but, somewhat astonishingly to modern eyes, for being too rational: Keats accuses Apollonius of being a cool and heartless philosopher – and philosophy, Keats thinks, ruins things. 'Philosophy will clip an Angel's wings / Conquer all mysteries by rule and line,' he wrote. Philosophy will 'Unweave a rainbow'. Today, these lines are largely remembered for containing a sideswipe at Newton, who had revealed the prismatic cause of rainbows.[65] What is much less often remembered is that their main target was not Newton at all, but Apollonius: in Keats' eyes, it was Apollonius who could unweave the rainbow.

Keats had argued the danger of Apollonius was that he was too logical. But the real danger of Apollonius was, for Christianity, precisely the reverse. The real danger was that he was too magical, too – to use the Christian word – miraculous. Apollonius' life was touched by miracles and shone with the borrowed glory of heaven. He lived in a world in which gods were made incarnate in mortal women, in which the sick were healed, the dead were raised, and in which one man, the son of a god, ascended into heaven. He was a mortal rebuke to the idea that Christ had been in any way unique. So Keats was right and he was wrong: Apollonius could destroy great mysteries – but not through logic. It was through his miracles that Apollonius could clip an angel's wings. Through his miracles, Apollonius could unweave the rainbow.

Chapter Seventeen

ST AUGUSTINE AND THE SPIDER

'It is to satisfy this unhealthy curiosity that . . . men are led to investigate the secrets of nature, which are irrelevant to our lives.'

St Augustine, *Confessions*, X.35, 4th century AD

One day, towards the end of the fourth century, while sitting at home, St Augustine found himself distracted by a spider.

Little was new about that; ancient authors had been having their interest piqued by spiders and their webs for centuries. Three centuries earlier, the encyclopedically interested Pliny the Elder had gone into raptures over the spider, and into some detail on its habits. It is 'a creature which is worthy of our especial admiration', he wrote. 'How steadily does it work with its claws, how beautifully rounded and how equal are the threads as it forms its web . . . With what wondrous art does it conceal the snares that lie in wait for its prey in its chequered nettings!'[1] The ever-curious Greek philosopher Aristotle had, four or so centuries before that, been similarly absorbed by them. He had noted the methods of spiders' copulation, as well as where spiders laid their eggs (in a web) and what happened when a grub metamorphosed into a spider (it made a leap – and then immediately 'begins to spin his web').[2]

Other authors had drifted into metaphor. The first-century-BC Latin philosopher Lucretius had used spiders' webs as an analogy to support his grand theory of the composition of the universe. Lucretius was an atomist and, unlike those who believed the world had been made by the gods, he argued forcefully, and beautifully, that everything we see in the world is merely made of atoms coming together and moving apart. His argument was not merely a physical one but a theological one: if no god had made the world, he argued, mankind had no need to fear divine retribution from its creator. In his great poem on this topic, Lucretius explained that he wrote to 'loose from round the mind / The tightened coils of dread religion.'[3]

However, it is clear that Lucretius realized it might be hard for his readers to believe in atoms that were imperceptibly small. And so he went on to offer an analogy – and it is here that he turns to the spider. Just as we 'don't feel alighting on our frames the clinging dust, or chalk that settles soft; nor mists of night, nor spider's gossamer [when] its net entangles us' – well, in just the same way, atoms also exist, and 'clash, combine and leap apart in turn' – but we do not feel them.[4]

It is worth comparing these with the encounter with a spider that St Augustine records in his autobiographical *Confessions*, written at the end of the fourth century, after almost a century of Christian rule. In one way, when you read this work, it is possible to feel that little has changed. Here, too, is a ferociously intelligent and curious mind investigating the world in which it finds itself. Here, too, are reflections on a vast variety of topics, from how children best learn languages (with smiles and stories, thinks St Augustine, rather than fear and punishments), to the adolescent's embarrassment at going to the baths with a parent (acute), to what the nature of time might be (confusing). And, at one point in the *Confessions*, he – like Lucretius, Pliny and Aristotle before him – finds his attention caught by that spider. 'Often,' he writes, 'as I sit at home, I cannot turn my eyes from the sight of a lizard catching flies or a spider entangling them as they fly into her web.'[5]

But his reaction is different. For Augustine isn't enchanted by the spider, as Pliny was; nor does he carefully catalogue its habits, as Aristotle had. Instead, he is appalled by his interest in it. Why, he laments, is he allowing his attention to be caught by a spider, instead of concentrating upon God? 'Who can tell how many times each day our curiosity is tempted by the most trivial and insignificant matters?' he writes. 'Who can tell how often we give way?'

Augustine continues, for line after line, berating both himself and mankind for being tempted by the 'self-indulgence' of 'inquisitiveness'. This 'futile curiosity', he writes, 'masquerades under the name of science and learning' – but, to Augustine, it is instead a 'temptation, more dangerous than [others] because it is more complicated.' He goes on: 'unhealthy curiosity' leads to all kinds of ills, such as looking at 'freaks' in the theatre, or at a mangled corpse lying on the ground. Moreover, it is through 'curiosity' – and it is clear that, for Augustine, as for other Christian writers of this era, this is a far from positive trait – 'men are led to investigate the secrets of nature, which are irrelevant to our lives, although such knowledge is of no value to them and they wish to gain it merely for the sake of knowing.'[6]

The change that can be glimpsed taking place here is at once mild and profound. Here, too, there is a spider; here, too, there is a man who is interested in it. But no longer is the interest praiseworthy; no longer is the spider worthy of interest. Instead, it is a 'contemptible' thing which arouses a corrupting vice – 'curiosity' – and draws man from the one true object of contemplation: God.

Ancient Christians were emphatic. The moment of Christ's birth had transformed everything. Before Christ, mankind had been damned; after him, it might be saved. This transformation was considered so profound that, by the middle ages, Christian writers had developed a striking metaphor to illustrate it. They started to argue that the classical era – that time of Plato and Aristotle, of Horace and Virgil – had not (as people had once thought) been a great era; and certainly not any kind of 'golden age'. Instead those centuries had been a penumbral and benighted time when mankind had languished in 'darkness and the night of error'.[7] It had, Christian writers made clear, been a 'Dark Age'.

A powerful metaphor had been born, and would last for many centuries. Albeit, unfortunately for Christians, not with its original meaning. For, in the Renaissance, when writers such as Petrarch looked back and compared what they saw as the dreary and benighted medieval era with the brilliance of the classical world, they turned the meaning of that phrase on its head. Because, to Petrarch and his companions, it seemed that true darkness was not caused by the absence of spiritual enlightenment – but by an absence of the intellectual kind. That, they argued, was the real darkness. A new 'Dark Age' had been born and – to the ongoing distress of medieval scholars – it was Petrarch's term that stuck.[8]

Today, scholars tend to take a more measured, less Manichaean view of the pre- and post-Christian eras. What changed when Christianity gained power within the Roman Empire? It is complicated, scholars now argue. Some things changed and some did not – and, as the historian Ramsay MacMullen has argued, the advent of Christianity caused little change in many areas one might have expected. The love-thy-neighbour religion of Christianity seems to have spread less love to certain neighbours than many modern minds might suppose. The increasing power of Christianity seems, for example, to have had little effect on levels of slave ownership; nor does it seem to have caused any improvement in the treatment of slaves: if anything, there is evidence that punishments for erring slaves increased in savagery in the Christian era.[9]

Indeed, the first century of Christian rule saw a hardening of legal punishments in general: the number of crimes carrying the death penalty increased, while the penalties for so-called sexual immorality became startlingly ferocious.[10] On the other hand, in many ways Christians did work hard to alleviate the lot of others: charitable acts were performed; funds for the needy provided; and the bloody gladiatorial contests, which Christians considered barbaric, declined in these years and finally were outlawed (although it is not clear if their decline was due to piety or pragmatism: they were expensive to run).[11]

There is, however, one area in which Christian influence can clearly be seen, and that is in literature. What is written starts to change, almost immediately. In this newly pious Christian world, certain genres, such as the sermon, flourished while others, such as sexually explicit love poetry, fell wholly out of fashion.[12] Another thing that started to change was, quite simply, who was writing. As one historian has observed, by 'the middle Byzantine Era perhaps half the literate class of the Empire consisted of monks' – but changes in who is holding the pen can be seen far earlier than that.[13]

Look along a shelf of books from Rome's literary golden and silver ages and you might notice works by Virgil (a poet), Pliny the Elder (a naval commander and naturalist), Pliny the Younger (a lawyer and bureaucrat), Cicero (a lawyer and politician), Caesar (a soldier and politician), Lucretius (a philosopher) and Catullus (a sublimely beautiful – and frequently filthy – love poet). Scan a shelf of the great writers from the first century of Christian rule and you might, it is true, chance upon the works of the non-Christian writers Libanius (a teacher and rhetorician) or Ammianus Marcellinus (a former soldier and a historian). But you are far more likely to find works by writers such as St Augustine (a bishop), St Ambrose (a bishop), St John Chrysostom (an archbishop), Eusebius (a bishop) . . . and so on. And none of them wrote smutty poetry.

There were other literary changes. The way that histories were structured started to alter, too. Where once a history might have opened with the founding of this city, or the commencement of that war, now a fashion arose for history to be pegged to Christian time. One confident Christian history from the sixth century opens with the creation of man in chapter one ('Adam, the first man was made, or created by God from earth. He was six feet tall,' it explains, before adding the unexpected clarification, 'including his head'). It then moves swiftly past the flood (it was damp), the Tower of Babel (it was 'built by the men who had known how to construct the ark') and, rather surprisingly, the Trojan War (Odysseus had 'a long nose').[14] *The History of the Franks*, by Gregory of Tours, another bishop, begins with a similarly brisk first chapter on Adam and Eve ('These first human beings lived happily in the pleasant place of Paradise'), before bouncing over the flood in Chapter 4 and, in Chapter 10, 'The Crossing of the Red Sea' ('They say that the ruts which the chariot-wheels made remain to this day and that, as far as the eye can reach, they can be seen at the bottom of the sea').[15]

It is easy to smirk at such histories today, but it is worth remembering how Christian-centric even modern histories are, albeit obliquely. When, in the eighth century, the English historian the Venerable Bede came to write his history of the English peoples, he adopted a novel dating system to pinpoint events in time. Whenever he mentioned an event, Bede took to writing a number after it, then adding either the words 'before the birth of our Lord' or 'in the year of our Lord'. Thus, for Bede, Caesar's invasion of Britain had happened, 'sixty years before the birth of our Lord', while the emperor Marcus Aurelius had come to power, 'In the year of our Lord's Incarnation 156.'[16] This served a practical benefit for Bede – hitherto, dating had been a complex and chaotic mess – but it also served a spiritual one. By pinning each and every historical event to Jesus' birth, then, Bede wrote, 'the source of our hope might be the more evident to us.'[17] Time itself was starting to turn on a Christian axis.

Open any one of the volumes written by the great Christian writers of the fourth century and it is possible to see from the merest glance at their contents pages that something else has changed, too. A Victorian edition of Augustine's famous work, *The City of God*, offers summaries of what each book within that work covers – and, as always, they are telling. The summary for Book II explains that it offers, 'A review of the calamities suffered by the Romans before the time of Christ, showing that their gods had plunged them into corruption and vice', while the similarly pugnacious Book IV will show 'That empire was given to Rome not by the gods, but by the One True God'. The summary for Book I reads, with pleasing simplicity: 'Augustine censures the pagans.'[18]

There is some variation. Augustine's biographical *Confessions* do, it is true, offer a wider palette to the reader than *The City of God* – as well as some personal revelations, including that youthful wish that God might make him chaste (but not yet) – but it is worth noting that even sex in St Augustine is deployed in the service of the divine. Other works by other Christian authors are similarly wholesome. Open one of the most famous works of St Ambrose and you find yourself looking at such invigorating chapter headings as 'Chapter 20: If we are to preserve our modesty we must avoid fellowship with profligate men, also the banquets of strangers, and intercourse with women; our leisure time at home should be spent in pious and virtuous pursuits'.[19] None of these works are easily confused with Catullus.

Such a starchy literary style was not entirely new. Hectoring prose had existed before Christianity. Plutarch himself had produced a volume called *Moralia*, which included essays on everything from whether one should have large numbers of friends (one should not, thinks Plutarch, for 'just as rivers whose waters are divided among branches and channels flow weak and thin, so affection . . . if portioned out among many persons become utterly enfeebled'), to whether or not one should eat meat (once again, one should not, for 'what sort of dinner is not costly for which a living creature loses its life?'), to an essay that offers extensive 'Advice to a Bride and Groom'.[20] That last includes instructions on the best way for a husband and wife to make up after an argument (have sex with her, says Plutarch; that always cheers things up), as well as advice on how a woman should behave around her husband (submissively; smilingly), not to mention advice on how a wife should react if her husband happened to 'commit some peccadillo with a paramour or a maidservant' (she should not be indignant or angry, but should instead realize that 'it is respect for her which leads him to share his debauchery, licentiousness, and wantonness with another woman').*[21]

But Plutarch isn't merely a moralizing bore. That same volume of *Moralia* also includes some spellbinding essays, including a debate on whether or not bees and other animals were intelligent or merely 'as it were' seemed so (clearly they were, Plutarch thinks; to suggest otherwise was idiocy; and, besides, the 'as it were' argument was a weasel-worded one – for what, really, is the difference between seeming intelligent 'as it were' and being so?), as well as an engaging account of an Alexandrian elephant that fell in love with a flower girl. This elephant, Plutarch's essay explains, happened to be in love with the same flower girl as a grammarian who also lived in Alexandria – and the elephant's love was 'no less manifest' than the man's. Every time the elephant visited the flower girl, he always used to bring her fruit and stand next to her for a long time. Then, he would 'insert his trunk, like a hand, within her garments and gently caress her fair breasts.'[22]

Christianity, then, changed the genres of literature that were written: out went amorous poetry; in came preachy sermonizing. But the change it caused is both more subtle and more significant than that. For, in these years, Christianity started to find its way into almost all prose, regardless of the topic. Consider, for example, how different authors treat the question of the shape of the world. The idea that the world was round had,

---

* One of the most commonly used translations of this work contains a pleasing footnote from its early-twentieth-century translator: 'The modern bride', he writes, managing to make 'modern' sound like an accusation, 'will undoubtedly turn up her nose and shake her independent head in disapproval of Plutarch's suggestions about subordinating herself to her husband.' However, he continues, she and her independent head should think again, for 'she will find in Plutarch's short essay many suggestions regarding whole-souled co-operation and cheerful intellectual companionship with her husband, which *mutatis mutandis* hold as good to-day as they did when they were written, nearly two thousand years ago.' Quite so.

by the time Christianity gained power in the Roman Empire, been widely accepted for a millennium or so.

In the fourth century BC, Aristotle had concluded confidently that the shape of the earth 'must be spherical'. He had gone on to briskly list the reasons why, which included the shape of the eclipses of the moon and the way different stars were seen from different vantage points on earth. As Aristotle put it, this change in the heavenly field 'proves both that the earth is spherical and that its periphery is not large, for otherwise such a small change of position could not have had such an immediate effect.'[23] (It has been suggested that one reason Greek astronomy was so advanced was that the Greek diaspora was so widely dispersed, which meant that the peripatetic Greeks knew, from personal experience, that the stars changed as you moved from this Greek settlement in the north of the Mediterranean, to that one on the coast of Egypt.)

Other Greek writers had written on this topic too, adding their own thoughts and proofs. Plato had posited the idea that, if one walked around the world far enough, one would end up in a position where one's feet (*podes*, in Greek) would be opposite (*anti-*) the position that you had been in when you first started walking.[24] The notion of the 'Antipodes' had been born. By the time that Pliny the Elder came to consider the question of the shape of the earth in the first century AD, he was therefore able to observe that all educated men agreed the world was spherical and that there were antipodes.

'We always speak of the ball of the earth,' he wrote, and 'that human beings are distributed all round the earth and stand with their feet pointing towards each other, and that the top of the sky is alike for them all and the earth [is] trodden under foot at the centre in the same way from any direction.' He is clear that not everyone thinks this – as he observes, 'there is a mighty battle between learning on one side and the common herd on the other.' The common herd, he observes wearily, 'enquire why the persons on the opposite side don't fall off'. As if, scoffs Pliny, 'it were not reasonable that the people on the other side wonder that we do not fall off.'[25]

Pliny goes on to offer various proofs for how we may know the earth is a globe. Its spherical shape is why, he writes, 'the land is not visible from the deck of a ship when in sight from the masthead; and why as a vessel passes far into the distance, if some shining object is tied to the top of the mast it appears slowly to sink and finally it is hidden from sight.'[26] And besides, he adds, there is also the work of Greek investigators who 'greatly . . . to their glory, prove by subtle mathematical reasoning' the shape of the seas.

Such then was the classical view, in the first century AD, when Pliny was writing. It was not a view that all Christians would receive with enthusiasm. Five centuries after Pliny had outlined his beliefs in his *Natural History*, around a millennium after Plato and Aristotle had been writing, the Christian writer Cosmas Indicopleustes took up the debate in his *Christian Topography*. One might think, having sailed to the visible horizon and then over it many times, that Cosmas would agree with Pliny. Not a bit of it. Cosmas, as he explains in his *Topography*, had heard of such 'pagan' theories and regarded them as absurd – although that word doesn't quite do justice to the fervour of Cosmas' emotions.[27] His adversaries, he wrote, 'vomit out fictions and fables' about the solar system and the earth, and his book was thus designed 'to overthrow from the foundation the error of the pagan theories' and to thwart those pagan 'fable-mongers'.[28]

And so Cosmas goes on, in his inimitable way, to do so. The pagans thought that the heavens and the earth were spherical. They are no such thing, Cosmas wrote. On the contrary, the Bible gives ample proof of the shape of the heavens. These had four corners which were, like a tent, tethered to the four corners of the (flat) earth, so 'making the figure of a cube . . . while up above it curves round in the form of an oblong vault and becomes as it were a vast canopy.'[29] Cosmas then attacks the idea of the spherical earth using arguments drawn from the Bible. If the earth was round, he argues, how could Noah's flood have happened? For how could water have been held on a rotating sphere? It would have all drained off. Besides, how could people who were on the bottom of the earth stand upside down? Cosmas closes his argument with a jab at the 'pagans' and their nonsensical, spherical, revolving earth. 'Such', he writes, 'is our reply to your fictitious and false theories and to the conclusions of your reasonings which are capricious, self-contradictory, inconsistent, doomed to be utterly confounded, and to be whirled round and round even more than that unstable and revolving mythical sphere of yours.'[30] It was one way to conclude the debate.

It might be possible to argue that Cosmas – an energetic writer, but not perhaps a subtle one – was an aberration. But he does not give the impression that he believes himself to be alone. In his book (which opens with the words, 'In the name of the Father and of the Son and of the Holy Ghost') he repeatedly presents this debate as being one between Christians, who adhere to (or he thinks should adhere to) the flat-earth theory, and the pagans, who prefer their 'mythical' sphere.

For Cosmas, the debate over the shape of the earth is an 'us' and 'them' one, with the Christians as 'us' and pagans – and particularly their arrogant, idiotic philosophers – as 'them'. 'Is it not then false and fabulous what they say about the sun,' he asks at another moment, 'that he is greater than the earth?'[31] It is clear that Cosmas' opinions on the shape of the earth are not shared by all Christians: at one point he directs his ire against those 'double-faced' men who profess Christianity while at the same time 'bedeck themselves with . . . the diversity of the errors of this world' – in other words, with those 'pagan' theories about the shape of heaven and earth.[32] But, on the whole, he clearly implies that there are beliefs which are good 'Christian' ones – and ones which are, to say the least, not.

Cosmas is an eccentric enough author that his work – and his views on what 'pagans' and Christians believe – should be read with a certain scepticism. However, the idea that a spherical earth is somehow 'pagan', and its opponents Christian, crops up in several other authors, too. The fourth-century Christian author Lactantius – a man whose intellect and education were rated highly enough that he was appointed as tutor to the son of the emperor Constantine – also considered the idea of a spherical world to be pagan bunk. In a typically zesty passage, after Lactantius has laid into Socrates ('many of his actions are not only undeserving of praise, but also most deserving of censure') and had a good go at Plato (his arguments are 'impossible' and 'unjust'), Lactantius turns his attention to the idea of a spherical world.[33]

'They' – and again it seems that by this he means pagan philosophers – appear to think that 'the world is round like a ball'. It is, he explains, one of the many 'ridiculous things' that 'they' believe. Who could believe in such a fiction as a round earth? If a round earth existed, Lactantius thinks, the Antipodes would also exist – and that, as Lactantius makes clear, is simply preposterous. 'Is there anyone so senseless as to believe that there are men whose footsteps are higher than their heads?' he scoffs. 'Or that the things which with us are in a recumbent position, with them hang in an inverted direction? That the crops and trees grow downwards? That the rains, and snow, and hail fall upwards to the earth?' Lactantius is of course just teasing; he knows full well that there are such people: they are called pagan philosophers. It is the philosophers, he writes, who 'make hanging fields, and seas, and cities, and mountains'. However, he explains, the origin of their error 'must also be set forth by us' – by which it appears he means the Christians. What the pagans need, he explains, is 'divine instruction; for that only is wisdom.'[34]

Echoes of Lactantius' reasoning on the Antipodes can be heard in the writings of St Augustine, too. A little while after Lactantius had scoffed at the philosophers, St Augustine took on the same idea in his *City of God*. Augustine's argument here is not particularly for or against the idea of a spherical earth. This he merely introduces in order to get onto what, for him, was manifestly a more pressing concern: namely, are there people dangling off the bottom of the earth? Augustine had clearly heard of the idea of a spherical world. 'The earth, they say, is suspended in the sphere of the heavens,' he writes – note that 'they' again. And though he seems a little ambivalent about this idea here (elsewhere he sounds keener), he doesn't spend much time on it.[35] Instead, he moves swiftly on to the idea that he really wishes to attack: namely, the idea of the Antipodes. 'As for the fabled "antipodes", that is, men who occupy the other side of the earth,' he writes, 'who plant their footsteps opposite ours: there is no reason to believe that such men exist.'[36] Those who believe in such things, he writes, follow mere 'conjecture' based on a certain line of 'reasoning'.

And as Augustine makes clear, he has a surer guide: scripture, for 'there is no falsehood of any kind in Scripture.'[37] And there are no Antipodeans in the Bible. As he makes clear, God made Adam on 'this' side of the world and it 'would be too absurd to say that some men might have sailed from one side of the earth to the other, arriving there having crossed the immense tract of the ocean, so that the human race, descended from the one first man, should be established there also.'[38] Having satisfactorily proved the Greek idea of the Antipodes to be 'too absurd', Augustine moves on to the more serious business of who begat whom after the flood: 'Shem begat Arphaxad,' he writes. 'When he was 135 years old, Arphaxad begat Cainan. When Cainan was 130 years old, he begat Salah . . .' And so on.[39]

The Antipodes are given similarly short shrift by other Christian authors. The acerbic St Jerome scoffed at the 'witless "wisdom"' of the philosophers who argued there were people suspended beneath the earth; the late-sixth- and early-seventh-century writer and archbishop Isidore of Seville argued that the idea there were Antipodeans suspended beneath the earth was 'by no means to be believed . . . it is the poets, in a kind of quasi-reasoning, who make such conjectures'; while the Venerable

Bede considered that 'no credence whatsoever' was to be given to tales of Antipodeans. Today, writers tend to squabble over whether or not ancient Christians believed in a flat earth, but what really seemed to exercise ancient writers was whether or not there were Antipodeans – and, for many, the answer was a flat 'no'.*

Eventually, Christian writers would start to promulgate the 'pagan' view of a spherical world more wholeheartedly, and by the thirteenth century writers such as Thomas Aquinas and Johannes de Sacrobosco were enthusiastically arguing (and indeed using 'pagan' texts to do so) for the truth of a spherical earth. Though, it is worth noting that the first Christians in this period to advocate for the Antipodes were denounced as heretics. It was, all in all, a somewhat slow start.

What is interesting in all of this is less whether or not ancient Christians believed that the earth was spherical – it is absolutely clear that, just as with non-Christians, some did and some did not. And, contrary to what modern arguments might claim, it is absolutely impossible to know what proportions of pagans and Christians believed in which: if the ancient world offers no statistics to the modern reader, it certainly does not offer any opinion polls.

What is more interesting is that certain beliefs – beliefs that would appear to modern minds to be little related to religion – were starting to be infused with a powerful religious charge. More than that: they were increasingly considered to lie under divine instruction and jurisdiction. In the eighth century, Pope Zachary would declare in a letter that the 'perverse and wicked doctrine' that there was 'another world and other men beneath

* The two questions – of whether or not the earth was round, and whether or not there were Antipodeans – were not necessarily linked in ancient minds. Some Christians were willing to accept the former but not the latter, which, for them (since it threatened the truth of Adam and Eve), was more concerning.

the earth' was so unorthodox that a priest who promulgated such an idea would be kicked out of the Church.

What difference did Christianity make? In one sense, very little: in the writings of Augustine and other authors, the same ideas were being discussed; the same topics considered; the same spiders looked at. And so, in one way, nothing changed. And yet, nonetheless, everything had started to feel so very, very different. The world was being overlain by a fine web of religious thought.

Chapter Eighteen

TO EXTIRPATE THE ADVERSARIES OF FAITH

'Give me the earth purged of heretics and I will give you heaven in return.'

Archbishop Nestorius to the emperor Theodosius II,
Socrates, *Ecclesiastical History*, VII.29

The violence that happened in Rome that year was so terrible that it would be remembered for centuries. It was AD 366 and the cause of the rioting was, at first sight, trivial.[1] The role of Bishop of Rome had become vacant and there was a dispute over who should fill it. Two Christians, named Damasus and Ursinus, both wanted it. Or rather, as the historian Ammianus Marcellinus puts it, their 'passionate ambition to seize the episcopal throne passed all bounds'. Their efforts to seize it would result in 'bloodshed and death'.[2]

Later, much later, the Bishop of Rome would start to be known as 'the Pope' – the 'father' – of the Church, and would become famous for habits that were frequently somewhat unfatherly. In the ninth century, for example, Pope Stephen VI put one of his predecessors, Formosus, on trial. If that sounds unremarkable, it is worth remembering that the papacy is held for life and so the predecessor was, by then, a corpse. Formosus' decomposing body was exhumed; dressed in full regalia; put on trial; found guilty; then punished by having three of its fingers chopped off and being tossed into the Tiber.[3]

In the time of the Borgias, the apostolic palace became infamous for debauchery: Cesare Borgia, the son of Pope Alexander VI, was said to have held a party for fifty prostitutes in his apartments. Naturally, they danced naked.[4] Another pope, as he was dying, is rumoured to have taken the blood of three young boys in an attempt to prolong his life. It didn't work for him, and wasn't wonderful for the boys either, who died. (This particular pope had previously been so ill that his only diet had been to drink mere drops of milk from the breast of a young woman – for health reasons, naturally.)

The role of pope is now so established that it is hard to remember that its appearance in the pages of history is something of a surprise. The gospels do not demand popes or pomp or cathedrals or chasubles or golden robes or men in mitres – and they certainly don't advocate prostitutes and papal apartments. And indeed, in the earliest years of the Church, bishops were not men of worldly influence – or even that much heavenly influence either. Their role had, initially, been little more than a tedious administrative one: it was the job of a bishop to oversee the funds that came into the Christian communities. Spiritual leadership was undertaken by other, more inspired, less bureaucratic individuals.[5]

But money has a habit of leaving a residue on the hands of those counting it and, by the middle of the first century of Christian rule, and certainly by its end, bishops had started to become very powerful men indeed. By the late fourth century, some of the most famous were sanctified celebrities: emperors inclined their ears to them; crowds cheered them, parted before them and rioted at their command. Bishops walked along porticoes that glittered with jewels and gleamed with gold; consecrated virgins chanted around them – and sometimes not so virginal women performed other services for them. Or so the rumours said.[6]

Such high living shocked some of the more modest clergy. One bishop, in distress, wrote that he did not know 'that we ought to ride on splendid horses, and drive in magnificent carriages, and be preceded by a procession and surrounded by applause, and have everyone make way for us, as if we were wild beasts.'[7] St Augustine modestly disdained such glitter: the honour of this world, he wrote humbly, is fleeting.[8] Still, he acknowledged, it was nice while it lasted.

The glitter didn't escape the notice of cynical non-Christian observers. As one pagan observer drily put it: 'make me bishop of Rome and I will be a Christian tomorrow.'[9] The non-Christian historian Ammianus similarly noted that any man who achieved the divine office of bishop was rewarded by some very earthly luxury. Such men were 'assured of rich gifts from ladies of quality; they can ride in carriages, dress splendidly, and outdo kings in the lavishness of their table.'[10] Ammianus, in his usual arch way, queried whether their desire was wise: such men, he wrote, 'might be truly happy if they would pay no regard to the greatness of the city, which they make a cloak for their vices, and follow the example of some provincial bishops, whose extreme frugality in food and drink, simple attire, and downcast eyes demonstrate to the supreme god and his true worshippers the purity and modesty of their lives.'[11]

The bishops themselves, however, generally begged to differ. And so, in these first decades of Christian rule, their power continued to grow. Some bishops started to control gangs of young Christian men. The muscle of these men was, in theory, gathered to perform good deeds – the carrying of the sick, the burying of the dead – but these de facto militias became infamous for doing bad ones. Cities lived in fear of their massed presence and of their violence: at the start of the fifth century, some of these men acted so violently that the law stepped in to rule that their numbers 'shall not be more than five hundred.'[12] It was a forbidding 'limitation'.

Other bishops were even blunter in their use of authority. Eschewing de facto armies, they instead simply opted – or so their critics said – for the real kind. The Christian writer John Chrysostom recorded, in disgust, that some of his followers had been bloodily attacked in church by just such soldiers. Bishops, he wrote in anger, were now 'not ashamed to have officers marching ahead of them in place of deacons.'[13]

And now, in Rome, in AD 366, men were massing once again as two men vied for the most desirable bishopric of all. To know precisely what happened in that infamous election in Rome is difficult: the sources are scant, inadequate, and the whiff of bias is often detectable. Accusations of heresy swirled. What is known is that whatever happened was very bloody indeed. First one contender, and then the next, had themselves ordained as bishop. Then the men's supporters started to mass. Then violence broke out. What followed was, more or less, chaos. The episode concluded with some Christians barricading themselves in one basilica, while Damasus set to work outside it. First, he summoned his muscle: gladiators, charioteers, gravediggers, as well as members of the clergy. Then, armed with hatchets, swords and clubs, they besieged the basilica.[14] A papal contest had turned into a battle.

The doors of the basilica were broken down, a fire was set underneath, and then, as some of Damasus' men attacked at ground level, others started tearing tiles off the roof of the building and hurling them onto the Christians huddling below. Eventually, Damasus and his men, 'rushing in, slaughtered 160 people, women and men alike; they wounded even more, many of whom later died.'[15] That chronicle is a little breathless – but even Ammianus puts the figure of the dead only a little lower: it is, he wrote, 'certain that in the basilica . . . 137 corpses were found on a single day.'[16] Whichever it was it was a bloody start to the episcopate of Pope Damasus – or, as he would later be called, St Damasus.

The 'peace of the Church' is the name given to the period following Constantine's conversion. But as academics have observed, the name was a misnomer.[17] When one ancient historian wrote an account of one small part of the violence that started to unfurl between Christians in this era, he called his work 'The Civil War' and given the bitterness and, in places, the violence that followed, it has been pointed out that that title feels apt.

The irony of what happened when Christianity gained control of the Roman Empire was not lost on its classical critics. Within half a century of Christian rule, as the Emperor Julian wrote, in disgust, large numbers of so-called 'heretics' were 'sent into exile, prosecuted, and cast into prison.' That was the least of it. As Julian continues, 'many whole communities of those who are called "heretics" were actually butchered, as at Samosata and Cyzicus, in Paphlagonia, Bithynia, and Galatia, and among many other tribes also villages were sacked and completely devastated'; so-called 'heretics' were 'slaughtered'.[18] Such people claimed to be doing the work of God, but, as Julian acerbically observed, these massacres had nothing to do with their religion. They were, he wrote, 'your own doings; for nowhere did either Jesus or Paul hand down to you such commands.'[19]

It is possible that Julian is exaggerating: the state generally preferred to exile rather than execute to avoid creating martyrs. But without doubt there was violence between various Christian groups in this period – and North Africa was the scene of some of the worst (or, at any rate, it was best recorded there). At the turn of the fourth century, one dissident bishop in North Africa complained that other Christians in that region had 'tortured us and our fathers without ever stopping through a hundred years and more.' He listed the horrors that had been inflicted by other Christians: the 'great number of venerable bishops killed and others thrown into exile, Christians tortured far and wide, sacred virgins raped, wealthy men proscribed, the poor pillaged, basilicas seized.' These Christian persecutors, he wrote, 'threw off great heights Christians who were trying to escape their grasp . . . and rained blows on those who tried to resist them.' In one village, he went on, they had committed mass slaughter of their fellow Christians.[20]

As always, trying to understand precisely what happened is hard: Christians did not hurry to preserve the accounts of the violence they had inflicted on their brethren. Yet, as the historian Peter Brown has also observed, 'Religious coercion on a large scale was mainly practised by Christians on other Christians.'[21] Nonetheless, when trying to understand what happened in these years, the historian must rely on snippets – a mention in a letter here, a sideswipe in a sermon there. However, for all that the historical record starts to become thin, vivid moments are preserved.

In Carthage, in the middle of the AD 340s, some Christians had been pursued by the local governor. One of them, Maximian, was arrested and tortured, beaten with lead-tipped scourges until his limbs dislocated, and 'this mangling of the limbs created one big wound.'[22] Other Christians were executed en masse, in a manner that was, even in a vicious period, notably cruel. They were put in boats, rowed out 'into the billows of the sea', then two casks of sand were tied around each person – one around the neck, one around the feet – and they were dumped into the water: a brutal method of execution, but one that would, as their executioners knew, prevent other Christians finding their bodies then reverencing them as martyrs.[23] Non-Christians looked on in disgust at what they saw as barbaric violence – as did many Christians. It is likely that the vast majority of Christians of all kinds were far less interested in religious difference than the rhetoric or the violence of their rulers might make them seem.

Even Constantine himself seems to have been taken aback by Christianity's bitter sectarianism. He had embraced one form of this religion imagining that, in doing so, he embraced unity: one God, one emperor. Instead, in Christianity he found himself with a fissile, feuding mass, and the more he exerted pressure on it, the more it seemed to fracture – much to his irritation. Like a father forced to referee between warring children, Constantine shows every sign of being less interested in these squabbles than deeply irritated by them, later raging against the 'malignant perversity and disloyalty' of the Christians who were fighting with each other in North Africa.[24] He was often conspicuously uninterested in the theological nitty-gritty of their debates and even counselled people against harming their heretical neighbours, for 'it is one thing to take on willingly the contest for immortality, quite another to enforce it with sanctions.'[25]

Although, rarely did those perpetrating such violence call it violence. Instead, both heretics and the Church wrapped a comforting cloak of metaphor around such acts, arguing that they were not cruel at all, but necessary, even loving. Medical metaphors bloomed as the Church Fathers explained why to be cruel was to be kind; why to harm someone was in fact to heal them. Epiphanius' virulent treatise against heretics is called 'the medicine chest' (the *Panarion*) because it provided 'antidotes' to the heretics 'to counteract their poison.'[26] In simile after simile, a web of words was woven ever tighter around the heretics.

Hagiographies recorded with enthusiasm how holy men 'cured' the misbeliefs of the erring, liberating them from their sins (and frequently also 'liberating' them of their churches and their possessions too). Such works celebrated these 'healers' in passionate prose. The account of a late-fourth-century bishop of Edessa called Rabbula records with enthusiasm how Rabbula ('this great and most glorious doctor') had, during his time, 'forced' many 'false religions' to the truth. When Rabbula took office, the whole land was 'entirely overgrown in the thickets of sin.'[27] The energetic Rabbula was undeterred by such a challenge. Instead, 'anxious in every way to wrest people from sin and to make them partakers in righteousness', he set to work, to 'pull up entangling weeds.'[28]

As his hagiography records with satisfaction, he was 'at all times like an experienced doctor', diagnosing what remedy was necessary against 'diseases of the soul' and lancing 'with a sharp blade the putrefaction of an abscess, to cause suffering and to restore to life.'[29] What the feeling of his flock was when they saw Rabbula approaching with his 'sharp blade' is not recorded. Doubtless some must have been terrified, for some heretics he 'hurled . . . with great compassion into monasteries for the rest of their lives', while others he 'forbade . . . to be found ever again in his province.' This was perhaps 'healing'; it was also exile and life imprisonment without trial.[30] But it worked. As the *Life of Rabbula* joyfully records, the 'evil doctrine' of heresy was 'conquered' and 'thousands of Jews and myriads of heretics he converted to the Messiah during all of the years of his priesthood.'[31]

The great German theologian Walter Bauer was sceptical of this account. There might, he wrote, have been tens of thousands of heretics 'pressing for baptism at the hands of Rabbula'.[32] But, he adds, one might also want to read such a life with caution, warning that 'we find ourselves in a period in which the power of the state also was already deliberately cooperating in the suppression of outspoken heresy'.[33] Rabbula's methods were, Bauer observes, 'rather coarse', and he is scornful of what 'the tyrant of Edessa' – as one Christian called him – really achieved. The thousands of conversions were, Bauer wrote, 'at best only the outward submission of people whose buildings had been torn down, whose scriptures had been burned, whose community goods had been confiscated, and who found themselves subjected to the worst kind of harassment, including danger to life and limb.'[34]

Through his weeding of the ungodly, the holy Rabbula gained not merely souls, but also a great deal of property and wealth. The *Life of Rabbula* records how some Arian 'heretics' were cured by Rabbula when he 'broke down their house of prayer and brought them to his own'.[35] It then goes on to explain how, after he had 'quietly' destroyed the heretical meeting places, he then went on 'to carry and bring all of its treasure[s] into his church until he had even taken all its stones for [his] use.'[36] Another group of heretics, the 'perfidious' Audians (who considered that, as God had made man in his own image, God must have a human form), found that they too lost not only their dignity but also their property when Rabbula 'disbanded their congregation, exiled them from their temple and expelled them from it. He settled in their place [our] brothers.'[37]

The appropriation of the buildings is worth noting, for another recurring theme that can be glimpsed in the texts of this period is that of money and property. Across the empire, long-running disputes between 'heretics' and the 'true Church' often ignited around church buildings, which, in those days of rapidly increasing numbers of Christians, were much in demand. It was a common complaint that the Church persecuted less from a love of righteousness than from a love of real estate.[38]

In these years, the magnificent religious variety that had once flourished within the Roman Empire starts to decline. The vast and striking profusion of those early Christianities – sects that worshipped one divine being, or two, or a male–female deity, or a Jesus who had laughed during the crucifixion – starts to fade away. Not always due to hostile forces: some of these sects would have needed no suppression and would have died anyway. Some were already moribund; simply because a religion is born does not mean that it will survive.

Indeed, some sects seemed almost designed for extinction. Augustine himself recorded that, in the countryside near him, in Hippo, 'there is also one rural heresy' – and then he corrects himself '– or rather, there was one. For growing smaller little by little it only survived in one small hamlet, in which there were a very small number of such persons, even if they were the sum total.'[39] As Augustine explains what the sect's beliefs were, it becomes clear why they might not have flourished. 'These men did not have sex with their wives,' he writes, 'although it was not permitted for them to live without wives from the same sect in their belief.' Instead of bringing up their own children, the celibate couple then adopted a son and a daughter, 'and by this sort of agreement they furnished their future descendants.'[40]

Though clearly, given their diminishing numbers, it didn't furnish them that well. However, as Augustine makes clear, it was not merely their odd habits that were causing these 'heretics' of North Africa to die out. They had been shrinking because of these habits, certainly – but it was something else that finished them off, and it is this that Augustine hints at in a sentence that is more ominous because it is so calmly noted. 'By now,' Augustine writes, 'all of them have been corrected and have been made Catholics, so that nothing of that former error now remains.'[41]

We will never know what these long-forgotten Christians thought of their 'correction' at the hands of the Church; we will never know what form their correction took, nor how their 'error' was quashed. Were they preached to? Fined? Flogged? Merely persuaded by the kindly words of Augustine or some other preacher? We have no idea. We will never know how these men and women – who had given their life to celibacy in tandem, and to the raising of other people's children – felt about the fact that they had 'all' now been 'corrected' and 'made Catholics'. Because they have gone.

So much has been lost. Almost all the information we have on the Christian sects that once existed comes only from the form of Christianity that suppressed them. Take the long legal lists in the Theodosian Code which name, one after another, all the heresies that were now forbidden. They were included in the code because their ideas were to be wiped out.

But, ironically, the Code now acts as their epitaph, too. To read the Code now is to read a catalogue of the dead, as the law lists those sects whom it will eventually destroy: the Novatians and the Sabbatians, the Eunomians and the Valentinians, the Priscillianists and the Phrygians, the Borborites and the Messalians and the Enthusiasts and the Donatists and the Audians and the Hydroparastatae and the Tascodrogitae and the Photinians and the Paulians and the Marcellians . . . On and on and on, naming and preserving, destroying and erasing, all in one.

Chapter Nineteen

THAT NO MEMORIAL BE LEFT

'We decree that the aforesaid books shall be diligently and zealously sought out and publicly burned . . .'

Theodosian Code, AD 435

It had been a long journey to the top of the precipice.

On 29 November, in AD 347, a bleak and ill-fitting group could be seen making their way up a sharp-sided peak in North Africa.[1] The majority of them were military men – the group comprised not only guards, but even, or so it was said, an entire division of soldiers. But at their centre was a civilian, a single prisoner: a bishop named Marculus.

Later, when people wrote about Marculus – for he was venerated for years afterwards – they would speak glowingly of his virtues. He was clever – he had once worked as a lawyer in the magistrates' courts – but he was also modest, and he had been more interested in a life that served God than in making money. It was because of this that he had left the law and come instead to the 'true Teacher, Christ'.[2] He had even been made a bishop; yet, despite his virtues, despite his status, he remained humble. Throughout his life, there was something that drew people to him: as one text recorded, his appearance had an almost spiritual charm.[3]

However, on that November day, his appearance must have been a little less imposing, his demeanour a little less aristocratic. Because, for months now, Marculus had been held captive by officials sent from the emperor himself – or, as this Christian chronicle would put it, from 'the Antichrist'.[4] And, before coming to that precipice, Marculus had been beaten, brutally, by the soldiers who had arrested him. In order to stop him from slipping away from their blows, they had tried to tie him to a post with rough ropes. Marculus, however, had gone one step further: so eager was he to suffer for his faith, ropes were not enough for him. Instead, he took the chains that were on him and fastened his own fetters to the column, 'so that no punishment could tear him away.'[5]

Then the beatings had begun. The wicked soldiers of the Antichrist 'raged' against him, smashing his 'sacred limbs' with their cudgels, raining down blow after blow.[6] The beating over, the soldiers untied him and 'dragged him with them through the other cities of Numidia, as some sort of public spectacle of their cruelty.'[7] The band of soldiers then took Marculus to Nova Petra, a citadel that lay near a sharp precipice.

The agents of the Antichrist were taking no chances with this particular execution, which is why not merely a guard, but an entire division of soldiers is reported to have marched him up the steep path to where the execution was to take place. Nonetheless, Marculus seemed serene. As he trod that steep path, it was as if, as one account later recorded, 'he approached heaven and the stars'.[8]

There were so many soldiers there that executing Marculus should have been simple. And yet, when the group reached the summit, something went wrong. The soldiers' nerve seemed to fail. For, as if they suddenly felt this crime was beyond them, they started pulling back. In the end, despite the large numbers of men who had climbed the hill, it was only the executioner, sword in hand, who stepped forward.[9]

This is one of those accounts – of a brutal Roman emperor and cruel Roman soldiers and tortured noble Christians – that feels so familiar, it hardly seems worth reading. Tale after similar tale had been told and would be told for centuries more about the wicked 'pagan' emperors and the tortures they inflicted upon their Christian victims. But this story isn't quite the same, because this time both soldiers and victim were Christians, and the wicked emperor – the Antichrist – was himself a Christian too.

It had, in so many ways, been a long journey to the top of the precipice.

*

It is not hard to know, broadly, what happened in these years. It is known that almost all heretical groups – some quickly, some slowly – died out within the Roman Empire as the Church became that 'greatest organized persecuting force in human history', as de Ste. Croix saw it.[10] And yet, to write about this period is nonetheless very difficult. So much has gone. No heretical churches survived in the Western Roman Empire to remind modern readers about their mistreatment or to reverence their mistreated martyrs; the libraries of Christendom did not hasten to preserve texts by the loathed heretics.[11] But it wasn't merely that such things were lost because they were not actively preserved; some were lost because they were actively destroyed. Such suppression was not unique to Christianity. The reliably intolerant Plato had recommended censorship for his ideal state; the Roman emperor Augustus had exiled the poet Ovid for merely a 'poem and a mistake'.[12] But book-burning in the classical period had tended to be piecemeal and sporadic – and, as writers at the time wryly noted, only tended to make those banned books more popular.

Christianity was far more thorough. From the second century onwards, Christian writers had warned the faithful to avoid reading 'heretical' or 'pagan' works that could act as a contagion and poison pure minds. It was still warning them against them when, in the sixteenth century, it formalized its disapproval into the Inquisition. Many of that organization's workers set about their task with an admirable enthusiasm; as Robert Bellarmine, a sixteenth-century cardinal, Jesuit and inquisitor, put it, 'I myself hardly ever read a book without feeling in the mood to give it a good censoring.'[13] The magnificently comprehensive *Index Librorum Prohibitorum* – the Index of Prohibited Books – was first drafted in 1557 and didn't cease production until 1966. Catholics who went to school in Britain in the fifties routinely used books bearing the *Imprimatur* – 'let it be printed' – stamp of the Catholic Church signifying that a book was suitable for faithful eyes to read.

The *Index* banned faithful Catholics not only from reading works by Gibbon, but also by Copernicus, Galileo, Erasmus, Hume, Hobbes, Locke, Voltaire, Rousseau, Kant, Milton and, indeed, God, for numerous translations of the Bible found their way onto the list. History was an early target. As the historian Robin Vose has observed, to those compiling such lists history was considered 'perhaps the most dangerous of the so-called "humanities" disciplines.'[14] History books that were considered 'unorthodox' were among the first to be forbidden.

The realization that history mattered came early to Christianity. Eusebius records how Constantine – the 'gentlest, mildest, and kindest man there ever was' – had actively suppressed not merely heretics, but also their books.[15] As Constantine observed in a characteristically peppery imperial letter, since 'protracted neglect allows healthy people to be infected with an epidemic disease', then not only should meeting places of the heretics be confiscated and handed over to the Catholic Church, but he also, Eusebius observes, 'required the books of these persons to be hunted out.'[16]

Another letter of Constantine's shows a similar understanding of the power of the written word. This letter is directed chiefly against one single heretic, named Arius. Arius would eventually become infamous in the ancient world as the archetype of the wicked heretic – although, at the heart of the Arian heresy was a difference of opinion that, to modern eyes, can seem rather mild. Arius, an Alexandrian cleric, had argued that, since fathers must come before sons, and since God was the father and Jesus the son, then God must have existed when Jesus did not.[17] This was not mild to ancient eyes – Arius was so disliked that Theodosius II is said to have erected a statue of him in the forum of Constantinople, so that passers-by could 'shit, piss and spit' on him.[18] As another letter by Constantine makes clear, this loathing began early. 'If anyone finds a book authored by [Arius] or agreeing with him,' Constantine wrote in a letter dated to around AD 330, 'he shall throw it into the fire.' And, he added, 'If anyone is found guilty of concealing such books and of not having immediately denounced and burnt them, then death shall be his penalty and decapitation.'[19]

The capital punishment is what people tend to notice in this letter. In fact, the more significant phrase is the one that comes just a little before – for Constantine, as he rules that Arius' writings should be consigned to the flames, also gives the reason why he is doing this. As Constantine clearly states: it is 'in order that no memory of Arius or of the doctrine which he had introduced might circulate.'[20] Books are not being burned merely to bring about control today: they are being burned for posterity; they are being burned to control the memory of the future.

Such prohibitions worked: little now remains of Arius' writings; academics who wish to study him work with mere scraps. Other writers suffered similarly. That same letter on Arius also mentions the books of the writer Porphyry – that philosopher who had so heartily and bawdily mocked Christianity. Constantine, as his letter makes clear, didn't find him funny. 'Porphyry, the enemy of piety, has composed unlawful books against religion,' he wrote, 'and therefore found a deserved compensation, namely that he became shameful for the future, was infected with the worst reputation, and his sacrilegious books were obliterated.'[21] Once again, it worked well: academics who study Porphyry have only fragments (he survives in quotations caught in other authors) to work with.

Even if all the books written in this period had survived, it would still be difficult for a modern reader to understand what was going on. The past is not merely today in togas; it is far odder and more eccentric than we often expect. Consider the religious crackdown that took place under the rule of the emperor Theodosius II. This was, it is true, in part caused by religious zeal. It was also caused by a panic about the weather. Why, lamented a peevish Emperor Theodosius, in a law dated to 31 January AD 438, 'has the springtime resigned its wonted charm, why does the summer with its scanty harvests mock the hopes of the toiling husband-man, why have the rigours of winter condemned the fruitful soil to barrenness?' Why, the law continued, has 'the intemperate ferocity of winter with its piercing cold doomed the fertility of the lands with the disaster of sterility?' Why all these things, 'unless nature has transgressed the decree of its own law to avenge such impiety?'[22]

Today, 'the heavens' and 'heaven' have been so successfully peeled apart into two different realms – one meteorological, one theological – that it seems oddly simplistic to conflate them as Theodosius II seems to in these laws. But such a separation is a very recent idea. In these centuries, the divine was everywhere: in the air, in the clouds, in the sun that shone on dappled forests and in the rain that fell on the leaves of the trees. Or didn't fall. Weather was a barometer of divine displeasure: if it didn't rain, or it rained too much, or if crops were destroyed by hail, then suspicions of divine anger clouded the minds of all, pagan and Christian alike. This had been the case for centuries. If something goes wrong, wrote the second-century Christian writer Tertullian, 'If the Tiber reaches the walls, if the Nile does not rise to the fields, if the sky doesn't move or the earth does, if there is famine, if there is plague, the cry is at once: "The Christians to the lion!" '[23]

In the first century BC, the Latin philosopher Lucretius had used the intricate, astonishing complexity of nature to argue vehemently against a divine creator and in favour of his atomic view of the universe.[24] Now, Christians (who had scant time for Lucretius or the atomists) used the magnificent complexity of the natural world to argue precisely the reverse: that there must be a God. Or, as the Theodosian Code put it, in its inimitable way: 'who is so demented, so damned by the enormity of strange savagery, that, when he sees the heavens . . . [or] when he sees the movements of the stars which control the benefits of life, the earth richly endowed with the harvests, the waters of the sea, and the vastness of this immense achievement confined within the boundaries of the natural world, he does not seek the author of so great a mystery, of so mighty a handiwork?'

Lest there be any confusion in the mind of the reader over who this law was referring to, or who might be 'so demented', it made this point very clear: 'the Jews, with blinded senses, the Samaritans, the pagans, and the other breeds of heretical monsters dare to do this.'[25] The law went further: 'Shall we endure longer that the succession of the seasons be changed, and the temper of the heavens be stirred to anger, since the embittered perfidy of the pagans does not know how to preserve these balances of nature?'[26] Once again, it was a rhetorical question: we shall not. It was cold in Constantinople because God was angry. And it was the job of Theodosius to make him less so.[27] And the solution to this was, to Theodosius II, clear: a religious crackdown must begin – and that included books.

As the first century of Christian rule rolled on, other laws mandated the destruction of other heretical works. In AD 398, a new law was directed at the writings of the 'heretics' Eunomius and Montanus (who the Church found distressing for many reasons, not least because of their scandalous habit of recognizing women as bishops): their books were to be burned and anyone who was found to have hidden them away was to be executed. Books by the 'heretics' Eutyches or Apollinaris (Christians who, to orthodox eyes, considered that Jesus was both too divine and too little human) were later also ruled against: 'All papers of this kind, and all books which contain the pernicious dogmas of Eutyches and Apollinaris, shall be committed to the flames.'[28]

Manichaeans, who had been brutally targeted under pagan rule, were targeted once again by the Christians. As another law records, 'Books in any way related to the ungodly error of the Manichaeans' were to be burned and their owners punished.[29] A slightly later law, of AD 435, would target the writings of yet another 'heretic'. 'Nor indeed', it states, 'shall any person dare to have or to read or to copy the impious books of the nefarious and sacrilegious Nestorius, written against the venerable sect of the orthodox . . . We decree that the aforesaid books shall be diligently and zealously sought out and publicly burned.'[30]

Sometimes destruction was legislated for by emperors. At other times, control happened at a more local level, from zealous local enforcers. The thuggish Rabbula had laid down commands on what books his own monks might possess. As Rule 10 in one of his lengthy lists of instructions ordered, 'Books outside of the faith of the church may not be in the monasteries'. That is unremarkable. However, what is interesting about this collection of rules is that they are also clearly aimed at controlling the books of everyone else, too. So, Rule 50 of another set of injunctions orders his clerics to 'Search for the writings of heretics and their books in every place, and as you are able, either let us have them or burn them in fire.'[31] Note that 'in every place'. No longer is this a Church concerned with correcting those within its own walls. This is a Church that is concerned with actively combatting heresy – choice – everywhere it can be found.

However, by far the most efficient way of silencing an opponent is not to write anything about them in the first place – as Christian authors clearly knew. The historian Sozomen, after praising the learning of a certain heretic, then defended his choice in doing so – but reassured his readers that he would not go into discussions on this man's heretical doctrines: 'I have not been set forth to record such matters, nor is it befitting in history.'[32] The historian Eusebius piously explained that, in his history, he would similarly include 'only those things by which first we ourselves, then later generations, may benefit.'[33]

Evidence about what went on within the Church, and in its meetings and synods, could also be carefully controlled. At one infamous church council, the end document seemed to show that all the bishops present had agreed on the matters being discussed. We did no such thing, the bishops later said. They had signed the final official document – but they had signed merely blank pages that were filled in later. They had done so because 'force with beatings' was used and 'soldiers were standing around and threatening us with clubs and swords. We subscribed from terror. With clubs and swords, what kind of synod is it?'[34] At this council, notaries working for one bishop were approached by the notaries of another bishop, who 'came up and erased their tablets and almost broke their fingers trying to seize them and the pens. And', laments the bishop, 'I did not get the record of the proceedings, nor do I know what became of it.'[35]

But the problems with writing about this period are deeper than a lack of sources, or a lack of books. The problem is that it is hard to imagine history might have been otherwise, that the heretics might ever have survived. It is hard, in short, to imagine they ever even mattered. Walk through a town in Italy or France or England today and you will pass Protestant churches, and Catholic ones, and Methodist ones – but you will not walk past churches preaching that there were two gods, or that the God of the Old Testament was an evil interloper, or that there are 365 heavens, or (perhaps thankfully) that you should have sex with other Christians as a form of worship. The 'heretics' have gone. The Christian persecution of heretical competition has largely been forgotten, but not because it didn't happen, or because it was mild, or ineffective – it has been forgotten because it was so very successful.

Take that account of the execution of Marculus that began this chapter. It is an astonishing historical rarity: an account of persecution that was written not by the winning side, but the losing one.* It comes from a collection of similar North African accounts by and about Christians who would become classified as 'heretics'. These accounts are manifestly biased and partial – and, at many points, frankly fantastical. But they are also invaluable: they are accounts about early Christianity written by one of the losing sides. And yet, despite their importance, most of them were not translated into English until 1996. As the

* The Christians whose martyrdoms it recounts were recognized as full heretics a few decades after their martyrdoms were written.

academic who eventually did translate them, Maureen Tilley, observed, 'Winning a religious war has much in common with being the victor in a military battle. Those who finally hold power enjoy carte blanche in writing the history of the campaign.'[36]

In her translation of the account, the end of the holy Marculus comes when the executioner steps forward and pushes him off the side of that mountain, ostensibly to his death. Marculus starts to fall – but he never strikes the ground. Those watching do not hear any noise as his body hits the rocks below. There is just the sound of the rushing wind as he falls, 'tumbling through the rushing rustle of the agitated air.'[37] His body disappears, never to be seen again. The heretic – pursued, tortured, beaten, executed – is not seen to die. Instead, he simply vanishes, into thin air.

Epilogue

In the course of his long life and his long travels along the silk roads, Marco Polo had seen many things. He had narrowly escaped death at the hands of robbers in Persia, he had felt the monsoon rains freshen the air of India and he had admired the complexion of the concubines of Kublai Khan (whose selection process involved, he noted, not merely ensuring that the women had sweet faces, but also a test to ensure they had sweet-smelling breath – and that they didn't snore).[1] He was, in other words, not a man who was easily impressed; yet even he seems to have been struck by a story that he heard while he was in Persia.

For, in that region, as *The Travels* records, lay the city of Saveh. This was the city from which – or so the locals believed – the three magi who had gone to worship Christ had set out. The magi were now buried there and the townspeople had built three sepulchres 'of great size and beauty' to worship them.*[2] Fascinated by this, Marco Polo had asked the people of the city of Saveh more about their magi, but no one could tell him anything.

Disappointed in his efforts, he moved on. Then, three days later, he came across a town named Kala Atashparastan, 'that is to say, Town of the Fire-Worshippers.' And, *The Travels* continues, 'that is no more than the truth; for the men of this

---

* This was a declaration that would later cause some distress to German Christians, who believed the remains of the magi lay in Cologne Cathedral.

town do worship fire. And I will tell you why they worship it.' The entire story is then recounted. The inhabitants of the Town of the Fire-Worshippers declare that, 'in days gone by three kings of this country went to worship a newborn prophet, taking with them three offerings, namely gold, frankincense and myrrh, in order to establish whether that prophet was God, an earthly king or a physician.'

According to *The Travels*, these gifts were a kind of test. 'For they said: "If he takes the gold, he is an earthly king; if he takes the frankincense, he is God; and if he takes the myrrh, he is a healer."' However, when the magi arrived at the birthplace of this newborn prophet, things did not go according to plan. First, 'the youngest of the three kings set off on his own to see him. He found that the infant resembled himself, for he seemed to be of the same age and appearance, and he came out filled with wonder.'

As if that were not strange enough, then the second magus went in. He was 'a man of middle age'. Yet the same thing happened again: 'the infant seemed to him, as he had to the other, to be of his own appearance and age. He, too, came away quite amazed.' The third and oldest magus went in and, once again, 'just the same thing happened to him as to the other two. And he emerged deep in thought.' The magi told each other what they had just seen, and, 'marvelling greatly, decided they would all go in together. So all three went together before the infant, and they found him with his own features and looking his real age, which is to say just thirteen days old. Then they worshipped him and offered him the gold, frankincense and myrrh.'

The remarkable infant then 'took all three offerings, and in return he gave them a closed casket. And upon receiving it the three kings set out to return to their own country.' They rode for several days before curiosity overcame them. They 'resolved to take a look at what the infant had given them. So they opened the casket, and inside they found a stone. They were greatly puzzled as to what it might be. The infant had given it to them to signify that they should be firm as rocks in the faith they had embarked upon.' When the infant had taken all three of their gifts, the kings had concluded that he was not merely a god, or a king, or a physician – but all three in one. 'And because the infant knew that the three kings had this faith, he gave them the stone as a sign that they should be firm and constant in their belief.'

However, the three kings did not understand this. Instead, piqued at what they considered to be a pitiful gift, they took the stone 'and tossed it into a well. The stone had barely fallen into the well when a burning flame descended from heaven and directly struck the well into which they had thrown the stone.' As soon as they saw this, 'they were greatly dismayed and repented the act of throwing away the stone, for they saw clearly that it was a great and beneficent portent.' The men 'immediately gathered some of the fire and carried it to their country, where they placed it in one of their churches, a magnificent and ornate building.'

And, to this day, *The Travels* records, 'They keep it perpetually burning and worship it as God. And every time they make a sacrifice or holocaust, they roast it in this fire. If it ever happens that the fire goes out, they pay a visit to others who share their faith and who also worship the fire, obtain from them some of the fire that burns in their church, and go back to rekindle their fire. On no account would they take it unless it came from the fire I have told you about. And often they make a journey of ten days to procure this fire. Now I have told you the reasons why the people of this country worship fire. And I assure you there are a great many of them.'[3]

Such, at any rate, is the story told by Marco Polo.

There is no one ending to this story – chiefly because there is no one story. This is the story of many, many different religions, and cults, and sects, and beliefs, and heresies, and schisms – and each one has its own tale, each its own ending. For, wherever Christianity travelled, it changed, blending here with wizardry, there with sorcery; here with astronomy and astrology; here with 'paganism' and Buddhism and fire worship and Greek philosophy; on and on and on, changing and changing and changing again. And each sect that was formed was convinced that it alone was the 'true' Church, it alone was right.

Some of these sects and groups lasted for almost no time at all. Others lingered on for centuries, even for a millennium or more, and ideas that were destroyed within the Roman Empire continued to flourish, for hundreds of years, beyond it. Manichaeism, that religion which blended the teachings of Christ with those of Zoroaster and of Buddha, might have been extirpated from Roman cities – but it survived far better in China. There are signs that Manichaeism still existed there in the closing years of the nineteenth century; it is entirely possible that the last surviving Manichaean might have died in the twentieth century. Other places preserved other forms. In Ethiopia, Christians still read books containing stories of how Christ resurrected cockerels. Those communities of Mandaeans,whom Wilfred Thesiger had been so struck by, still live in Iraq.

But perhaps it is wrong to look at this story in such black and white terms, of death and life, extinction and survival. Much was lost and much was destroyed – but the total extirpation that the laws of Rome demanded did not happen. Groups were scattered, books were burned – but ideas lived on. 'Forbidden' books continued to be read; 'forbidden' ideas continued to be spread. Other ideas grew up, afresh. And other ideas lived on, unexpectedly, far past their time.

For, in Europe, the cult of the Virgin Mary – inspired by that strange gospel which told of a miraculous birth in a cave, and a vagina that could burn human flesh – spread and grew and flourished. In churches across the world, people still listen to how, during the reign of the emperor Augustus – the great, divine Augustus, son of god and saviour, who brought peace upon the earth – yet another son was born to yet another god, and to another mortal woman, and how that saviour came to bring peace to the world.

This is a story about how ideas are born, and how they die. It is also a story about how they survive. It is about how ancient stories linger, and divine whispers persist. It is about how religions change and change again, as they travel, and age, and spread into other lands, and other ages. It is about how long memory is, and how short. It is about what was, and what might have been. It is also about what is. And it is about why, when midwinter falls, and cribs are set out, an ox and an ass stand and watch over the baby Jesus in the manger.

Acknowledgements

There are so many. Thanks as always to George Morley, who was magnificent, and made me laugh, and was unspeakably kind while I was writing it (so slowly, and at first with a newborn). Thank you. To Patrick Walsh, whose good humour and help has been invaluable. To Laura Carr, who is just superb. To Francesca Stavrakopoulou, who read it all not once, but twice, and offered clever comments every time. To Natalie Haynes, who knew that what I really needed on that cold dark night in midwinter was to be taken for a toasted cheese sandwich on the cheese barge. Of course it was. To Nat and Francesca together for good holy-trinity work. To Anne and Mima (whose name, it turns out, is still there) for excellence over two entire decades. To my family, for listening to me talk about this. And last but not least, to Tom. For everything. The handwriting-deciphering. The wood-chopping that keeps me warm. Thank you.

Finally: hearty thanks to the academics who have read this and saved me from my worst excesses. To Hal Drake, for superb comments on Constantine and the Theodosian Code – and for a shared enthusiasm for Walter Bagehot, of all things. To Dirk Rohmann, for reading so much and for detailed comments on heretics and more besides. To Candida Moss, for clever and funny comments on everything from gospels to Roman darkness. To Vivian Nutton, for wonderful writings on ancient medicine and for reading my chapters on the same. To David Brakke for, as always, excellent thoughts on so many things. To Justin Meggitt, for reading my chapters on ancient magic (and for supervision excellence). To Jacob Dahl, who was superb and droll on ancient epics. To Tony Burke, who was superbly helpful on early Christian texts. To Sam Lieu, who was super on Marco

Polo. To Michele R. Salzman, for insightful comments on the Code and Christianization. To Harry Sidebottom, for excellent thoughts on Roman travel (and stasis). Thank you all. All mistakes are my own.

Bibliography

ABBREVIATIONS

ANF Ante-Nicene Fathers
NPNF Nicene and Post-Nicene Fathers

PRIMARY SOURCES

Ambrose, *Epistles*, in *Some of the Principal Works of St. Ambrose*, tr. H. De Romestin, E. De Romestin and H. T. F. Duckworth (Oxford: J. Parker & Co., 1896)

—, *On the duties of the clergy*, in *Some of the Principal Works of St. Ambrose*, tr. H. De Romestin, E. De Romestin and H. T. F. Duckworth (Oxford: J. Parker & Co., 1896)

Ammianus Marcellinus, *The Later Roman Empire (AD 354–378)*, tr. W. Hamilton, intr. A. Wallace-Hadrill (London: Penguin, 1986)

Anonymous, *An Apostolic Gospel: The 'Epistula Apostolorum' in Literary Context*, tr. F. Watson. Society for New Testament Studies; 179 (Cambridge: Cambridge University Press, 2020)

—, *Ancient Roman Statutes: A Translation with Introduction, Commentary, Glossary, and Index*, tr. Johnson et al. (Lawbook Exchange, 2012)

—, *Historia Augusta*, Volume I, tr. D. Magie, revised D. Rohrbacher. Loeb Classical Library 139 (Cambridge, MA: Harvard University Press, 2022)

—, *The Greek Magical Papyri in Translation, Including the Demotic Spells*, ed. H. D. Betz (Chicago; London: University of Chicago Press, 1986)

—, *Manichaean Texts from the Roman Empire*, ed. S. Lieu and I. Gardner (Cambridge: Cambridge University Press, 2004)

—, *Prester John: The Legend and Its Sources*, tr. K. Brewer. Crusade Texts in Translation (Routledge, 2015)

Antony, *The Letters of St Antony: Monasticism and the Making of a Saint*, ed. S. Rubenson (Minneapolis: Fortress Press, 1995)

Apostolic Fathers, tr. R. Grant (New York; Camden, NJ: T. Nelson, 1964)

Apuleius, *Apologia, Florida, De Deo Socratis*, ed. and tr. C. P. Jones, Loeb Classical Library 534 (Cambridge, MA: Harvard University Press, 2017)

—, *The Apologia and Florida of Apuleius of Madaura*, tr. H. E. Butler (Oxford: Clarendon Press, 1909)

—, *The Golden Ass*, tr. E. J. Kenney (London: Penguin, 2004)

—, *The Letter of Aristeas*, tr. H. St. J. Thackeray (London: Macmillan, 1904)

Aristotle, *De Caelo* in *The Works of Aristotle*, ed. W. D. Ross, tr. J. L. Stocks et al. (Oxford: Clarendon, 1970)

—, *On the Heavens*, tr. W. K. C. Guthrie Loeb Classical Library 338 (Cambridge, MA: Harvard University Press, 1939)

—, *Historia Animalium* in *The Works of Aristotle*, tr. D'Arcy Wentworth Thompson Volume IV (Oxford: Clarendon Press, 1910)

Arnobius, *The Seven Books of Arnobius adversus gentes*, tr. A. H. Bryce and Hugh Campbell (Edinburgh: T. & T. Clark, 1871)

Athanasius, *Life of Antony*, in *Early Christian Lives*, tr. C. White (London: Penguin, 1998)

Augustine, *City of God*, tr. M. Dods (Edinburgh: T. & T. Clark, 1913)

—, *City of God: An abridged version from the translation by Gerald Walsh et al.*, ed. V. J. Bourke (New York: Image Books, 1958)

—, *City of God*, vol. III, in *Books 8–11*, tr. D. S. Wiesen, Loeb Classical Library 413 (Cambridge, MA: Harvard University Press, 1968)

—, *The City of God against the Pagans*, tr. R. W. Dyson, Cambridge Texts in the History of Political Thought (Cambridge: Cambridge University Press, 1998)

—, *Confessions*, tr. R. S. Pine-Coffin (Harmondsworth: Penguin, 1961)

—, *Confessions*, tr. F. J. Sheed, M. P. Foley, 2nd ed. (Indianapolis: Hackett, 2006)

—, *Letters*, tr. J. G. Cunningham, in *Letters of Augustine*, tr. Cunningham, vol. 1 (Edinburgh: T. & T. Clark, 1872); vol. 2 (Edinburgh: T. & T. Clark, 1875)

—, *Tractates on the Gospel according to St John*, tr. J. Gibb, in *Nicene and Post-Nicene Fathers*, first series, vol. 7, ed. Schaff (Buffalo, NY: Christian Literature Publishing Co., 1888)

—, *Vingt-six sermons au peuple d'Afrique; retrouvés à Mayence*, ed. F. Dolbeau (Paris: Institut d'études augustiniennes, 1996)

—, *The Writings Against the Manichaeans*, tr. R. Stothert and A. H. Newman, and *Against the Donatists*, tr. J. R. King and Rev. C. D. Hartranft (Buffalo, NY: Christian Literature Co., 1887)

Marcus Aurelius, *Meditations* in *Marcus Aurelius*, tr. C. R. Haines, Loeb Classical Library 58 (Cambridge, MA: Harvard University Press, 1916)

—, *Meditations*, tr. R. Hard (Oxford: Oxford University Press, 2011)

Bagehot, W., *Biographical Studies by the Late Walter Bagehot*, ed. R. H. Hutton (London: Longmans, Green, and Co., 1881)

Basil, *Address to Young Men on Reading Greek Literature*, in *The Letters*, vol. IV: *Letters*, tr. R. J. Deferrari and M. R. P. McGuire, Loeb Classical Library 270 (Cambridge, MA: Harvard University Press, 1934)

—, *Address to Young Men on the Right Use of Greek Literature*, in *Essays on the Study and Use of Poetry by Plutarch and Basil the Great*, tr. F. M. Padelford, in Yale Studies in English 15 (New York: Henry Holt & Company, 1902)

—, *Epistles*, in *Nicene and Post-Nicene Fathers*, second series, vol. 8, tr. Blomfield Jackson, ed. Philip Schaff and Henry Wace (Buffalo, NY: Christian Literature Publishing Co., 1895), available online at newadvent.org/fathers

Basil of Ancyra, *The Synodal Letter of the Council of Ancyra*, in Radde-Gallwitz, A. and Muehlberger, E., *The Cambridge Edition of Early Christian Writings* (Cambridge: Cambridge University Press, 2017)

Bede, *A History of the English Church and People*, tr. L. Sherley-Price (Harmondsworth: Penguin, 1955)

—, *The Reckoning of Time*, tr. F. Wallis. Translated Texts for Historians; 29 (Liverpool: Liverpool University Press, 1999)

Besa, *The Life of Shenoute*, tr. D. N. Bell (Collegeville, MN: Cistercian Publications, 1983)

Betz, H. D. (tr.), *The Greek Magical Papyri in Translation, Including the Demotic Spells* (Chicago; London: University of Chicago Press, 1986)

Bīrūnī, *The Chronology of Ancient Nations: An English Version of the Arabic Text of the Athâr-ul-bâkiya of Albîrûnî, or 'Vestiges of the Past'*, tr. E. Sachau (London: W. H. Allen & Co., 1879)

Caesar, *The Gallic War*, tr. H. J. Edwards, Loeb Classical Library 72 (Cambridge, MA: Harvard University Press, 1917)

Catullus, *The Poems of Catullus*, tr. P. Whigham (Harmondsworth: Penguin, 1966)

—, *The Poems of Gaius Valerius Catullus*, tr. F. W. Cornish (Cambridge: Cambridge University Press, 1904)

Celsus, *On the True Doctrine: A Discourse Against the Christians*, tr. R. J. Hoffmann (New York; Oxford: Oxford University Press, 1987)

—, *On Medicine*, Volume I: Books 1–4, tr. W. G. Spencer. Loeb Classical Library 292 (Cambridge, MA: Harvard University Press, 1935)

Celsus, Aulus Cornelius, *On Medicine*, tr. W. G. Spencer, Loeb Classical Library 292, 304, 336 (Cambridge, MA; London: Harvard University Press, 1935)

Chariton, *Callirhoe*, tr. G. P. Goold, Loeb Classical Library 481 (Cambridge, Mass: Harvard University Press, 1995)

Charles, R. H., *The Book of Enoch* (Oxford: Clarendon, 1912)

Chrysostom, John, *Against the Games and Theatres*, in *John Chrysostom*, W. Mayer and P. Allen (London; New York: Routledge, 2000)

—, *Discourses Against Judaizing Christians*, tr. P. W. Harkins (Washington, DC: Catholic University of America, 1979)

—, *The Homilies of John Chrysostom: Archbishop of Constantinople, on the Statues, or To the People of Antioch* (Oxford: J. H. Parker, 1842)

Cicero, *Letters to Atticus*, tr. D. R. Shackleton Bailey, vol. 5, 48–45 B.C. 211–354 (Books XI–XIII). Cambridge Classical Texts and Commentaries; 4 (Cambridge: Cambridge University Press, 1966)

—, *Letters to Atticus*, vol. 3, tr. E. O. Winstedt. Loeb Classical Library 97 (London; Heinemann, 1918)

—, *Letters to Friends*, vols. I–III, ed. and tr. D. R. Shackleton Bailey, Loeb Classical Library 216 (London: Harvard University Press, 2001)

—, *Letters to Friends*, vol. III, ed. and tr. E.O. Winstedt (Cambridge, MA: Harvard University Press, 1967)

—, *On the Nature of the Gods*, tr. H. Rackham, Loeb Classical Library 268 (Cambridge, MA: Harvard University Press, 1933)

—, *On the Republic. On the Laws*, tr. C. W. Keyes, Loeb Classical Library 213 (Cambridge, MA: Harvard University Press, 1928)

Clement, *Stromata*, in *Fathers of the Second Century: Hermes, Tatian, Athenagoras, Theophilus, and Clement of Alexandria etc.*, ed. A. Roberts, J. Donaldson and A. Coxe, *Ante-Nicene Fathers*, vol. 2 (Buffalo, NY: Christian Literature Publishing Co., 1885)

—, *The Epistles of Clement in The Ante-Nicene Fathers: The Writings of the Fathers down to A.D. 325*, vol. 9, tr. J. Keith (Peabody, Mass.: Hendrickson, 1995)

—, *The Writings of Clement of Alexandria*, tr. W. Wilson, in the *Ante-Nicene Christian Library*, vols. 4, 12 (Edinburgh: T. & T. Clark, 1867–9)

Collectio Avellana in *The Collectio Avellana and Its Revivals*, eds. R. Lizzi Testa and G. Marconi (Newcastle upon Tyne: Cambridge Scholars Publishing, 2019)

Cosmas Indicopleustes, *The Christian Topography of Cosmas, an Egyption Monk*, tr. J. W. McCrindle (Cambridge: Cambridge University Press, 2010)

Cyprian, *On the Lapsed*, *On the Mortality* and *On the Unity of the Church*, in *The Writings of Cyprian, Bishop of Carthage*, tr. R. E. Wallis (Edinburgh: T. & T. Clark, 1868–9)

Dalley, S. (tr.), *Myths from Mesopotamia: Creation, The Flood, Gilgamesh, and Others*, Oxford World's Classics, revised ed. (Oxford: Oxford University Press, 2008)

Damascius, *The Philosophical History*, ed. P. Athanassiadi (Athens: Apamea Cultural Association, 1999)

Dio Cassius, *Roman History, Volume V: Books 46–50*, tr. E. Cary and H. B. Foster, Loeb Classical Library 82 (Cambridge, MA: Harvard University Press, 1917)

Diodorus Siculus, *Library of History, Volume II: Books 2.35–4.58*, tr. C. H. Oldfather, Loeb Classical Library 303 (Cambridge, MA: Harvard University Press, 1935)

—, *Library of History, Volume XI: Fragments of Books 21–32*, tr. F. R. Walton, Loeb Classical Library 409 (Cambridge, MA: Harvard University Press, 1957)

Diogenes Laertius, *Lives of Eminent Philosophers*, vol. I: books 1–5, tr. R. D. Hicks, Loeb Classical Library 184 (Cambridge, MA: Harvard University Press, 1925); vol. II: books 6–10, tr. R. D. Hicks, Loeb Classical Library 185 (Cambridge, MA: Harvard University Press, 1925)

Dobschütz, E. von (ed.), *De Libris Recipiendis Et Non Recipiendis*; *Das Decretum Gelasianum: De Libris Recipiendis Et Non Recipiendis*, Texte Und Untersuchungen Zur Geschichte Der Altchristlichen Literatur (Leipzig: Hinrichs, 1912)

Edelstein, E. and Edelstein, L. (eds.), *Asclepius: A Collection and Interpretation of the Testimonies* (New York: Arno, 1975)

Ehrman, B. D. and Pleše, Z., *The Apocryphal Gospels: Texts and Translations* (New York: Oxford University Press, 2011)

—, *The Other Gospels: Accounts of Jesus from outside the New Testament* (New York: Oxford University Press, 2014)

Elliott, J. K. and James, M. R., *The Apocryphal New Testament: A Collection of Apocryphal Christian Literature in an English Translation* (Oxford: Clarendon, 1993; reprinted 2009)

Epictetus, *Discourses, Books 3–4, Fragments, The Enchiridion*, tr. A. Oldfather, Loeb Classical Library 218 (Cambridge, MA: Harvard University Press, 1928)

Epiphanius, *The Panarion of Epiphanius of Salamis: Book I (Sects 1–46)*, tr. F. Williams, second edition, revised and expanded, Nag Hammadi and Manichaean Studies 63 (Leiden: Brill, 2008); *Books II and III*, tr. F. Williams, second, revised edition, Nag Hammadi and Manichaean Studies 79 (Leiden; Boston: Brill, 2012)

Eunapius, *Lives of the Philosophers and Sophists*, tr. W. C. Wright, Loeb Classical Library 134 (Cambridge, MA: Harvard University Press, 1921)

Euripides, *Alcestis*, tr. T. Hughes (London: Faber, 1999)

Eusebius, *The History of the Church from Christ to Constantine*, tr. G. A. Williamson (London: Penguin, 1989)

—, *The History of the Martyrs in Palestine*, tr. W. Cureton (London: Williams & Norgate, 1861)

—, *The Life of the Blessed Emperor Constantine, in four books, from* AD *306 to 337* (London: S. Bagster & Sons, 1845)

—, *Life of Constantine*, tr. A. Cameron and S. G. Hall (Oxford: Clarendon Press, 1999)

—, *Oration in Praise of Constantine*, in *Eusebius Pamphilius: Church History, Life of Constantine, Oration in Praise of Constantine*, ed. P. Schaff, tr. Richardson et al. (New York: Christian Literature Publishing, 1890)

—, *The Preparation for the Gospel*, tr. E. H. Gifford (n.p.: Aeterna Press, 2015)

—, *Reply to Hierocles*, in *Philostratus: Apollonius of Tyana, Volume III*, ed. and tr. C. P. Jones, Loeb Classical Library 458 (Cambridge, MA: Harvard University Press, 2006)

Evagrius Ponticus, *The Praktikos: Chapters on Prayer*, tr. J. E. Bamberger (Spencer, MA: Cistercian Publications, 1972)

—, *Talking Back: A Monastic Handbook for Combating Demons*, tr. D. Brakke (Trappist, KY; Collegeville, MN: Cistercian Publications, 2009)

Firmicus Maternus, *The Error of the Pagan Religions*, tr. C. A. Forbes (New York: Newman Press, 1970)

Galen, *On Anatomical Procedures*, tr. C. Singer (London: Oxford University Press, 1956)

Gellius, *Attic Nights*, vol. II, books 6–13, tr. J. C. Rolfe, Loeb Classical Library 200 (Cambridge, MA: Harvard University Press, 1927)

Gibbon, E., *History of the Decline and Fall of the Roman Empire, with the notes by H. H. Milman* (London: Methuen & Co., 1896–1900)

—, *The History of the Decline and Fall of the Roman Empire*, ed. J. B. Bury (London: Methuen, 1909)

—, *Memoirs of My Life and Writings; illustrated from his letters, with occasional notes and narrative by John, Lord Sheffield* (Keele: Ryburn Publishing, Keele University Press, 1994)

—, *A Vindication of Some Passages in the Fifteenth and Sixteenth Chapters of the History of the Decline and Fall of the Roman Empire* (Dublin: W. & H. Whitestone, 1779)

Gregory Nazianzen, *Select Orations of Saint Gregory Nazianzen*, tr. C. G. Browne and J. E. Swallow, in *Nicene and Post-Nicene Fathers*, second series, vol. 7, ed. P. Schaff and H. Wace (Buffalo, NY: Christian Literature Publishing Co., 1894)

Gregory, *The History of the Franks*, tr. L. G. M. Thorpe (Harmondsworth: Penguin, 1974)

Herodotus, *The Histories*, tr. A. D. Godley, Loeb Classical Library (Cambridge, MA: Harvard University Press, 1920)

—, *The Histories*, tr. A. de Sélincourt, revised J. Marincola (London: Penguin, 1996)

Hesiod, *Theogony*, in *Hesiod: Theogony and Works and Days* and *Theognis: Elegies*, tr. D. Wender (Harmondsworth: Penguin, 1976)

Hippocrates, *On Airs, Waters and Places*, in *The Genuine Works of Hippocrates*, tr. F. Adams (London: Baillière, Tindall & Cox, 1939)

Hippolytus, *The Refutation of All Heresies*, tr. J. H. MacMahon and S. D. F. Salmond, in the *Ante-Nicene Christian Library*, vol. 5 (Edinburgh: T. & T. Clark, 1868)

—, *The Refutation of All Heresies*, tr. J. H. MacMahon and S. D. F. Salmond, in the *Ante-Nicene Christian Library*, vol. 6 (Edinburgh: T. & T. Clark, 1868)

Homer, *Iliad*, tr. M. Hammond (Harmondsworth: Penguin, 1987)

—, *Odyssey*, tr. E. V. Rieu, revised D. Rieu (London: Penguin, 2003)

—, *Odyssey*, tr. E. Wilson (New York: W. W. Norton and Company, 2018)

Horace, *The Odes and Carmen Sæculare*, tr. J. Conington (London: George Bell and Sons, 1882)

—, *Odes and Epodes*, tr. N. Rudd, Loeb Classical Library 33 (Cambridge, MA: Harvard University Press, 2004)

—, *Satires*; *Epistles*; *Art of Poetry*, tr. H. Rushton Fairclough, Loeb Classical Library 194 (Cambridge, MA: Harvard University Press, 1926)

Ignatius, *Epistle of Ignatius to the Ephesians*, in *The Writings of the Apostolic Fathers*, tr. Roberts, Donaldson and Crombie, in the *Ante-Nicene Christian Library*, vol. 1 (Edinburgh: T. & T. Clark, 1867)

Irenaeus, *Against the Heresies*, tr. D. J. Unger, J. Dillon, Ancient Christian Writers 65 (New York: Paulist Press, 1992)

James (attrib.), *Protoevangelium of James*, in *Ante-Nicene Fathers. Volume 8: The Twelve Patriarchs, Excerpts and Epistles* etc., *Ante-Nicene Fathers*, ed. A. Roberts, J. Donaldson, rev. A. Cleveland Coxe (Buffalo, NY: Christian Literature Publishing Co., 1886)

James, M. R., *The Apocryphal New Testament: Being the Apocryphal Gospels, Acts, Epistles, and Apocalypses, with other narratives and fragments* (Oxford: Clarendon Press, 1924)

—, *The Apocryphal New Testament: Being the Apocryphal Gospels, Acts, Epistles, and Apocalypses with Other Narratives and Fragments* (corrected edn) (Oxford: Clarendon Press, 1975)

Jerome, *Letters*, in *The Principal Works of St. Jerome*, tr. W. H. Freemantle, G. Lewis and W. G. Martley, in *A Select Library of Nicene and Post-Nicene Fathers of the Christian Church*, second series, vol. 6 (Oxford: Parker, 1893)

John, Bishop of Nikiu, *The Chronicle of John, Bishop of Nikiu*, tr. R. H. Charles (London: Williams & Norgate, for the Text and Translation Society, 1916)

John of Ephesus, *The Third Part of the Ecclesiastical History of John, Bishop of Ephesus*, tr. R. P. Smith (Oxford: Oxford University Press, 1860)

Julian, *Against the Galilaeans*, in *Julian*, vol. III, tr. W. C. Wright, Loeb Classical Library 157 (Cambridge, MA: Harvard University Press, 1923)

Julian, *Orations 6–8, Letters to Themistius . . .* , tr. W. C. Wright. Loeb Classical Library 29 (Cambridge, MA: Harvard University Press, 1913)

Justin Martyr, *The Apology*, in *The Writings of Justin Martyr and Athenagoras*, tr. M. Dods, G. Reith and B. Pratten, in the *Ante-Nicene Christian Library*, vol. 2 (Edinburgh: T. & T. Clark, 1867)

—, *The Apology*, in *The Ante-Nicene Fathers: Translations of the Writings of the Fathers down to AD 325. Volume 1, The Apostolic Fathers, with Justin Martyr and Irenaeus*, ed. A. Roberts and J. Donaldson, revised A. Cleveland Coxe (Grand Rapids, MI: Wm. B. Erdmanns Pub. Co., 1979)

Justinian, *Annotated Justinian Code*, tr. F. H. Blume, ed. T. Kearley, second edition (George W. Hopper Library of the University of Wyoming, online at uwyo.edu / lawlib / blume-justinian)

—, *The Codex of Justinian: A new annotated translation, with parallel Latin and Greek text based on a translation by Justice Fred H. Blume*, ed. B. W. Frier et al. (Cambridge; New York: Cambridge University Press, 2016)

—, *The Digest of Justinian*, tr. and ed. A. Watson (Philadelphia, PA: University of Pennsylvania Press, 1995)

Juvenal, *The Sixteen Satires*, tr. P. Green (London: Penguin, 1967)

—, *Sixteen Satires*, in *Juvenal and Persius*, tr. S. Morton Braund, Loeb Classical Library 91 (Cambridge, MA: Harvard University Press, 2004)

Lactantius, *Divine Institutes* in *The Fathers of the Third and Fourth Centuries: Lactantius,* Venantius . . . , tr. W. Fletcher, in the *Ante-Nicene Christian Library*, vol. 7 (Edinburgh: T. & T. Clark, 1885)

—, *On the Anger of God*, in *The Works of Lactantius, Vol. 2*, tr. W. Fletcher and R. Skinner, in the *Ante-Nicene Christian Library*, vol. 22 (Edinburgh: T. & T. Clark, 1871)

—, *On the Deaths of the Persecutors*, ed. and tr. J. L. Creed (Oxford: Clarendon, 1984)

Pope Leo XIII, Encyclical, *On the Nature of Human Liberty* (1888, now available online, published by Libreria Editrice Vaticana)

Libanius, *Oration 18*, in *Selected Orations, Volume I: Julianic Orations*, tr. A. F. Norman (Cambridge, MA: Harvard University Press, 1969)

—, *Oration 30*, in *Selected Orations, Volume II*, tr. A. F. Norman, Loeb Classical Library 452 (Cambridge, MA: Harvard University Press, 1977)

Livy, *The Early History of Rome*, tr. A. de Sélincourt (London: Penguin, 2002)

Locke, John, 'A Letter Concerning Toleration', in *John Locke: Political Writings*, ed. D. Wootton (Indianapolis, IN: Hackett Publishing, 2003)

Lucian, *Alexander the False Prophet*, in Lucian, *Anacharsis or Athletics etc.*, tr. A. M. Harmon, Loeb Classical Library 162 (Cambridge, MA: Harvard University Press, 1925)

—, *Demonax*, in *Lucian*, vol. I, tr. A. M. Harmon, Loeb Classical Library 14 (Cambridge, MA: Harvard University Press, 1913)

—, *The Descent into Hades*, in Lucian, *Anacharsis or Athletics etc.*, tr. A. M. Harmon, Loeb Classical Library 162 (Cambridge, MA: Harvard University Press, 1925)

—, *The Lover of Lies*, in *Lucian*, vol. III, tr. A. M. Harmon, Loeb Classical Library 130 (Cambridge, MA: Harvard University Press, 1921)

—, *The Passing of Peregrinus*, in *Lucian*, vol. V, tr. A. M. Harmon, Loeb Classical Library 302 (Cambridge, MA: Harvard University Press, 1936)

—, *Menippus or The Descent into Hades in Anacharsis or Athletics* . . . , tr. A. M. Harmon. Loeb Classical Library 162 (Cambridge, MA: Harvard University Press, 1925)

—, *Philopseudes*, in *The Works of Lucian of Samosata*, tr. H. W. Fowler and F. G. Fowler (Oxford: Clarendon Press, 1905)

—, *True History*, tr. F. Hickes, illustrated by W. Strang, J. B. Clark, A. Beardsley (London: A. H. Bullen, 1902)

Lucretius, *On the Nature of Things: A Metrical Translation*, tr. W. E. Leonard (London: Dent, 1916)

—, *On the Nature of Things*, tr. W. H. D. Rouse, revised M. F. Smith, Loeb Classical Library 181 (Cambridge, MA: Harvard University Press, 1924)

Malalas, *The Chronicle of John Malalas*, tr. E. Jeffreys, M. Jeffreys and R. Scott (Melbourne: Australian Association for Byzantine Studies; Sydney, NSW: Department of Modern Greek, University of Sydney, 1986)

Polo, Marco, *The Travels*, tr. N. Cliff (London: Penguin, 2015)

Marinus, *Life of Proclus*, in *Life, Hymns & Works*, tr. K. S. Guthrie (North Yonkers, NY: Platonist Press, 1925)

Mark the Deacon, *The Life of Porphyry, Bishop of Gaza*, tr. G. F. Hill (Oxford: Clarendon Press, 1913)

Martial, *Epigrams, Volume II: Books 6–10*, tr. D. R. Shackleton Bailey, Loeb Classical Library 95 (Cambridge, MA: Harvard University Press, 1993)

Mead, G. R. S. (tr.), *Pistis Sophia: A Gnostic Gospel* (Cambridge: Cambridge University Press, 2012)

Meyer, M., *The Nag Hammadi Scriptures: The Revised and Updated Translation of Sacred Gnostic Texts Complete in One Volume* (New York: HarperOne, 2009)

Milton, John, *The Poetical Works of John Milton, Vol. I: Paradise Lost* (Oxford: Oxford University Press, 2013)

Minucius Felix, *The 'Octavius'*, tr. J. H. Freese (London: SPCK; New York: Macmillan, 1919)

Moschos, John, *The Spiritual Meadow*, tr. J. Wortley (Kalamazoo, MI: Cistercian Publications, 1992)

Musurillo, H. (tr.), *The Acts of the Christian Martyrs* (Oxford: Clarendon Press, 1972)

Nixon, C. E. V. & Saylor Rodgers, B. (trs.), *In Praise of Later Roman Emperors: The Panegyrici Latini*; Transformation of the Classical Heritage XXI (Berkeley: University of California Press, 1994)

Optatus, *Against the Donatists*, in *The Work of St. Optatus, Bishop of Milevis, Against the Donatists*, tr. O. R. Vassall-Phillips (London: Longmans, Green, and Co., 1917)

—, *The Work of St. Optatus, Bishop of Milevis, against the Donatists*, tr. O. R. Vassall-Phillips (London: Longmans, Green and Co., 1917)

Origen, *Contra Celsum*, tr. F. Crombie, from *Ante-Nicene Fathers*, vol. 4, ed. A. Roberts, J. Donaldson and A. Cleveland Coxe (Buffalo, NY: Christian Literature Publishing Co., 1885)

—, *Contra Celsum*, tr. H. Chadwick (Cambridge: Cambridge University Press, 1953)

—, *Commentary on the Gospel of Matthew*, tr. Patrick, in *The Gospel of Peter, the Diatessaron of Tatian, the Apocalypse of Peter, the Vision of Paul* etc., *Ante-Nicene Fathers*, vol. 9, eds. A. Roberts and J. Donaldson, rev. A. Cleveland Coxe (New York: Christian Literature Publishing Co., 1896–7)

Orosius, Paulus, *Seven Books of History against the Pagans*, tr. A. T. Fear (Liverpool: Liverpool University Press, 2010)

Ovid, *The Art of Love*, tr. R. Humphries (Bloomington, IN: Indiana University Press, 1957)

—, *The Art of Love*, in *The Erotic Poems*, tr. P. Green (Harmondsworth: Penguin, 1982)

—, *Fasti*, tr. J. G. Frazer, rev. G. P. Goold, Loeb Classical Library 253 (Cambridge, MA: Harvard University Press, 1931)

—, *Heroides*, tr. H. Isbell (London; New York: Penguin; Viking Penguin, 1990)

—, *Metamorphoses*, tr. F. J. Miller, rev. G. P. Goold, Loeb Classical Library 42 (Cambridge, MA: Harvard University Press, 1916)

—, *Metamorphoses*, tr. A. S. Kline, 2000, viewed September 2021 (https://www.poetryintranslation.com/PITBR/Latin/Metamorph.php)

—, *Tristia; Ex Ponto*, tr. A. L. Wheeler, 2nd edition, rev. G. P. Goold, Loeb Classical Library 151 (Cambridge, MA: Harvard University Press, 1996)

Pachomius, *The Life of Saint Pachomius*, tr. Schodde (London; New York: T&T Clark, 1885)

—, *The Life of Saint Pachomius*, tr. Apostolos N. Athanassakis; introduction by Birger A. Pearson (Missoula, MT: Scholars for the Society of Biblical Literature, 1975)

—, *The Life of Saint Pachomius and His Disciples, Pachomian Koinonia*, tr. A. Veilleux, vol. 1 (Kalamazoo, Mich.: Cistercian Publications, 1980)

Palladas, *The Greek Anthology, Volume III: Book 9*, tr. W. R. Paton, Loeb Classical Library 84 (Cambridge, MA: Harvard University Press, 1917)

Petronius, *The Satyricon*, in *Petronius, Seneca: Satyricon, Apocolocyntosis*, tr. M. Heseltine, W. H. D. Rouse, rev. E. H. Warmington, Loeb Classical Library 15 (Cambridge, MA: Harvard University Press, 1913)

Philo, *On the Embassy to Gaius, General Indexes*, tr. F. H. Colson; index by J. W. Earp, Loeb Classical Library 379 (Cambridge, MA: Harvard University Press, 1962)

—, *On Rewards and Punishments*, in *On the Special Laws, Book 4. On the Virtues. On Rewards and Punishments*, tr. F. H. Colson, Loeb Classical Library 341 (Cambridge, MA: Harvard University Press, 1939)

Philostratus, *Apollonius of Tyana, Letters of Apollonius, Ancient Testimonia, Eusebius's Reply to Hierocles*, ed. and tr. C. Jones, Loeb Classical Library 458 (Cambridge, MA: Harvard University Press, 2006)

—, *Life of Apollonius*, tr. C. P. Jones, abridged and introduced by G. Bowersock (London: Penguin, 1970)

—, *The Life of Apollonius of Tyana: The Epistles of Apollonius and the Treatise of Eusebius*, vols. 1 and 2, tr. F. C. Conybeare, Loeb Classical Library (London: Heinemann, 1912)

Pindar, *Nemean Odes, Isthmian Odes, Fragments*, ed. and tr. W. H. Race, Loeb Classical Library 485 (Cambridge, MA: Harvard University Press, 1997)

Plato, *Phaedo*, in *Euthyphro; Apology; Crito; Phaedo; Phaedrus*, tr. H. N. Fowler, Loeb Classical Library 36 (Cambridge, MA; London: Harvard University Press; Heinemann, 1914)

—, *Phaedo*, tr. D. Gallop, Clarendon Plato Series (Oxford, 1975)

—, *Protagoras*, ed. N. Denyer (Cambridge: Cambridge University Press, 2008)

—, *Timaeus*, in *Timaeus; Critias; Cleitophon; Menexenus; Epistles*, tr. R. G. Bury, Loeb Classical Library 234 (Cambridge, MA: Harvard University Press, 1929)

Pliny the Elder, *Natural History, Volume I–X*, tr. H. Rackham, W. H. S. Jones, D. E. Eichholz, Loeb Classical Library 330 (Cambridge, MA: Harvard University Press, 1938–63)

—, *The Natural History of Pliny, Translated with Copious Notes and Illustrations* (6 vols.), tr. J. Bostock and H. T. Riley (London: n.p., 1855)

Pliny the Younger, *The Letters of the Younger Pliny*, tr. J. B. Firth (London: Walter Scott, 1910)

—, *The Letters of the Younger Pliny*, tr. B. Radice (Harmondsworth: Penguin, 1963)

Plutarch, *De Sollertia Animalium*, in *Moralia, Volume XII: Concerning the Face Which Appears in the Orb of the Moon etc.*, tr. H. Cherniss and W. C. Helmbold, Loeb Classical Library 406 (Cambridge, MA: Harvard University Press, 1957)

—, *Life of Alexander*, in *Plutarch's Lives*, B. Cohoon and J. W. Perrin, Loeb Classical Library 46 (London: Heinemann, 1914)

—, *On the Delay of the Divine Justice*, tr. Peabody (Boston: Little, Brown, and Company, 1885)

—, *On the Delays of the Divine Vengeance*, in *Plutarch, Moralia, Volume VII: On Love of Wealth, On Compliancy &* c, tr. P. H. De Lacy and B. Einarson, Loeb Classical Library 405 (Cambridge, MA: Harvard University Press, 1959)

—, *On Superstition*, in *Moralia*, vol. 2, tr. F. C. Babbitt, Loeb Classical Library 222 (Cambridge, MA: Harvard University Press, 1928)

—, *Whether Land or Sea Animals Are Cleverer*, in *Moralia*, Volume XII, tr. H. Cherniss, W. C. Helmbold. Loeb Classical Library 406 (Cambridge, MA: Harvard University Press, 1957)

Polo, Marco, *The Travels of Marco Polo*, ed. and tr. R. E. Latham (London: Penguin Classics, 1982)

Polyhistor, Alexander, in *Cory's Ancient Fragments of the Phoenician, Carthaginian, Babylonian, Egyptian and Other Authors*, rev. E. R. Hodges (London: Reeves & Turner, 1876)

Porphyry, *Against the Christians*, ed. and tr. R. M. Berchman (Leiden: Brill, 2005)

—, *A Chronological Account of the Life of Pythagoras, and of Other Famous Men His Contemporaries* (London: printed by J. H. for H. Mortlock and J. Hartley, 1699)

Procopius, *History of the Wars*, tr. H. B. Dewing (London; New York: Heinemann; Macmillan, 1914)

—, *The Secret History*, tr. G. A. Williamson (London: Penguin, 2004)

Propertius, *Elegies*, ed. and tr. G. P. Goold, Loeb Classical Library 18 (Cambridge, MA: Harvard University Press, 1990)

Prudentius, *Crowns of Martyrdom*, in *Prudentius*, vol. II, tr. H. J. Thomson, Loeb Classical Library 398 (Cambridge, MA: Harvard University Press, 1953)

—, *Preface. Daily Round. Divinity of Christ. Origin of Sin. Fight for Mansoul. Against Symmachus 1*, tr. H. J. Thomson, Loeb Classical Library 387 (Cambridge, MA: Harvard University Press, 1949)

Quintilian, *The Orator's Education, Volume V: Books 11–12*, ed. and tr. D. A. Russell, Loeb Classical Library 494 (Cambridge, MA: Harvard University Press, 2002)

Quodvultdeus, *Livre des Promesses et des Prédictions de Dieu*, tr. R. Braun (Paris: Cerf, 1964)

Rabbula, *The Rabbula Corpus: Comprising the Life of Rabbula, His Correspondence, a Homily Delivered in Constantinople, Canons, and Hymns*, tr. R. Phenix and C. Horn, Writings from the Greco-Roman World 17 (Atlanta, GA: Society of Biblical Literature, 2017)

Reymond, E. A. E. and Barns, J. W. B. (eds.), 'The Martyrdom of S. Coluthus', in *Four Martyrdoms from the Pierpont Morgan Coptic Codices* (Oxford: Clarendon, 1973)

Rouge, J. (tr.), *Expositio totius mundi et gentium* (Paris: Éditions du Cerf, 1966)

Rufinus of Aquileia, *The Church History of Rufinus of Aquileia: books 10 and 11*, tr. P. R. Amidon (New York; Oxford: Oxford University Press, 1997)

Schneemelcher, W. (ed.), *New Testament Apocrypha, vol. 1, Gospels and related writings* (Cambridge: James Clarke, 1991)

—, *New Testament Apocrypha, vol. 2, Writings related to the apostles, apocalypses and related subjects*, tr. R. McL. Wilson (London: Lutterworth, 1965)

Schaff, P. (ed.), *The Confessions and Letters of St. Augustin, with a Sketch of His Life and Work, A Select Library of the Nicene and Post-Nicene Fathers of the Christian Church*, vol. 1 (Edinburgh: Grand Rapids, Mich.: T. & T. Clark; W. B. Eerdmans, 1988)

Schoff, W. H. (tr.), *The Periplus of the Erythraean Sea: Travel and Trade in the Indian Ocean by a Merchant of the First Century* (New York; London: Longmans, Green, 1912)

Seneca, *Apocolocyntosis*, in Petronius, *Seneca. Satyricon. Apocolocyntosis*, tr. M. Heseltine, W. H. D. Rouse, rev. E. H. Warmington, Loeb Classical Library 15 (Cambridge, MA: Harvard University Press, 1913)

—, *Epistles, Volume I: Epistles 1–65*, tr. R. M. Gummere, Loeb Classical Library 75 (Cambridge, MA: Harvard University Press, 1917)

Shenoute, *Let Our Eyes*, tr. Emmel, in 'The Study of Religion in Late Roman Egypt', in *From Temple to Church: Destruction and Renewal of Local Cultic Topography in Late Antiquity*, eds. J. Hahn, S. Emmel, U. Gotter (Leiden; Boston, MA: Brill, 2008)

—, *Open Letter to a Pagan Notable*, in 'Shenute as a Historical Source', tr. J. Barnes, in J. Wolski (ed.), *Actes du Xe Congrès International de Papyrologues* (Varsovie / Cracovie, 1961), pp. 156–8, with suggested alterations by Gaddis (2005), pp. 151–2

—, *Selected Discourses of Shenoute the Great: Community, Theology, and Social Conflict in Late Antique Egypt*, ed. and tr. D. Brakke, A. Crislip (Cambridge: Cambridge University Press, 2015)

Socrates Scholasticus, *The Ecclesiastical History of Socrates Scholasticus: Comprising a history of the church from A.D. 323 to A.D. 425*, tr. A. C. Zenos (Oxford: Parker, 1891)

Solomon, *Odes of Solomon*, tr. J. R. Harris (Cambridge: Cambridge University Press, 1909)

Soranus, *Gynaecology*, tr. O. Temkin (Baltimore, MA: Johns Hopkins University Press, 1991)

Sozomen, *The Ecclesiastical History*, tr. C. D. Hartranft, in *A Select Library of the Nicene and Post-Nicene Fathers of the Christian Church*, ed. P. Schaff and H. Wace, vol. 2 (Oxford: Parker, 1890)

Statius, *Thebaid, Volume I: Thebaid: Books 1–7*, ed. and tr. D. R. Shackleton Bailey, Loeb Classical Library 207 (Cambridge, MA: Harvard University Press, 2004)

Strabo, *Geography*, volume I, books 1–2, tr. H. L. Jones, Loeb Classical Library 49 (Cambridge, MA: Harvard University Press, 1917)

—, *Geography*, tr. D. W. Roller (Cambridge: Cambridge University Press, 2014)

Suetonius, *Lives of the Caesars*, vol. II, tr. J. C. Rolfe, Loeb Classical Library 38 (Cambridge, MA: Harvard University Press, 1914)

—, *The Lives of the Twelve Caesars*, tr. A. Thomson, T. Forester (London: H. G. Bohn, 1855)

—, *The Twelve Caesars*, tr. R. Graves, rev. J. B. Rives (London: Penguin Classics, 2007)

Sulpicius Severus, *Life of St. Martin of Tours*, in *Early Christian Lives*, tr. C. White (London; New York: Penguin, 1998)

Symmachus, *Memorandum 3*, in *Pagans and Christians in Late Antiquity: A Sourcebook*, ed. A. D. Lee (London: Routledge, 2000)

Tacitus, *Annals*, tr. C. Damon (London: Penguin, 2012)

—, *The Annals of Imperial Rome*, tr. M. Grant (London: Penguin, 2003)

—, *The Histories*, tr. C. H. Moore, Loeb Classical Library 111 (Cambridge, MA: Harvard University Press, 1925)

—, *The Histories*, tr. C. H. Moore, J. Jackson, Loeb Classical Library 249 (London; Cambridge, MA: W. Heinemann; Harvard University Press, 1962)

Tertullian, *The Address of Q. Sept. Tertullian to Scapula Tertullus, Proconsul of Africa*, tr. D. Dalrymple (Edinburgh: Murray & Cochrane, 1790)

—, *Apology* in *Tertullian, Minucius Felix. Apology. De Spectaculis. Minucius Felix: Octavius*, tr. T. R. Glover, G. H. Rendall, Loeb Classical Library 250 (Cambridge, MA: Harvard University Press, 1931)

—, *The Apology, The Crown* and *Spectacles*, in *Christian and Pagan in the Roman Empire: The Witness of Tertullian*, ed. R. Sider (Washington, DC: The Catholic University of America Press, 2001)

—, *De Spectaculis*, in *The Writings of Q. S. F. Tertullianus*, tr. S. Thelwall (Edinburgh: T. & T. Clark, 1869)

—, *On the Prescription against Heretics*, in *The Writings of Q. S. F. Tertullianus*, tr. P. Holmes (Edinburgh: T. & T. Clark, 1870)

Themistius, *Speech 5*, in *Pagans and Christians in Late Antiquity: A Sourcebook*, ed. A. D. Lee (London: Routledge, 2000)

Theocritus, *Hymn to the Dioscuri*, in *Greek Bucolic Poets*, ed. and tr. J. M. Edmonds, Loeb Classical Library 28 (Cambridge, MA: Harvard University Press, 1912)

Theodoret, *Ecclesiastical History*, in *Theodoret, Jerome, Gennadius and Rufinus: Historical Writings*, in *Nicene and Post-Nicene Fathers*, second series, vol. 3, ed. P. Schaff and H. Wace (Oxford: Parker, 1892)

—, *A History of the Monks of Syria*, tr. R. M. Price (Kalamazoo, MI: Cistercian Publications, 1985)

Theodosius, *The Theodosian Code and Novels: And the Sirmondian Constitutions*, tr. C. Pharr, in collaboration with T. S. Davidson and M. B. Pharr (Princeton, NJ: Princeton University Press, 1952)

Thomas, Bishop of Marga, *The Book of Governors: The Historia Monastica of Thomas, Bishop of Margâ, A.D. 840*, tr. E. A. Wallis Budge (London: Kegan Paul, Trench, Trübner & Co., 1893)

Thucydides, *The History of the Peloponnesian War*, tr. R. Crawley (repr.) (London: J. M. Dent, 1936)

—, *The History of the Peloponnesian War*, tr. C. F. Smith, Loeb Classical Library 108 (Cambridge, MA; London: Harvard University Press, 2003)

Tibullus, *Elegies*, in *Catullus. Tibullus. Pervigilium Veneris*, tr. F. W. Cornish, J. P. Postgate, J. W. Mackail, rev. G. P. Goold, Loeb Classical Library 6 (Cambridge, MA: Harvard University Press, 1913)

Tilley, M. A. (tr.), *Donatist Martyr Stories: The Church in Conflict in Roman North Africa* (Liverpool: Liverpool University Press, 1996)

Virgil, *The Aeneid*, in *Eclogues, Georgics, Aeneid: Books 1–6*, tr. H. Rushton Fairclough, rev. G. P. Goold, Loeb Classical Library 63 (Cambridge, MA: Harvard University Press, 1916)

Vitruvius, *The Architecture of Marcus Vitruvius Pollio*, tr. J. Gwilt (London: Lockwood, 1874)

Vööbus, A. (tr.), *Didascalia Apostolorum*, Corpus Scriptorum Christianorum Orientalium. Scriptores Syri 175, 176 (Louvain: Secrétariat Du Corpus SCO, 1979)

Voragine, Jacobus de, *The Golden Legend: Readings on the Saints*, tr. W. Granger Ryan, intr. E. Duffy (Princeton, NJ; Oxford: Princeton University Press, 2012)

Ward, B. (tr.), *Apophthegmata Patrum, The Sayings of the Desert Fathers: the Alphabetical Collection* (Collegeville, MN: Cistercian Publications, 1975)

Zachariah of Mytilene, *The Life of Severus*, tr. L. Ambjörn (Piscataway, NJ: Gorgias Press, 2008)

Zosimus, *The History of Count Zosimus, sometime advocate and chancellor of the Roman Empire* (London: J. Davis, 1814)

SECONDARY SOURCES

Aasgaard, R., *The Childhood of Jesus: Decoding the Apocryphal Infancy Gospel of Thomas* (Cambridge: James Clarke & Co., 2010)

Abraham, A., 'The Geography of Culture in Philostratus' *Life of Apollonius of Tyana*', in *Classical Journal*, vol. 109, no. 4 (2014), pp. 465–80

Alter, R., 'The Glories and the Glitches of the King James Bible', in H. Hannibal and N. W. Jones, *The King James Bible after Four Hundred Years Literary, Linguistic, and Cultural Influences* (Cambridge: Cambridge University Press, 2013)

Anderson, G., 'Folklore Versus Fakelore: Some Problems in the Life of Apollonius', in *Theios Sophistes: Essays on Flavius Philostratus'* Life of Apollonius, ed. K. Demoen and D. Praet (Leiden: Brill, 2009), pp. 211–24

Arnold, B., 'The Literary Experience of Vergil's Fourth "Eclogue"', in *Classical Journal*, vol. 90, no. 2 (1994), pp. 143–60

Ashwin-Siejkowski, P., 'Chapter Five: The Docetic View Of Christ', in *Clement of Alexandria on Trial* (Leiden: Brill, 2010)

Atiya, A. S., *A History of Eastern Christianity* (London: Methuen, 1968)

Attwater, D., *The Penguin Dictionary of Saints* (Harmondsworth: Penguin, 1965)

Bagnall, R. and Frier, B., *The demography of Roman Egypt*, Cambridge Studies in Population, Economy and Society in Past Time, 23 (Cambridge: Cambridge University Press, 1994)

Barclay, J. M. G., 'Mirror-Reading a Polemical Letter: Galatians as a Test Case', in *Journal for the Study of the New Testament*, vol. 10(31) (1987), pp. 73–93

Barnard, L. W., 'The Background of St. Ignatius of Antioch', in *Vigiliae Christianae*, vol. 17, no. 4 (1963), pp. 193–206

—, 'Athanasius and the Meletian Schism in Egypt', in *Journal of Egyptian Archaeology*, vol. 59 (1973), pp. 181–9

Barnes, T. D., 'Sossianus Hierocles and the Antecedents of the "Great Persecution"', in *Harvard Studies in Classical Philology*, vol. 80 (1976), pp. 239–52

—, *Constantine and Eusebius* (Cambridge, MA; London: Harvard University Press, 1993)

—, 'Scholarship or Propaganda? Porphyry Against the Christians and its Historical Setting', in *Bulletin of the Institute of Classical Studies*, vol. 39, issue 1 (December 1994), pp. 53–65

—, *Constantine: Dynasty, Religion and Power in the Later Roman Empire*, Blackwell Ancient Lives (Chichester: Wiley Blackwell, 2014)

Barrett, A. A., 'Claudius' British Victory Arch in Rome', in *Britannia*, vol. 22, Society for the Promotion of Roman Studies, Cambridge University Press (1991), pp. 1–19

Barton, J., *The Old Testament: Canon, Literature and Theology*, Society for Old Testament Study Monograph (Aldershot: Ashgate, 2007)

Bauer, W., *Orthodoxy and Heresy in Earliest Christianity*, New Testament Library (London: SCM, 1972)

Bawer, B., 'What Is Truth?' in *Hudson Review*, vol. 53, no. 4 (2001), pp. 685–92

Beard, M., *Emperor of Rome* (London: Profile, 2023)

Beard, M., 'The Sexual Status of Vestal Virgins', in *Journal of Roman Studies*, vol. 70 (1980), pp. 12–27

—, 'Frazer, Leach, and Virgil: The Popularity (and Unpopularity) of the Golden Bough', in *Comparative Studies in Society and History*, vol. 34, no. 2 (1992), pp. 203–24

Beard, M., North, J., Price, S. R. F., *Religions of Rome: Volume 1, A History* (Cambridge: Cambridge University Press, 2000)

—, *Religions of Rome: Volume 2, A History* (Cambridge: Cambridge University Press, 2000)

Beck, R., 'The Mysteries of Mithras: A New Account of Their Genesis', in *Journal of Roman Studies*, vol. 88 (1998), pp. 115–28

—, 'Ritual, Myth, Doctrine, and Initiation in the Mysteries of Mithras: New Evidence from a Cult Vessel', in *Journal of Roman Studies*, vol. 90 (2000), pp. 145–80

Beck, R. and Rice, B., 'If So, How?: Representing "Coming Back to Life" in the Mysteries of Mithras', in *Coming Back to Life: The Permeability of Past and*

Present, Mortality and Immortality, Death and Life in the Ancient Mediterranean, ed. F. S. Tappenden and C. Daniel-Hughes, 2nd ed. (Montreal: McGill University Library, 2017), pp. 129–52

Beckley, Frederic A., 'Why Pears? The Role of Little Sins in Augustine's Confessions', in *Augustiniana*, vol. 43, no. 1/2 (1993), pp. 53–75

Belayche, N., '*Deus deum . . . summorum maximus* (Apuleius): Ritual expressions of distinction in the divine world in the imperial period', in S. Mitchell and P. Van Nuffelen (eds.), *One God: Pagan Monotheism in the Roman Empire* (Cambridge: Cambridge University Press, 2010), pp. 141–66

Benefiel, R. R. and Sypniewski, H. M., 'The Greek Graffiti of Herculaneum', *American Journal of Archaeology*, vol. 122, no. 2 (2018), pp. 209–44

Benko, S., 'The Libertine Gnostic Sect of the Phibionites, According To Epiphanius', in *Vigiliae Christianae*, vol. 21.1 (1967), pp. 103–19

—, *Pagan Rome and the Early Christians* (London: B. T. Batsford, 1984)

Bennett, A., *The History Boys* (London: Faber & Faber, 2008)

Betts, E., *Senses of the Empire: Multisensory Approaches to Roman Culture* (London; New York: Routledge, 2017)

Blackburn, B., *Theios Anēr and the Markan Miracle Traditions: A Critique of the Theios Anēr Concept as an Interpretative Background of the Miracle Traditions Used by Mark* (Tübingen: J. C. B. Mohr (Paul Siebeck), 1991)

Bliquez, L. J., 'The Tools of Asclepius: Surgical Instruments in Greek and Roman Times', in *Studies in Ancient Medicine* 43 (Leiden: Brill, 2015)

Bonner, C., 'A Papyrus Describing Magical Powers', in *Transactions and Proceedings of the American Philological Association*, vol. 52 (1921), pp. 111–18

—, 'A Dionysiac Miracle at Corinth', in *American Journal of Archaeology*, vol. 33, no. 3 (1929), pp. 368–75

Bourne, E., 'The Messianic Prophecy in Vergil's Fourth Eclogue', in *Classical Journal*, vol. 11, no. 7 (1916), pp. 390–400

Bowersock, G. W., *Augustus and the Greek World* (Oxford: Clarendon, 1965)

—, *Fiction as History: Nero to Julian*, Sather Classical Lectures, vol. 58 (Berkeley; London: University of California, 1994)

—, 'Polytheism and Monotheism in Arabia and the Three Palestines', in *Dumbarton Oaks Papers* 51 (1997), pp. 1–10

Bradshaw, H., 'Rome: A Note on Housing Conditions, Etc.', in *Town Planning Review*, vol. 10, no. 1 (1923), pp. 53–5

Brakke, D., 'Canon Formation and Social Conflict in Fourth-Century Egypt: Athanasius of Alexandria's Thirty-Ninth "Festal Letter" ', in *Harvard Theological Review*, vol. 87, no. 4 (1994), pp. 395–419

—, *Demons and the Making of the Monk: Spiritual Combat in Early Christianity* (Cambridge, MA: Harvard University Press, 2006)

—, *The Gnostics: Myth, Ritual, and Diversity in Early Christianity* (Cambridge, MA: Harvard University Press, 2010)

Bremmer, J., 'Why did Early Christianity Attract Upper-Class Women?', in *Fructus Centesimus: Mélanges Offerts À Gerard J. M. Bartelink À L'occasion De Son Soixante-cinquième Anniversaire* (Dordrecht: In Abbatia Sancti Petri Steenbrugis; Kluwer Academic, 1989)

—, 'Magic in the Apocryphal Acts of the Apostles', in *The Metamorphosis of Magic from Late Antiquity to Early Modern Period*, ed. J. N. Bremmer and J. R. Veenstra (Leuven: Peeters, 2002), pp. 51–70

—, 'Christian Hell: From the Apocalypse of Peter to the Apocalypse of Paul', in *Numen*, vol. 56, no. 2/3 (2009), pp. 298–325

—, *Initiation into the Mysteries of the Ancient World* (Berlin: De Gruyter, 2014)

Brown, P., 'St. Augustine's Attitude to Religious Coercion', in *Journal of Roman Studies*, vol. 54 (1964), pp. 107–16

—, 'The Diffusion of Manichaeism in the Roman Empire', in *Journal of Roman Studies*, vol. 59, no. 1/2 (1969), pp. 92–103

—, 'The Rise and Function of the Holy Man in Late Antiquity', in *Journal of Roman Studies*, vol. 61, Society for the Promotion of Roman Studies (Cambridge University Press, 1971), pp. 80–101

—, *The Body and Society: Men, Women and Sexual Renunciation in Early Christianity* (New York: Columbia University Press, 1988)

—, *Power and Persuasion in Late Antiquity: Towards a Christian Empire* (Madison, WI: University of Wisconsin Press, 1992)

—, *The Rise of Western Christendom: Triumph and Diversity* AD *200–1000* (Oxford: Basil Blackwell, 1996)

—, 'Christianization and Religious Conflict', in *The Cambridge Ancient History*, vol. 13, ed. A. Cameron and P. Garnsey (Cambridge: Cambridge University Press, 1997), pp. 632–64

—, *Augustine of Hippo: A Biography*, forty-fifth anniversary edition (Berkeley, CA: University of California Press, 2000)

—, *Through the eye of a needle: Wealth, the fall of Rome, and the making of Christianity in the West, 350–550* AD (Princeton, NJ: Princeton University Press, 2014)

—, 'Don't Blame Him', in *TLS*, vol. 37, no. 8 (23 April 2015)

Budge, E. A. Wallis, *The Rise and Progress of Assyriology* (London: Martin Hopkinson, 1925)

—, *Egyptian Magic* (London; New York: Routledge, 2009)

Bultmann, R. and Marsh, J., *The History of the Synoptic Tradition* (Oxford: Blackwell, 1963)

Bundy, D., *Early Asian and East African Christianities*, in A. Casiday and F. Norris (eds.), *The Cambridge History of Christianity* (Cambridge: Cambridge University Press, 2007), pp. 118–48

Burkitt, F. Crawford, *Early Christianity outside the Roman Empire*, Two Lectures Delivered at Trinity College, Dublin (Cambridge: Cambridge University Press, 1899)

—, 'The Decretum Gelasianum', in *Journal of Theological Studies*, vol. 14 (1913), pp. 469–71

Burriss, E. E., 'The Religious Element in the Satires of Juvenal', in *Classical Weekly*, vol. 20, no. 3 (1926), pp. 19–21

Burrus, V., 'The Heretical Woman as Symbol in Alexander, Athanasius, Epiphanius, and Jerome', in *Harvard Theological Review*, vol. 84(3) (1991), pp. 229–48

—, *The Making of a Heretic: Gender, Authority, and the Priscillianist Controversy*, Transformation of the Classical Heritage, 24 (Berkeley, CA: University of California Press, 1995)

Cameron, A., 'Palladas and Christian Polemic', in *Journal of Roman Studies*, vol. 55, no. 1/2 (1965), pp. 17–30

—, *Christianity and the Rhetoric of Empire: The Development of Christian Discourse* (Berkeley, CA; Oxford: University of California Press, 1994)

—, 'Sacred and Profane Love: Thoughts on Byzantine Gender', in James, L. (ed.), *Women, Men, and Eunuchs: Gender in Byzantium* (London; New York: Routledge, 1997)

—, 'Constantine and the "Peace of the Church"', in *The Cambridge History of Christianity*, vol. 1, ed. M. Mitchell and F. Young (Cambridge: Cambridge University Press, 2006), pp. 538–51

—, *The Last Pagans of Rome* (New York: Oxford University Press, 2011)

Carr, E. H., *What is History?* (London: Penguin Modern Classics, 2018)

Carlyle, T., *The French Revolution: A History*, vol. 2 (Charles C. Little and James Brown, 1838)

Cartlidge, D. J. and Elliott, J. K., *Art and the Christian Apocrypha* (London: Routledge, 2001)

Casson, L., 'Speed under Sail of Ancient Ships', in *Transactions and Proceedings of the American Philological Association*, vol. 82 (1951), pp. 136–48

—, 'Trade in the Ancient World', in *Scientific American*, vol. 191, no. 5, a division of Nature America, Inc. (1954), pp. 98–105

—, *Ships and Seamanship in the Ancient World* (Princeton, NJ: Princeton University Press, 1972)

—, 'Rome's Trade with the East: The Sea Voyage to Africa and India', in *Transactions of the American Philological Association*, vol. 110 (1980), pp. 21–36

Chaniotis, A., 'Megatheism: The search for the almighty god and the competition of cults', in S. Mitchell and P. Van Nuffelen (eds.), *One God: Pagan Monotheism in the Roman Empire* (Cambridge: Cambridge University Press, 2010), pp. 112–40

Chartrand-Burke, T., 'Completing the Gospel: The Infancy Gospel of Thomas as a Supplement to the Gospel of Luke', in DiTommaso, L., Kannengiesser, C., and Turcescu, L., *The Reception and Interpretation of the Bible in Late Antiquity: Proceedings of the Montréal Colloquium in Honour of Charles Kannengiesser* (Leiden: Brill, 2008)

Chesterton, G. K., *The Everlasting Man* (Peabody, MA: Hendrickson, 2007)

Cioffi, R. and Trnka-Amrhein, Y., 'What's in a Name? Further Similarities between Lollianos' *Phoinikika* and Apuleius' *Metamorphoses*', in *Zeitschrift Für Papyrologie Und Epigraphik*, vol. 173 (2010), pp. 66–8

Clark, E. A., 'Women, Gender, and the Study of Christian History', in *Church History*, vol. 70, no. 3 (2001), pp. 395–426

Clauss, M., *The Roman Cult of Mithras: The God and His Mysteries* (Edinburgh: Edinburgh University Press, 2000)

Cloke, G., *'This female man of God': Women and spiritual power in the Patristic Age, 350–450* (London: Routledge, 1995)

Collins, D., 'Mapping the Entrails: The Practice of Greek Hepatoscopy', in *American Journal of Philology*, vol. 129, no. 3 (2008), pp. 319–45

Conybeare, F. C., 'Christian Demonology III', in *Jewish Quarterly Review*, vol. 9, no. 3 (1897), pp. 444–70

Cooper, K., 'Insinuations of Womanly Influence: An Aspect of the Christianization of the Roman Aristocracy', in *Journal of Roman Studies*, vol. 82 (1992), pp. 150–64

—, *Band of Angels: The Forgotten World of Early Christian Women* (London: Atlantic Books, 2013)

Corley, K. E., *Women & the Historical Jesus: Feminist Myths of Christian Origins* (Santa Rosa, CA: Polebridge, 2002)

Crüsemann, M., 'Irredeemably Hostile to Women: Anti-Jewish Elements in the Exegesis of the Dispute About Women's Right To Speak (1 Cor. 14.34–35)', in *Journal for the Study of the New Testament*, vol. 23(79) (2002), pp. 19–36

Cueva, E. P., 'Plutarch's Ariadne in Chariton's *Chaereas* and *Callirhoe*', in *American Journal of Philology*, vol. 117, no. 3 (Fall 1996), pp. 473–84

Dąbrowa, E., 'The Date of the Census of Quirinius and the Chronology of the Governors of the Province of Syria', in *Zeitschrift Für Papyrologie Und Epigraphik*, vol. 178 (2011), pp. 137–42

Dalrymple, W., *From the Holy Mountain: A Journey in the Shadow of Byzantium* (London: HarperCollins, 1997)

Darwin, C. R., *Journal of researches into the natural history and geology of the countries visited during the voyage of H.M.S. Beagle round the world, under the Command of Capt. Fitz Roy, R.N*, second edition (London: John Murray, 1845)

De Souza, P., 'Rome's Contribution to the Development of Piracy', in *Memoirs of the American Academy in Rome. Supplementary Volumes*, vol. 6 (2008), pp. 71–96

De Ste. Croix, G. E. M., Whitby, M., Streeter, J., *Christian Persecution, Martyrdom, and Orthodoxy* (Oxford: Oxford University Press, 2006)

Declercq, G., *Anno Domini: The Origins of the Christian Era* (Turnhout: Brepols, 2000)

DeConick, A. D., *'Codex Judas Papers', Proceedings of the International Congress on the Tchacos Codex Held at Rice University, Houston, Texas, March 13–16, 2008*, Nag Hammadi and Manichaean Studies (Leiden: Brill, 2009)

Deissmann, A., *New Light on the New Testament, From Records of the Graeco-Roman Period*, tr. Lionel R. M. Strachan (Edinburgh: T. & T. Clark, 1908)

—, *St. Paul: A Study in Social and Religious History*, tr. Lionel R. M. Strachan (London: Hodder & Stoughton, 1912)

Denzey, N., and Blount, J. A., 'Rethinking the Origins of the Nag Hammadi Codices', in *Journal of Biblical Literature*, vol. 133, no. 2 (2014), pp. 399–419

Denzey Lewis, N., 'Death on the Nile: Egyptian Codices, Gnosticism, and Early Christian Books of the Dead', in DeConick, April D., Shaw, Gregory, Turner, John D. (eds.), *Practicing Gnosis* (Leiden: Brill, 2013)

DiTommaso, L., Kannengiesser, C., and Turcescu, L., *'The Reception and Interpretation of the Bible in Late Antiquity', Proceedings of the Montréal Colloquium in Honour of Charles Kannengiesser, 11–13 October 2006* (Leiden: Brill, 2008)

Doresse, J., 'A Gnostic Library from Upper Egypt', in *Archaeology*, vol. 3, no. 2 (1950), pp. 69–73

Dossey, L., 'Shedding Light on the Late Antique Night' in A. Chaniotis (ed.), *La Nuit: Imaginaire et Réalités Nocturnes dans le Monde Gréco-romain*, Entretiens Sur L'Antiquité Classique (series); Tome 64 (2018)

Drake, H. A., *Constantine and the Bishops: The Policy of Intolerance*, Ancient Society and History (Baltimore, MD; London: Johns Hopkins University Press, 2000)

—, 'The Church, Society and Political Power', in *The Cambridge History of Christianity*, vol. 2, ed. A. Casiday and F. W. Norris (Cambridge: Cambridge University Press, 2007), pp. 403–28

—, 'Intolerance, Religious Violence, and Political Legitimacy in Late Antiquity', in *Journal of the American Academy of Religion*, vol. 79, no. 1 (2011), pp. 193–235

—, *A Century of Miracles: Christians, Pagans, Jews, and the Supernatural, 312–410* (New York: Oxford University Press, 2017)

Dresken-Weiland, J., 'Visual Art and Iconography', in Dupont, A., Boodts, S., Partoens, G., and Leemans, J. (eds.), *Preaching in the Patristic Era: Sermons, Preachers, and Audiences in the Latin West* (Leiden: Brill, 2018)

Drower, E. S., 'Mandaean Polemic', in *Bulletin of the School of Oriental and African Studies, University of London*, vol. 25, no. 1/3 (1962), pp. 438–48

Dunn, G. D., 'Mary's Virginity "in partu" and Tertullian's Anti-Docetism in "De Carne Christi" Reconsidered', in *Journal of Theological Studies*, vol. 58, no. 2 (2007), pp. 467–84

Dzielska, M., 'Apollonius of Tyana in Legend and History', in *Problemi E Ricerche Di Storia Antica*, vol. 10 (Roma: Bretschneider, 1986)

Edwards, C., *The Politics of Immorality in Ancient Rome* (Cambridge: Cambridge University Press, 2002)

Ehrman, Bart D., *The Orthodox Corruption of Scripture: The Effect of Early Christological Controversies on the Text of the New Testament* (New York; Oxford: Oxford University Press, 1996)

—, *Lost Christianities: The battle for Scripture and the Faiths we never knew* (New York; Oxford: Oxford University Press, 2003)

—, *How Jesus Became God: The Exaltation of a Jewish Preacher from Galilee* (New York: HarperOne, 2014)

Ehrman, B. D., and Pleše, Z., *The Apocryphal Gospels: Texts and Translations* (New York: Oxford University Press, 2011)

Elliott, J., 'A synopsis of the apocryphal nativity and infancy narratives', in *New Testament tools and studies*, vol. 34 (Leiden: Brill, 2002)

Elzey, W., ' "What Would Jesus Do?" "In His Steps" and The Moral Codes of the Middle Class', in *Soundings: An Interdisciplinary Journal*, vol. 58, no. 4 (1975), pp. 463–89

Epp, E. J., *Junia: The First Woman Apostle*, foreword by Gaventa, B. (Minneapolis, MN: Fortress, 2005)

Eshleman, K., 'Becoming Heretical: Affection and Ideology in Recruitment to Early Christianities', in *Harvard Theological Review*, vol. 104, no. 2 (2011), pp. 191–216

Eve, E., 'Spit in Your Eye: The Blind Man of Bethsaida and the Blind Man of Alexandria', in *New Testament Studies*, vol. 54(1) (2008), pp. 1–17

Evola, J., 'Sol Invictus: Encounters Between East and West in the Ancient World', in *East and West*, vol. 8, no. 3 (1957), pp. 303–6

Favro, D., ' "Pater Urbis": Augustus as City Father of Rome', in *Journal of the Society of Architectural Historians*, vol. 51, no. 1 (1992), pp. 61–84

Fernando, L., Gispert-Sauch, G., *Christianity in India: Two Thousand Years of Faith* (New Delhi: Viking, 2004)

Ferngren, G. B., 'Early Christianity as a Religion of Healing', in *Bulletin of the History of Medicine*, vol. 66 (1992), pp. 1–15

Finkel, Y. I., *The Ark before Noah: Decoding the Story of the Flood* (London: Hodder & Stoughton, 2014)

Flannery, F., '"Talitha Qum! An Exploration of the Image of Jesus as Healer-Physician-Savior in the Synoptic Gospels in Relation to the Asclepius Cult', in *Coming Back to Life: The Permeability of Past and Present, Mortality and Immortality, Death and Life in the Ancient Mediterranean*, ed. Tappenden, F. and Daniel-Hughes, C. (Montreal: McGill University Library, 2017), pp. 407–34

Flemming, R., 'Galen and the Plague', in *Galen's Treatise Περὶ Ἀλυπίας (De Indolentia) in Context: A Tale of Resilience*, ed. C. Petit, vol. 52 (Leiden; Boston, MA: Brill, 2019), pp. 219–44

Flohr, M., 'The sensory landscape of the Roman fullonica', in Betts, E. (ed.), *Senses of the Empire: Multisensory Approaches to Roman Culture* (Abingdon: Routledge, 2017)

Forrest, M., 'The Abolition of Compulsory Latin and Its Consequences', in *Greece & Rome*, vol. 50 (2003), pp. 42–66

Fowden, G., 'Bishops and Temples in the Eastern Roman Empire AD 320–435', in *Journal of Theological Studies*, ser. 2, 29 (1978), pp. 53–78

—, 'The Pagan Holy Man in Late Antique Society', in *Journal of Hellenic Studies*, vol. 102 (1982), pp. 33–59

—, *Empire to Commonwealth: Consequences of Monotheism in Late Antiquity* (Princeton, NJ: Princeton University Press, 1993)

Frankopan, P., *The Silk Roads: A New History of the World* (London: Bloomsbury, 2016)

Fredriksen, P., 'Mandatory Retirement: Ideas in the Study of Christian Origins Whose Time Has Come to Go', in *Studies in Religion/Sciences Religieuses*, vol. 35, no. 2 (June 2006), pp. 231–46

Frend, W. H .C., *The Early Church: From the Beginnings to 461* (Fortress Press, 1991)

Frey, J., 'Texts about Jesus: Non-canonical Gospels and Related Literature', in *The Oxford Handbook of Early Christian Apocrypha*, ed. Gregory, A., and Tuckett, N., et al. (Oxford; New York: Oxford University Press, 2015)

Frykenberg, R. E., *Christianity in India: From Beginnings to the Present* (Oxford; New York: Oxford University Press, 2008)

Gaddis, M., *There is No Crime for Those Who Have Christ: Religious Violence in the Christian Roman Empire*, Transformation of the Classical Heritage 39 (Berkeley, CA: University of California Press, 2005)

Gaisser, J. H., *The Fortunes of Apuleius and the Golden Ass, a Study in Transmission and Reception*, American Council of Learned Societies (Princeton, NJ: Princeton University Press, 2008)

Garbe, R., 'St Thomas in India', in *Monist*, vol. 25, no. 1 (1915), pp. 1–27

Garnsey, P., 'The Lex Iulia and Appeal under the Empire', in *Journal of Roman Studies*, vol. 56 (1966), pp. 167–89

Georgia, D., 'Bultmann's Theology of the New Testament Revisited', in *Bultmann, Retrospect, and Prospect: The Centenary Symposium at Wellesley, Harvard Theological Studies, no. 35* (Philadelphia, PA: Fortress Press, 1985)

Gero, S., 'The Infancy Gospel of Thomas: A Study of the Textual and Literary Problems', in *Novum Testamentum*, vol. 13, no. 1 (1971), pp. 46–80

Gleason, M., 'Shock and awe: the performance dimension of Galen's anatomy demonstrations', in Wilkins, J., Whitmarsh, T., and Gill, C., *Galen and the World of Knowledge* (Cambridge: Cambridge University Press, 2009)

Globe, A., 'Some Doctrinal Variants in Matthew 1 and Luke 2, and the Authority of the Neutral Text', in *Catholic Biblical Quarterly*, vol. 42, no. 1 (1980), pp. 52–72

Godeau, A., *Histoire De L'Eglise, Quatriéme Edition Reveuë Corrigée & De Beaucoup Augmentée Par L'autheur* (Paris: Thomas Jolly, 1672)

Gordon, R. L., '"Straightening the Paths": Inductive Divination, Materiality, and Imagination in the Graeco-Roman Period', in *Memoirs of the American Academy in Rome. Supplementary Volumes*, vol. 13 (2017), pp. 119–43

Grant, R. M., *The Apostolic Fathers, A New Translation and Commentary*, Volume IV: *Ignatius of Antioch*, tr. R. M. Grant (Wipf and Stock, 2020)

Green, P., *Alexander the Great* (London: Weidenfeld & Nicolson, 1970)

Grimes, J., 'Tree(s) of Knowledge in the Junius Manuscript', in *Journal of English and Germanic Philology*, vol. 112, no. 3 (2013), pp. 311–39

Guthrie, W., 'The Presocratic World-Picture', in *Harvard Theological Review*, vol. 45(2) (1952), pp. 87–104

Gutjahr, P. C., *Bestsellers in Nineteenth-Century America: An Anthology* (London: Anthem Nineteenth Century Studies, 2016)

Hagg, T., *The Novel in Antiquity* (Berkeley, CA: University of California Press, 1983)

Hall, I. H., 'The Newly Discovered Apocryphal Gospel of Peter', in *Biblical World*, vol. 1, no. 2 (1893), pp. 88–98

Hambye, E. R., 'Saint Thomas the Apostle, India and Mylapore: Two Little Known Documents', *Proceedings of the Indian History Congress*, vol. 23 (1960), pp. 104–10

Hamilton, N. Q., 'Resurrection Tradition and the Composition of Mark', in *Journal of Biblical Literature*, vol. 84, no. 4 (1965), pp. 415–21

Hanrahan, M., 'Paganism and Christianity at Alexandria', in *University Review*, vol. 2, no. 9 (1962), pp. 38–66

Hardin, J., *Galatians and the imperial cult: A critical analysis of the first-century social context of Paul's letter* (Tübingen: Mohr Siebeck, 2008)

Harnack, A. von, 'Medicinisches Aus Der Ältesten Kirchengeschichte', in *Texte Und Untersuchungen Zur Geschichte Der Altchristlichen Literatur*, Bd. 8, Hft. 4 (Leipzig: J. C. Hinrichs, 1892)

—, *The Expansion of Christianity in the First Three Centuries*, tr. Moffatt, J., Theological Translation Library, vol. 19 (London: Williams & Norgate, 1904)

Harris, W. V., *Ancient Literacy*, American Council of Learned Societies (Cambridge, MA: Harvard University Press, 1989)

Harvey, S. A., and Hunter, D., *The Oxford Handbook of Early Christian Studies* (New York; Oxford: Oxford University Press, 2009)

Hasel, G. F., 'The Meaning of "Let Us" in Gn 1:26', in *Andrews University Seminary Studies* (AUSS), vol. 13.1 (1975)

Heilig, C., *Hidden Criticism?: The Methodology and Plausibility of the Search for a Counter-Imperial Subtext in Paul* (Tübingen: Mohr Siebeck, 2015)

Heuser, M., and Klimkeit, H.-J., *Studies in Manichaean Literature and Art*, Nag Hammadi and Manichaean Studies; 46 (Leiden: Brill, 1998)

Hijmans, S., 'Sol Invictus, the Winter Solstice, and the Origins of Christmas', in *Mouseion: Journal of the Classical Association of Canada*, vol. 3, no. 3 (2003), pp. 377–98

Himmelfarb, M., *Tours of Hell: An Apocalyptic Form in Jewish and Christian Literature* (Philadelphia, PA: University of Pennsylvania Press, 1983)

Hirschfeld, N., 'The Ship of Saint Paul: Historical Background (Part I)' in *The Biblical Archaeologist* 53 (1990): 25–30

Hobbs, E., *Bultmann, Retrospect, and Prospect: The Centenary Symposium at Wellesley, Harvard Theological Studies, no. 35* (Philadelphia, PA: Fortress Press, 1985)

Hock, R. F., *The Infancy Gospels of James and Thomas: With Introduction, Notes, and Original Text Featuring the New Scholars Version Translation* (Santa Rosa, CA: Polebridge Press, 1995)

Hone, W., *Regency Radical: Selected Writings of William Hone*, ed. D. A. Kent and D. R. Ewen (Wayne State University Press, 2003)

Hone, W. and Jones, J., *The Apocryphal New Testament: Being All the Gospels, Epistles, and Other Pieces Now Extant, Attributed in the First Four Centuries to Jesus Christ, His Apostles and Their Companions and Not Included in the New Testament by Its Compilers* (London: W. Hone, 1820)

Hopkins, K., 'The Age of Roman Girls at Marriage', in *Population Studies*, vol. 18, no. 3 (1965), pp. 309–27

—, 'Contraception in the Roman Empire', in *Comparative Studies in Society and History*, vol. 8, no. 1 (1965), pp. 124–51

—, 'Christian Number and its implications', in C. Kelly (ed.), *Sociological Studies in Roman History*, Cambridge Classical Studies (Cambridge: Cambridge University Press, 2018), pp. 398–431

Horn, C., 'The Protoevangelium of James and Its Reception in the Caucasus', in *Status Quaestionis, Scrinium*, vol. 14(1) (2018), pp. 223–38

Hume, D., *Principal Writings on Religion: Including, Dialogues concerning Natural Religion; And The Natural History of Religion*, ed. Gaskin, J. C. A. (Oxford: Oxford University Press, 1998)

Hunt, E. D., 'Christians and Christianity in Ammianus Marcellinus', in *Classical Quarterly*, vol. 35(1) (1985), pp. 186–200

Huxley, H. H., 'Storm and Shipwreck in Roman Literature', in *Greece & Rome*, vol. 21, no. 63 (1952), pp. 117–24

Irwin, M. E., 'Odysseus' "Hyacinthine Hair" in "Odyssey" 6.231', in *Phoenix*, vol. 44, no. 3 (1990), pp. 205–18

Israelowich, I., 'The Rain Miracle of Marcus Aurelius: (Re-)Construction of Consensus', in *Greece & Rome*, vol. 55, no. 1 (2008), pp. 83–102

James, L., *Women, Men, and Eunuchs: Gender in Byzantium* (London; New York: Routledge, 1997)

James, M. R., *The Apocryphal New Testament: Being the Apocryphal Gospels, Acts, Epistles, and Apocalypses, with other narratives and fragments* (Oxford: Clarendon Press, 1924)

—, *The Apocryphal New Testament Being the Apocryphal Gospels, Acts, Epistles, and Apocalypses with Other Narratives and Fragments*, tr. James, M. R. (Oxford: Clarendon Press, 1975)

James, W., *The Varieties of Religious Experience: A Study in Human Nature* (New York; London: Penguin Books, 1985)

Jefferson, L. M., *Christ the Miracle Worker in Early Christian Art* (Minneapolis, MN: Augsburg Fortress Publishers, 2014)

Jenkins, P., *The Lost History of Christianity: The Thousand-Year Golden Age of the Church in the Middle East, Africa, and Asia – and How It Died* (New York: HarperOne, 2008)

—, *The Many Faces of Christ: The Thousand-Year Story of the Survival and Influence of the Lost Gospels* (New York: Basic Books, 2015)

Jensen, L. B., 'Royal Purple of Tyre', in *Journal of Near Eastern Studies*, vol. 22, no. 2 (1963), pp. 104–18

Jensen, R. M., *Understanding Early Christian Art* (London; New York: Routledge, 2000)

Johnson, A. P., 'The Author of the "Against Hierocles": A response to Borzi and Jones', in *Journal of Theological Studies*, vol. 64, no. 2 (2013), pp. 574–94

Johnson, M., 'Witches in Time and Space: "Satire" 1.8, "Epode" 5 and Landscapes of Fear', in *Hermathena*, no. 192 (2012), pp. 5–44

Jonas, H., *The Gnostic Religion: The Message of the Alien God and the Beginnings of Christianity*, 2nd ed., rev. ed. (London: Routledge, 1992)

Jones, C. P., 'An Epigram on Apollonius of Tyana', in *Journal of Hellenic Studies*, vol. 100, Society for the Promotion of Hellenic Studies (1980), pp. 190–4

Joyce, J., *A Portrait of the Artist as a Young Man*, ed. Belanger (Ware: Wordsworth Editions, 1992)

Kaegi, W. E., 'The Fifth-Century Twilight of Byzantine Paganism', in *Classica et Mediaevalia*, vol. 27 (1968), pp. 243–75

Kanavou, N., *Philostratus'* Life of Apollonius of Tyana *and its Literary Context* (München: C. H. Beck, 2018)

Kannengiesser, C., DiTommaso, L. and Turcescu, L., *'The Reception and Interpretation of the Bible in Late Antiquity', Proceedings of the Montréal Colloquium in Honour of Charles Kannengiesser, 11–13 October 2006* (Leiden: Brill, 2008)

Keats, J., *Lamia: Revolution and Romanticism, 1789–1834* (Oxford: Woodstock, 1990)

Kee, H. C., 'Aretalogy and Gospel', in *Journal of Biblical Literature*, vol. 92, no. 3, Society of Biblical Literature (1973), pp. 402–22

Keresztes, P., 'The Decian Libelli and Contemporary Literature', in *Latomus*, vol. 34, no. 3 (1975), pp. 761–81

Klauck, H., *Apocryphal gospels: An introduction* (London: T. & T. Clark International, 2003)

Klijn, A. F. J., *Acts of Thomas*, Supplements to Novum Testamentum, vol. 108 (Leiden; Boston: Brill, 2003)

Klimkeit, H.-J., *Gnosis on the Silk Road: Gnostic Texts from Central Asia* (San Francisco, CA: Harper San Francisco, 1993)

Knust, J., and Wasserman, T., *To Cast the First Stone: The Transmission of a Gospel Story* (Princeton, NJ: Princeton University Press, 2019)

Koester, H., 'Apocryphal and Canonical Gospels', in *Harvard Theological Review*, vol. 73, no. 1/2 (1980), pp. 105–30

—, *Ancient Christian Gospels: Their History and Development* (London: SCM Press, 1990)

Koskenniemi, E., 'Apollonius of Tyana: A Typical *θεῖος ἀνήρ*?', in *Journal of Biblical Literature*, vol. 117, no. 3 (1998), pp. 455–67

—, 'The Function of the Miracle-Stories in Philostratus' Vita Apollonii Tyanensis', in *Wonders Never Cease: The Purpose of Narrating Miracle Stories in the New Testament and Its Religious Environment*, ed. Labahn, M., and Lietaert Peerbolte, B. J. (London; New York: T. & T. Clark, 2006), pp. 71–83

—, 'Apollonius of Tyana, the Greek Miracle Workers in the Time of Jesus and the New Testament', in *Hermeneutik der frühchristlichen Wundererzählungen*, eds. B. Kollmann, Zimmermann, R. (Tübingen: Mohr Siebeck, 2014), pp. 165–81

Kraemer, R. S., *Her Share of the Blessings: Women's Religions among Pagans, Jews, and Christians in the Greco-Roman World* (New York; Oxford: Oxford University Press, 1993)

—, 'Becoming Christian', in James, Sharon L., and Dillon, S. (eds.), *A Companion to Women in the Ancient World*, Blackwell Companions to the Ancient World (Malden, MA: Wiley-Blackwell, 2015)

Kreitzer, L., 'Apotheosis of the Roman Emperor', in *Biblical Archaeologist*, vol. 53, no. 4 (1990), pp. 211–17

Kurtz, L. R., 'The Politics of Heresy', in *American Journal of Sociology*, vol. 88, no. 6 (1983), pp. 1085–115

Kyle, D. G., *Spectacles of Death in Ancient Rome* (London and New York: Routledge, 1998)

Kynaston, D., *Austerity Britain, 1945–51 (Tales of a New Jerusalem)* (London: Bloomsbury, 2007)

Kyrtatas, D. J., 'The Origins of Christian Hell', in *Numen*, vol. 56, no. 2/3 (2009), pp. 282–97

Lacarrière, J., *The God-Possessed* (London: Allen & Unwin, 1963)

Lane Fox, R., *Pagans and Christians* (New York: Knopf, 1989)

—, *Augustine: Conversions and Confessions* (London: Allen Lane, an imprint of Penguin Books, 2015)

Laqueur, T. W., *Making Sex: Body and Gender from the Greeks to Freud*, American Council of Learned Societies (Cambridge, MA: Harvard University Press, 1992)

Layton, B., 'Rules, Patterns, and the Exercise of Power in Shenoute's Monastery: The Problem of World Replacement and Identity Maintenance', in *Journal of Early Christian Studies*, vol. 15, no. 1 (2007)

Le Goff, J., *The Birth of Purgatory*, tr. Goldhammer, A. (Chicago: University of Chicago Press, 1984)

Le Nain De Tillemont, L.-S., *An Account of the Life of Apollonius Tyaneus*, tr. Jenkin, R. (London: S. Smith and B. Walford, 1702)

Lee, A. D., 'Traditional Religions', in *The Cambridge Companion to the Age of Constantine*, ed. Lenski, N., Cambridge Companions to the Ancient World (Cambridge: Cambridge University Press, 2005), pp. 159–80

Legrand, *Vie D'Apollonius De Tyane* (Paris: Chez L. Collin, 1807)

Leith, J. H., *Creeds of the Churches: A Reader in Christian Doctrine, from the Bible to the Present*, revised ed. (Atlanta, GA: John Knox, 1982)

LeMahieu, D. L., 'Malthus and the Theology of Scarcity', in *Journal of the History of Ideas*, vol. 40, no. 3 (1979), pp. 467–74

Lenski, N., 'Valens and the Monks: Cudgeling and Conscription as a Means of Social Control', in *Dumbarton Oaks Papers*, vol. 58, Dumbarton Oaks, Trustees for Harvard University (2004), pp. 93–117

—, 'The Significance of the Edict of Milan', in Siecienski, A. E. (ed.), *Constantine: Religious Faith and Imperial Policy* (London: Routledge, 2017)

Liddell and Scott, *A Lexicon, Abridged from Liddell and Scott's Greek–English Lexicon* (Oxford: Clarendon Press, 1996)

Lieu, J. M., 'The "attraction of Women" in/to Early Judaism and Christianity: Gender and the Politics of Conversion', in *Journal for the Study of the New Testament*, vol. 21(72) (1999), pp. 5–22

—, 'What Did Women Do for the Early Church? The Recent History of a Question', in *The Church on Its Past*, ed. Clarke, P. D., and Charlotte Methuen (2013), pp. 261–81

Lieu, S., 'Nestorians and Manichaeans on the South China Coast', in *Vigiliae Christianae*, vol. 34, no. 1 (Leiden: Brill, 1980), pp. 71–88

Lieu, S. N. C.,'Marco Spurio?: Marco Polo on the Church of the East in China' in E. C. D. Hunter (ed.), *Šalmūtā Šapīrtā – Festschrift for Rifaat Y. Ebied in honour of his contributions to Semitic Studies presented for his 85th birthday, 29th June 2023* (Piscataway, 2023), pp. 329–60

Lieu, S. N. C., with Eccles, L., Franzmann, M., Gardner, I. and K. Parry, *Medieval Christian and Manichaean Remains from Zayton (Quanzhou)*, Corpus Fontium Manichaeorum: Series Archaeologica et Iconographica 2 (Turnhout, 2012), pp. 25–52 and 208–211

Lillis, J. K., 'No Hymen Required: Reconstructing Origen's View on Mary's Virginity.' *Church History* 89, no. 2 (2020): 249–67.

Lim, R., *Public Disputation, Power, and Social Order in Late Antiquity*, American Council of Learned Societies (Berkeley, CA: University of California Press, 1995)

Lindenlauf, A., 'The Sea as a Place of No Return in Ancient Greece', in *World Archaeology*, vol. 35, no. 3 (2003), pp. 416–33

Lo Cascio, E., 'Did the Population of Imperial Rome Reproduce Itself?' in *Urbanism in the Preindustrial World: Cross-Cultural Approaches*, ed. G. R. Storey (Tuscaloosa, AL: University of Alabama Press, 2006)

—, 'Urbanization as a Proxy of Demographic and Economic Growth', in Bowman, Alan K., and Wilson, Andrew (eds.), *Quantifying the Roman Economy: Methods and Problems*, Oxford Studies on the Roman Economy (Oxford: Oxford University Press, 2009)

Löhr, W., 'Western Christianities', in A. Casiday and F. Norris (eds.), *The Cambridge History of Christianity* (Cambridge: Cambridge University Press, 2007), pp. 7–51

McCready, W. D., 'Isidore, the Antipodeans, and the Shape of the Earth', in *Isis*, vol. 87, no. 1 (1996), pp. 108–27

MacDonald, M. Y., 'Was Celsus Right? The Role of Women in the Expansion of Early Christianity', in *Early Christian Families in Context: An Interdisciplinary Dialogue*, ed. David L. Balch and Carolyn Osiek (Grand Rapids, MI: Wm. B. Eerdmans, 2003), pp. 157–84

Mace, E. R., 'Feminist Forerunners and a Usable Past: A Historiography of Elizabeth Cady Stanton's The Woman's Bible', in *Journal of Feminist Studies in Religion*, vol. 25(2) (2009), pp. 5–23

Mack, B. L., *A Myth of Innocence: Mark and Christian Origins* (Philadelphia, PA: Fortress Press, 1988)

McKechnie, P., *The First Christian Centuries: Perspectives on the Early Church* (Leicester: Apollos, 2001)

MacMullen, R., *Changes in the Roman Empire: Essays in the Ordinary* (Princeton, N.J.: Princeton University Press, 1990)

—, *Christianizing the Roman Empire: A.D. 100–400* (New Haven, CT; London: Yale University Press, 1984)

—, *Christianity and Paganism in the Fourth to Eighth Centuries* (New Haven, CT; London: Yale University Press, 1997)

—, *Paganism in the Roman Empire* (New Haven, Conn.: London: Yale University Press, 1981)

—, *Roman Social Relations, 50 B.C. to A.D. 284* (New Haven; London: Yale University Press, 1974)

Malthus, T. R., *An Essay on the Principle of Population, as It Affects the Future Improvement of Society: With Remarks on the Speculations of Mr. Godwin, M. Condorcet, and Other Writers* (London: printed for J. Johnson, 1798)

Marsh, J., *Word Crimes: Blasphemy, Culture, and Literature in Nineteenth-Century England* (Chicago, IL; London: University of Chicago Press, 1998)

Marzano, A., *Harvesting the Sea: The Exploitation of Marine Resources in the Roman Mediterranean*, Oxford Studies on the Roman Economy (Oxford: Oxford University Press, 2013)

Mathews, T. F., *The Clash of Gods: A Reinterpretation of Early Christian Art* (Princeton, NJ: Princeton University Press, reprinted 1999)

Mead, G. R. S., *Apollonius of Tyana: The Philosopher-Reformer of the First Century A.D.* (London: Theosophical Society, 1901)

Meijer., F. J., 'Cato's African Figs', in *Mnemosyne*, vol. 37, no. 1/2 (1984), pp. 117–24

Melcher, S., 'The Problem of Anti-Judaism in Christian Feminist Biblical Interpretation: Some Pragmatic Suggestions', in *CrossCurrents*, vol. 53(1) (2003), pp. 22–31

Merrill, E. T., 'The Attitude of Ancient Rome toward Religion and Religious Cults', in *Classical Journal*, vol. 15, no. 4 (1920), pp. 196–215

Methuen, C., '"For pagans laugh to hear women teach": Gender stereotypes in the Didascalia Apostolorum', in Swanson, R. N. (ed.), *Gender and Christian Religion: papers read at the 1996 Summer Meeting and the 1997 Winter Meeting of the Ecclesiastical History Society*, Studies in Church History, Ecclesiastical History Society 34 (Woodbridge, Suffolk; Rochester, NY: published for the Ecclesiastical History Society by the Boydell Press, 1998), pp. 23–35

Metzger, B. M., 'Considerations of Methodology in the Study of the Mystery Religions and Early Christianity', in *Harvard Theological Review*, vol. 48(1) (1955), pp. 1–20

—, *New Testament Studies: Philological, Versional, and Patristic, New Testament Tools and Studies*, vol. 10 (Leiden: Brill, 1980)

—, *The Canon of the New Testament: Its Origin, Development, and Significance* (Oxford: Oxford University Press, 2009)

Meyer, M. W., *The Gnostic Discoveries: The Impact of the Nag Hammadi Library* (Pymble, NSW; New York: HarperCollins, 2009)

Miles, G., 'Ominous Swans in Philostratus' Life of Apollonius (1.5)', in *Mnemosyne*, vol. 70, no. 5 (2017), pp. 758–74

Moehring, H. R., 'The Persecution of the Jews and the Adherents of the Isis Cult at Rome A.D. 19', in *Novum Testamentum*, vol. 3, no. 4 (1959), pp. 293–304

Moffett, S. H., *A History of Christianity in Asia: Vol. 1, Beginnings to 1500*, 2nd rev. and corrected ed. (Maryknoll, NY: Orbis, 2004)

Mommsen, T. E., 'Petrarch's Conception of the "Dark Ages"', in *Speculum*, the Mediaeval Academy of America, vol. 17 (1942), pp. 226–42

Montserrat, D., 'Reading Gender in the Roman World', in *Experiencing Rome: Culture, Identity and Power in the Roman Empire*, ed. Janet Huskinson (London: Routledge, 2000), pp. 153–82

Murdoch, B., *The Medieval Popular Bible: Expansions of Genesis in the Middle Ages* (Cambridge: D. S. Brewer, 2003)

Nash, M. L., *The History and Politics of Exhumation: Royal Bodies and Lesser Mortals* (Palgrave Macmillan, 2019)

Nedungatt, G., 'The Apocryphal "Acts of Thomas" and Christian Origins in India', in *Gregorianum*, vol. 92, no. 3 (2011), pp. 533–57

Nock, A. D., 'Greek Magical Papyri', in *Journal of Egyptian Archaeology*, vol. 15, no. 3/4 (1929), pp. 219–35

—, 'The Apocryphal Gospels', in *Journal of Theological Studies*, New Series, vol. 11, no. 1 (1960), pp. 63–70

—, *Early Gentile Christianity and Its Hellenistic Background* (New York: Harper & Row, 1964)

Noel, G., *The Renaissance Popes: Culture, Power, and the Making of the Borgia Myth* (London: Constable, 2016)

Norris, F., 'Greek Christianities', in Casiday, A., and Norris, F. (eds.), *The Cambridge History of Christianity* (Cambridge: Cambridge University Press, 2007), pp. 70–117

North, J. A., 'Religious Toleration in Republican Rome', *Proceedings of the Cambridge Philological Society*, vol. 25 (1979), pp. 85–103

—, 'The Limits of the "Religious" in the Late Roman Republic', in *History of Religions*, vol. 53, no. 3 (2014), pp. 225–45

Nothaft, C. P. E., 'The Origins of the Christmas Date: Some Recent Trends in Historical Research', in *Church History*, vol. 81, no. 4 (2012), pp. 903–11

Nunn, G. E., 'Ptolemy's Geography', in *Geographical Review*, vol. 24, no. 3 (1934), pp. 516–18

Nutton, V., *Ancient Medicine*, 2nd ed., Sciences of Antiquity (London: Routledge, 2013)

Obbink, D., and Rutherford, R. B. (eds.), *Culture in Pieces: Essays on Ancient Texts in Honour of Peter Parsons* (Oxford: Oxford University Press, 2011)

Ogden, D., *Drakōn: Dragon Myth and Serpent Cult in the Greek and Roman Worlds* (Oxford: Oxford University Press, 2013)

—, *In Search of the Sorcerer's Apprentice: The Traditional Tales of Lucian's Lover of Lies* (Swansea: Classical of Wales, 2007)

O'Grady, S., *And Man Created God: Kings, Cults, and Conquests at the Time of Jesus* (London: Atlantic, 2012)

Orlandi, T., 'A Catechesis against Apocryphal Texts by Shenute and the Gnostic Texts of Nag Hammadi', in *Harvard Theological Review*, vol. 75, no. 1 (1982), pp. 85–95

Orlin, E. M., 'Octavian and Egyptian Cults: Redrawing the Boundaries of Romanness', in *American Journal of Philology*, vol. 129, no. 2 (2008), pp. 231–53

Pagels, E. H., 'What Became of God the Mother? Conflicting Images of God in Early Christianity', in *Signs*, vol. 2,2 (1976), pp. 293–303

—, *The Gnostic Gospels* (London: Phoenix, 2006)

Paxton, J., and Paley, W., *Natural Theology: Or, Evidences of the Existence and Attributes of the Deity: Collected from the Appearances of Nature* (Boston, MA: Richardson, 1831)

Papadopoulos, J. K., and Ruscillo, D., 'A Ketos in Early Athens: An Archaeology of Whales and Sea Monsters in the Greek World', in *American Journal of Archaeology*, vol. 106, no. 2 (2002), pp. 187–227

Parkin, T. G., *Old Age in the Roman World: A Cultural and Social History* (Baltimore, MD; London: Johns Hopkins University Press, 2002)

Pearson, B. A., 'Gnosticism and Christianity in Roman and Coptic Egypt', in *Studies in Antiquity and Christianity* (New York: T. & T. Clark International, 2004)

Peppard, M., *The World's Oldest Church: Bible, Art, and Ritual at Dura-Europos, Syria* (New Haven, CT: Yale University Press, 2016)

Petersen, A. K., 'Imperial Politics in Paul: Scholarly Phantom or Actual Textual Phenomenon?', in *People under Power: Early Jewish and Christian Responses to the Roman Power Empire*, ed. Labahn, M., and Lehtipuu, O. (Amsterdam: Amsterdam University Press, 2015), pp. 101–28

Petridou, G., *Divine Epiphany in Greek Literature and Culture* (Oxford: Oxford University Press, 2015)

Pharr, C., 'The Interdiction of Magic in Roman Law', in *Transactions and Proceedings of the American Philological Association*, vol. 63 (1932), pp. 269–95

Piovanelli, P., 'Exploring the Ethiopic Book of the Cock, An Apocryphal Passion Gospel from Late Antiquity', in *Harvard Theological Review*, vol. 96 (2003), pp. 427–54

—, 'The Reception Of Early Christian Texts And Traditions In Late Antiquity Apocryphal Literature', in *Reception and Interpretation of the Bible in Late Antiquity*, DiTommaso, L., and Turcescu, L. (Leiden: Brill, 2008)

Pollard, E. A., 'Indian Spices and Roman "Magic" in Imperial and Late Antique Indomediterranean', in *Journal of World History*, vol. 24, no. 1 (2013), pp. 1–23

Pounds, N. J. G., 'The Urbanization of the Classical World', in *Annals of the Association of American Geographers*, vol. 59, no. 1 (1969), pp. 135–57

Price, S. R. F., 'Gods and Emperors: The Greek Language of the Roman Imperial Cult', in *JHS*, vol. 104 (1984), pp. 79–95

—, *Rituals and Power: The Roman Imperial Cult in Asia Minor* (Cambridge: Cambridge University Press, 1990)

—, *Religions of the Ancient Greeks*, Key Themes in Ancient History (Cambridge: Cambridge University Press, 1999)

—, 'Religious Mobility in the Roman Empire', in *Journal of Roman Studies*, vol. 102 (2012), pp. 1–19

Prudlo, D. A., *Companion to Heresy Inquisitions. Brill's Companions to the Christian Tradition*, Volume 85 (Boston: Brill, 2019)

Quickel, A. T., and Williams, G., 'In Search of Sibakh: Digging Up Egypt from Antiquity to the Present Day', in *Journal of Islamic Archaeology*, vol. 3(1) (2016), pp. 89–108

Quispel, G., 'The Original Doctrine of Valentinus the Gnostic', in *Vigiliae Christianae*, vol. 50, no. 4 (1996), pp. 327–52

Radde-Gallwitz, A., and Muehlberger, E., *The Cambridge Edition of Early Christian Writings* (Cambridge: Cambridge University Press, 2017)

Rahmouni, A., *Divine Epithets in the Ugaritic Alphabetic Texts* (Leiden: Brill, 2008)

Rahner, K., *Encyclopedia of Theology: A Concise Sacramentum Mundi* (London: Burns and Cates, 1975)

Rapp, C., *Holy Bishops in Late Antiquity: The Nature of Christian Leadership in an Age of Transition*. The Transformation of the Classical Heritage 37 (Berkeley, California: University of California Press, 2013)

Rawson, E., 'The Life and Death of Asclepiades of Bithynia', in *Classical Quarterly*, vol. 32, no. 2 (1982), pp. 358–70

Raynor, D. H., 'Moeragenes and Philostratus: Two Views of Apollonius of Tyana', in *Classical Quarterly*, vol. 34, no. 1 (1984), pp. 222–6

Rea, M. C., 'Polytheism and Christian Belief', in *Journal of Theological Studies*, New Series, vol. 57, no. 1 (2006), pp. 133–48

Rebillard, E., *Christians and Their Many Identities in Late Antiquity, North Africa, 200–450 CE*, 1st ed. (Ithaca, NY: Cornell University Press, 2012)

Rimell, V., 'The Best a Man Can Get: Grooming Scipio in Seneca Epistle 86', in *Classical Philology*, vol. 108, no. 1 (2013), pp. 1–20

—, *The Closure of Space in Roman Poetics: Empire's Inward Turn* (Cambridge: Cambridge University Press, 2015)

Rives, 'Legal Strategy and Learned Display', in Riess, Werner, *Paideia at Play: Learning and Wit in Apuleius* (Groningen: Barkhuis, Groningen University Library, 2008)

Robinson, J., *The Nag Hammadi library in English*, 3rd ed. (Leiden: E. J. Brill, 1988)

—, *The Nag Hammadi Story*, 2 vols. (Leiden: Brill, 2014)

—, *The Nag Hammadi Story from the Discovery to the Publication*, Nag Hammadi and Manichaean Studies 86 (Leiden; Boston: Brill, 2014)

Rohmann, D., 'Book Burning as Conflict Management in the Roman Empire (213 BCE – 200 CE)', in *Ancient Society*, vol. 43 (2013), pp. 115–49

—, 'Christianity, Book-Burning and Censorship in Late Antiquity: Studies in Text Transmission', in *Arbeiten Zur Kirchengeschichte*, vol. 135 (Berlin; Boston, MA: De Gruyter, 2016)

Russell, B., *The Collected Papers of Bertrand Russell Volume 29: Détente or Destruction, 1955–57*, ed. Bone, A. G. (London: Routledge, 2012)

—, 'Why I Am Not a Christian' in *Why I Am Not a Christian, and other essays on religion and related subjects* (United States, Simon & Schuster, 1953)

—, 'Free Thought and Official Propaganda', in *Uncertain Paths to Freedom: Russia and China, 1919–22*, ed. R. A. Rempel and B. Haslam (London: Routledge, 2000)

—, *The Scientific Outlook* (London: Routledge, 2017)

Sabin, P., van Wees, H., and Whitby, M., *The Cambridge History of Greek and Roman Warfare, Volume 2, Rome from the Late Republic to the Late Empire* (Cambridge: Cambridge University Press, 2007)

Salzman, M. R., 'The Evidence for the Conversion of the Roman Empire to Christianity in Book 16 of the "Theodosian Code"', in *Historia: Zeitschrift Für Alte Geschichte*, vol. 42, no. 3 (1993), pp. 362–78

Sayce, A. H., 'Polytheism in Primitive Israel', in *Jewish Quarterly Review*, vol. 2, no. 1 (1889), pp. 25–36

Schäfer, P., *Jesus in the Talmud* (Princeton, NJ: Princeton University Press, 2007)

Schäferdiek, K., 'Germanic and Celtic Christianities', in Casiday, A., and Norris, F. (eds.), *The Cambridge History of Christianity* (Cambridge: Cambridge University Press, 2007), pp. 52–69

Schneemelcher, W., *New Testament Apocrypha, Vol. 1: Gospel and Related Writings*, English, 2nd ed. (Cambridge: James Clarke, 1991)

—, *New Testament Apocrypha, Vol. 2: Writings Related to the Apostles, Apocalypses and related subjects*, 2nd ed. (Cambridge: James Clarke, 1992)

Schultz, C. E., 'The Romans and Ritual Murder', in *Journal of the American Academy of Religion*, vol. 78, no. 2 (2010), pp. 516–41

Schüssler Fiorenza, E., *In Memory of Her: A Feminist Theological Reconstruction of Christian Origins*, 2nd ed. (London: SCM, 1999)

Scott, D., 'Christian Responses to Buddhism in Pre-Medieval Times', in *Numen*, vol. 32, no. 1 (1985), pp. 88–100

Shaw, B. D., 'Bandits in the Roman Empire', in *Past & Present*, no. 105, Past and Present Society, Oxford University Press (1984), pp. 3–52

—, *Sacred Violence: African Christians and Sectarian Hatred in the Age of Augustine* (Cambridge: Cambridge University Press, 2011)

Shiner, W. T., and Kent, C., *Proclaiming the Gospel: First-Century Performance of Mark* (Harrisburg, PA: Trinity Press International, 2003)

Shoemaker, S. J., 'Between Scripture and Tradition: The Marian Apocrypha of Early Christianity', in Turcescu, L., et al., *The Reception and Interpretation of the Bible in Late Antiquity, Proceedings of the Montréal Colloquium in Honour of Charles Kannengiesser, 11–13 October 2006* (Leiden: Brill, 2008)

—, 'The Virgin Mary's Hidden Past: From Ancient Marian Apocrypha to the Medieval Vitae Virginis', in *Marian Studies*, vol. 60: *Telling Mary's Story: The "Life of Mary" Through the Ages* (2009), pp. 1–30

Simon, F. M., 'Celtic Ritualism from the (Graeco)-Roman 2007 Point of View', in Bonnet, C., et al., *Rites Et Croyances Dans Les Religions Du Monde Romain: Huit Exposés Suivis De Discussions: Vandoevres-Genève, 21–25 Août 2006*, Entretiens Sur L'Antiquité Classique (Ser.); T. 53 (Genève: Fondation Hardt, 2007)

Simon, M., 'From Greek Haeresis to Christian Heresy', in Schoedel, W., and Wilken, R. L., *Early Christian Literature and the Classical Intellectual Tradition: In Honorem Robert M. Grant, Théologie Historique*; 53 (Paris: Éditions Beauchesne, 1979)

Smith, A., 'The Pagan Neoplatonists' Response to Christianity', in *Maynooth Review / Revieú Mhá Nuad*, vol. 14 (1989), pp. 25–41

Smith, G., and Sayce, A., *The Chaldean Account of Genesis: Containing the Description of the Creation, the Fall of Man, the Deluge, the Tower of Babel, the Destruction of Sodom, the Times of the Patriarchs, and Nimrod* (Cambridge Library Collection – Archaeology, 1876)

Smith, H., 'The Laying-on of Hands', in *American Journal of Theology*, vol. 17, no. 1 (1913), pp. 47–62

Smith, H., and Smith, M., 'Heroes and Gods; Spiritual Biographies in Antiquity', in *Religious Perspectives*, vol. 13 (London: Routledge & Kegan Paul, 1965)

Smith, J. Z., *Drudgery Divine: On the Comparison of Early Christianities and the Religions of Late Antiquity* (London: School of Oriental and African Studies, University of London, 1990)

Smith, M., 'Prolegomena to a Discussion of Aretalogies, Divine Men, the Gospels and Jesus', in *Journal of Biblical Literature*, vol. 90, no. 2 (1971), pp. 174–99

—, *The Secret Gospel: The Discovery and Interpretation of the Secret Gospel According to Mark* (London: Gollancz, 1974)

—, *Jesus the Magician* (San Francisco, CA: Harper & Row, 1981)

Smith, T., Plantzos, D., *A Companion to Greek Art*, vol. 1 (Malden, MA; Oxford: Wiley-Blackwell, 2012)

Snyder, G. F., *Ante Pacem: Archaeological Evidence of Church Life before Constantine* (Macon, GA: Mercer University Press, 2003)

Snyder, H. G., 'Early Christianity', in Spaeth, S. (ed.), *The Cambridge Companion to Ancient Mediterranean Religions*, Cambridge Companions to Religion (Cambridge: Cambridge University Press, 2013)

Stark, E., 'Reconstructing the Rise of Christianity: The Role of Women', in *Sociology of Religion*, vol. 56, no. 3 (1995), pp. 229–44

Stark, R., *The Rise of Christianity: A Sociologist Reconsiders History* (Princeton, NJ: Princeton University Press, 1996)

Stein, R. H., 'The Ending of Mark', in *Bulletin for Biblical Research*, vol. 18, no. 1 (University Park, PA: Penn State University Press, 2008), pp. 79–98

Stewart, E., 'Domitian and Roman Religion: Juvenal, Satires Two and Four', in *Transactions of the American Philological Association* (1974–) vol. 124 (1994), pp. 309–32

Stichele, C. V., and Penner, T., *Contextualizing Gender in Early Christian Discourse: Thinking Beyond Thecla* (London: Bloomsbury T. & T. Clark, 2009)

Strycker, É. de and Quecke, H., *La Forme la plus Ancienne du Protévangile de Jacques*, Subsidia Hagiographica, 33 (Bruxelles: Société des Bollandistes, 1961)

Swancutt, D. M., 'Still Before Sexuality: "Greek" Androgyny, the Roman Imperial Politics of Masculinity and the Roman Invention of the Tribas', in Stichele and Penner (eds.), *Mapping Gender in Ancient Religious Discourse*, Biblical Interpretation Ser., vol. 84 (Leiden: Brill, 2007)

Swerdlow, N. M., 'Review Article: On the Cosmical Mysteries of Mithras', in *Classical Philology*, vol. 86, no. 1 (1991), pp. 48–63

Syme, R., *The Roman Revolution* (Oxford: Oxford University Press, 1960)

Thorley, J., 'Junia, a Woman Apostle', in *Novum Testamentum*, vol. 38, no. 1 (1996), pp. 18–29

Tiede, D., 'Religious Propaganda and Gospel Literature of the Early Christian Mission', in *ANRW* II.2.5.2, eds. Temporini and Haase (Berlin: Walter de Gruyter, 1984), pp. 1705–29

Tilg, S., *Chariton of Aphrodisias and the Invention of the Greek Love Novel* (Oxford: Oxford University Press, 2010)

Tillotson, J., *The Works of Dr. John Tillotson, with the Life of the Author* (J. F. Dove, 1820)

Torrey, C. C., 'A New Era in the History of the "Apocrypha"', in *Monist*, vol. 25, no. 2 (1915), pp. 286–94

Trevor-Roper, H., *The European witch-craze of the 16th and 17th centuries* (Harmondsworth: Penguin, 1969)

Tuckett, C. M., *The Oxford Handbook of Early Christian Apocrypha*, Oxford Handbooks (Oxford; New York: Oxford University Press, 2015)

Turkeltaub, D., 'Perceiving Iliadic Gods', in *Harvard Studies in Classical Philology*, vol. 103 (2007), pp. 51–81

Ulrich, E., 'The notion and definition of canon', in McDonald, L. M., and Sanders, J. A. (eds.), *The Canon Debate* (Peabody, MA: Hendrickson, 2002)

Unger, D., *Irenaeus: Against the Heresies*, rev. Dillon, J. (New York: Paulist Press, 1992)

Van Der Toorn, K., Becking, B., and Van Der Horst, P. W., *Dictionary of Deities and Demons in the Bible* (Leiden; Boston: Brill, 1998)

van Kooten, G., 'John's Counter-Symposium: "The Continuation of Dialogue" in Christianity—A Contrapuntal Reading of John's Gospel and Plato's Symposium', in *Intolerance, Polemics, and Debate in Antiquity*, ed. van Kooten, G., and van Ruiten, J. (Leiden: Brill, 2019)

Van Lommel, K., 'The Recognition of Roman Soldiers' Mental Impairment', in *Acta Classica*, vol. 56 (2013), pp. 155–84

Van Uytfanghe, M., 'La Vie D'Apollonius De Tyane Et Le Discours Hagiographique', in *Theios Sophistès* (Leiden: Brill, 2009)

Vermes, G., *Jesus the Jew: A Historian's Reading of the Gospels* (London, 1973)

Vose, R. J. E., *The Index of Prohibited Books: Four Centuries of Struggle over Word and Image for the Greater Glory of God* (London: Reaktion Books, 2022)

Wagemakers, B., 'Incest, Infanticide, and Cannibalism: Anti-Christian Imputations in the Roman Empire', in *Greece & Rome*, vol. 57, no. 2 (2010), pp. 337–54

Waldner, K., 'Hippolytus and Virbius: Narratives of Coming Back to Life and Religious Discourses in Greco-Roman Literature', in *Coming Back to Life: The Permeability of Past and Present, Mortality and Immortality, Death and Life in the Ancient Mediterranean*, eds. Tappenden, F. S. and Daniel-Hughes, C., with the assistance of Rice, B. N., 2nd ed. (Montreal: McGill University Library, 2017), pp. 345–74

Walsh, P. G., 'Making a Drama out of a Crisis: Livy on the Bacchanalia', in *Greece & Rome*, vol. 43, no. 2 (1996), pp. 188–203

Walzer, R., *Galen on Jews and Christians*, Oxford Classical & Philosophical Monographs (London: Oxford University Press, 1949)

Ward-Perkins, B., *The Fall of Rome: And the End of Civilization* (Oxford: Oxford University Press, 2006)

Warmington, B., 'The Vision of Constantine', in *Journal of Roman Archaeology*, vol. 16 (2003), pp. 237–59

Watson, L., *A Commentary on Horace's Epodes* (Oxford: Oxford University Press, 2003)

Werner, M., 'The Madonna and Child Miniature in the Book of Kells: Part I', in *Art Bulletin*, vol. 54, no. 1 (Taylor & Francis, Ltd., 1972), pp. 1–23

Whatham, A. E., 'The Polytheism of Gen., Chap. 1', in *Biblical World*, vol. 37, no. 1 (1911), pp. 40–7

Whitmarsh, T., *Battling the Gods: Atheism in the Ancient World* (London: Faber & Faber, 2015)

Williams, C., and Nussbaum, M., *Roman Homosexuality* (Oxford: Oxford University Press, 2010)

Williams, M., *Deforesting the Earth from Prehistory to Global Crisis: An Abridgment* (Chicago: University of Chicago Press, 2006)

Williams, R., *Arius: Heresy and Tradition* (London: SCM, 2001)

Wills, G., 'Augustine's Pears and the Nature of Sin', in *Arion: A Journal of Humanities and the Classics*, vol. 10, no. 1 (2002), pp. 57–66

Windon, B., 'The Seduction of Weak Men: Tertullian's Rhetorical Construction of Gender and Ancient Christian "Heresy" ', in *Mapping Gender in Ancient Religious Discourses*, eds. Penner, T., Vander Stichele, C., Biblical Interpretation Ser., vol. 84 (Leiden: Brill, 2007)

Winkler, J., 'Lollianos and the Desperadoes', in *Journal of Hellenic Studies*, vol. 100 (1980), pp. 155–81

Wiseman, T. P., 'Maecenas and the Stage', in *Papers of the British School at Rome*, vol. 84 (2016), pp. 131–55

Woolf, G., 'Isis and the Evolution of Religions', in *Power, politics and the cults of Isis: Proceedings of the Vth International Conference of Isis studies, 2011*, eds. Bricault, L., Versluys, M. J., Religions in the Graeco-Roman world, vol. 180 (Leiden: Brill, 2014)

Yamauchi, E. M., 'The Nag Hammadi Library', in *Journal of Library History (1974–87)*, vol. 22, no. 4, University of Texas Press (1987), pp. 425–41

Young, F. A., *A History of Exorcism in Catholic Christianity*, Palgrave Historical Studies in Witchcraft and Magic (Cham: Palgrave Macmillan, 2016)

Notes

Prologue

1. *Infancy Gospel of Thomas*, Greek A, 1:1–2:4, tr. Elliott.
2. Ibid., 3:1–2.
3. Ibid., 4:1.

Introduction

1. Epiphanius, *The Panarion of Epiphanius of Salamis*, Book I, 27.2, 2, tr. F. Williams.
2. For the pipe reference, see Valentinians, in Epiphanius, ibid., 31.7, 3.
3. See W. Schneemelcher (1991), p. 251.
4. Epistula Apostolorum, Ethiopic, 14, ed. Wilson, rev. Schneemelcher. Francis Watson's translation is similar: 'When I took the form of the angel Gabriel, I appeared to Mary and I spoke with her. Her heart received me, she believed, sh[e moul]ded me, I entered into her, I became flesh.' See Watson (2020), 179.
5. Suffer the little children: Matthew 19:14; lunatics . . . or idiots: *Acts of Thomas*, 12, tr. Elliott.
6. Epiphanius, *Panarion*, Book I, 24.3, 2. Epiphanius was not a disinterested witness, and, here and elsewhere, what he writes should be treated with due caution; though, in the absence of accounts from the heretics themselves (which have almost all been lost), such hostile sources are almost all that academics have to work with. There is a very plausible suggestion that this Jesus is a misunderstanding of the gnostic conception of Jesus, as seen in the Coptic gnostic *Apocalypse of Peter*, which told of how the real Jesus watched, 'glad and laughing', while nails were driven into the hands and feet of the fleshly body. See Pearson (2005), p. 23.
7. *Protoevangelium of James*, 20.1, tr. M. R. James.
8. Origen, *Contra Celsum*, I.50, tr. Chadwick.
9. Ibid., VII.9.
10. E. H. Carr (2018), pp. 5–20.
11. Codex Theodosianus, 16.4.1, tr. Pharr.

12. Ibid., 16.5.20.
13. Julian, Epistle 41, tr. W. C. Wright.
14. G. E. M. de Ste. Croix (2006), pp. 201–2.
15. Liddell and Scott (1996).
16. 'quos partim digessit ecclesia tamquam stercora.' Discussed in Shaw (2011), p. 339.
17. John Locke, 'A Letter Concerning Toleration', in Wootton (2003), p. 390.
18. Thomas Carlyle, *The French Revolution: A History*, vol. 2 (1838), p. 159.
19. The observation is indebted to Mary Beard in Beard (2023), p. 8.
20. Bagehot (1881), p. 4.
21. James (1902).
22. For example, *Greek Magical Papyri*, XIII.285–95. The story of the statue is dubious (it is in the untrustworthy *Historia Augusta*) but what is clearly true is that people continued worshipping ancient deities alongside the Christian one, and for a long time.
23. Solomon, Ode 19, *Odes of Solomon*, tr. J. R. Harris.

Chapter One: Antichrist

1. Philostratus, *Life of Apollonius of Tyana*, I.4, tr. C. P. Jones.
2. Ibid., I.5.
3. Ibid., IV.45.1.
4. Ibid.
5. Ibid., VIII.8. Apollonius was quoting at the time, but the sense remains.
6. Eunapius, quoted in C. P. Jones (1980), p. 193.
7. The estimation of popularity is that of V. Nutton (2013), p. 289; the imperial worshipper Julia Domna.
8. See M. Dzielska (1986), p. 157; also G. R. S. Mead (1901), p. 5, who reflects that 'the many have been taught to look upon our philosopher not only as a charlatan, but even as an anti-Christ.' To start a discussion on Apollonius in the way I have here has a long history. It was first done in the third century AD and the majority of authors who write on Apollonius in the modern day will include such a passage in which his life is compared with that of Jesus – see, for example, the excellent Bart D. Ehrman (2012), to which this is indebted.
9. Milton, *On the Morning of Christ's Nativity* (1645).
10. E. Gibbon (1909), chapter XV, p. 330.
11. E. H. Gombrich (2005), p. 94.
12. For the snake, see Plutarch, *Life of Alexander*, 2.6, tr. B. Perrin.
13. Quoted in Macarius, *Apokritikos*, 3.3, in Berchman (2005), fr. 176.

14. C. S. Lewis (1970); though it has been raised by others before.
15. Quoted in Macarius, *Apokritikos*, 3.15, in Berchman (2005), fr. 181.
16. Ibid.
17. Pliny the Elder, *Natural History*, 28.2.
18. Origen, *Contra Celsum*, II.58, tr. Chadwick.
19. Porphyry, in Jerome, *Tractatus de Psalmo* 81. in J. H. Gaisser (2008), p. 24.
20. Eusebius, *Reply to Hierocles*, 2.1, tr. C. P. Jones.
21. Ibid., 2.2.
22. Origen, *Contra Celsum*, VII.9, tr. Chadwick.
23. Ibid.
24. Ibid.
25. Matthew 24:24, KJV.
26. Origen, *Contra Celsum*, VI.11, tr. Chadwick.
27. Porphyry, as summarized by Augustine, Epistle 102.8, fr. 112, Berchman (2005), fr. 112.
28. Quoted in Jerome, Epistulae 133, in Berchman (2005), fr. 106.
29. Porphyry, in Macarius, *Apokritikos*, 4.3, in Berchman (2005), fr. 197.
30. Justin Martyr, First Apology, 21, ANF, vol. 2.
31. Augustine, *The City of God against the Pagans*, VI.9, tr. R. W. Dyson.
32. Hippolytus, *The Refutation of All Heresies*, VI.3, ANF, vol. 5.
33. Lucian, *Alexander the False Prophet*, 8, tr. A. M. Harmon.
34. Lucian, *Alexander the False Prophet*, 3, tr. A. M. Harmon.
35. Ibid.
36. Lucian, *Alexander the False Prophet*, 9, tr. A. M. Harmon.
37. Dzielska (1986), p. 32; Bowersock (1970), p. 10; Jones (2005), p. 8.
38. Philostratus, *Life of Apollonius of Tyana*, I.4, tr. C. P. Jones.
39. Luke 1:30–2, ESV.
40. Matthew 2:2, KJV; Philostratus, *Life of Apollonius of Tyana*, IV.45.1, tr. C. P. Jones.
41. Philostratus, *Life of Apollonius of Tyana*, IV.1, tr. C. P. Jones.
42. Matthew 4.20, ESV.
43. Luke 7:12, ESV.
44. Luke 7:13, ESV.
45. Luke 7:14, ESV.
46. Philostratus, *Life of Apollonius of Tyana*, VII.41, tr. C. P. Jones.
47. Luke 22.70, ESV.
48. Matthew 27:24, ESV.
49. Philostratus, *The Life of Apollonius of Tyana*, VIII.9, tr. F. C. Conybeare.
50. John 20:27, ESV.
51. Philostratus, *The Life of Apollonius of Tyana*, VIII.12, tr. Conybeare.
52. See N. Kanavou (2018), V.32.

53. Dzielska (1986), p. 91. See Raynor (1984) on Philostratus' view of Moeragenes. For a simple summary of the debate over the way in which Apollonius was seen, see Rives (2008), p. 33ff; for dates, see Hagg (2012), p. 324.
54. N. Kanavou (2018), V.32.

Chapter Two: To Heal the Blind and Cure the Lame

1. Paul, Seven Books, 6,45, quoted in the as ever superb V. Nutton (2013), pp. 302–3, to which this section is indebted.
2. Frier (2000), p. 788 (though he notes the enormous caveats of making assumptions on the scanty data that is available).
3. V. Nutton (2013), pp. 21–2.
4. Pliny, *Natural History*, 30.8 (22), in Edelstein and Edelstein (1945), T.369.
5. Soranus, *Gynaecology*, IV.II.9, under the horrifying heading, 'On Extraction by Hooks and Embryotomy'.
6. Origen, *Contra Celsum*, I.68, tr. Chadwick.
7. Homer, *Iliad*, 1.49ff. Plagues, which are dramatic, sudden and affect everyone, are an honourable exception to the lack of medical writing, and they pockmark the history of the era, appearing in the writings of Thucydides and Galen and others, with great detail, zest and abundant use of the word 'scab'.
8. This estimate is quoted in D. Rohmann (2016), p. 8.
9. V. Nutton (2013), p. 391, n. 21.
10. A. von Harnack (1892), p. 96.
11. Herodas, *Mimiambi*, IV, 16–19, Edelstein and Edelstein (1945), T.482.
12. *Inscriptiones Graecae*, IV2, 1, nos. 121–22.9, 35 and 37, in Edelstein and Edelstein (1945), T.423.
13. Suetonius mentions this (*Vespasian*, 4); the historian Tacitus, writing at about the same time, also noted it. See Tacitus, *Histories*, V.8.3: 'the prophecy that this was the very time when the East should grow strong and that men starting from Judaea should possess the world'. Hume would later discuss it and note the reliability of Tacitus.
14. See, for example, Tacitus, *Histories*, V.13.1.
15. Suetonius, *Vespasian*, 7, tr. A. Thomson, T. Forester.
16. Ibid.
17. Mark 8:22–5, ESV.
18. Justin, *Apologia*, 22.6, in Edelstein and Edelstein (1945), T.94.
19. Acts 14:8–13, ESV.

20. For making the mute speak, see *Inscriptiones Graecae*, IV2, 1, nos. 121–2, in Edelstein and Edelstein (1945), T.423.5; for the story of the lame man and his stolen crutch, see ibid., 16.
21. For white raiment, see *Inscriptiones Graecae*, IV, 1, no. 128, 20ff, i, i–ii, 26, quoted in Edelstein and Edelstein (1945), T.296; for being enthroned in the sky, see Aelius Aristides, Oratio L, 56 in ibid., T.302; for 'saviour' see *Inscriptiones Creticae*, I, xvii, no. 24 [2–1st c. BC] in ibid., T.441.
22. *Inscriptiones Graecae*, IV2, 1, nos. 121–2, in Edelstein and Edelstein (1945), T.423.23.
23. For healing the abscess, see ibid., T.423.27; for the cure for lice, see ibid., T.423.28.
24. Aelius Aristides, Oratio XLVII, 32, quoted in ibid., T.544.
25. Herodotus, *The Histories*, IV.95, tr. A. de Sélincourt.
26. Ibid., IV.95–6.
27. Monkeys: Pliny the Elder, *Natural History*, 8.54, tr. H. Rackham; for griffins, see ibid., 7.2.6; for habits of Arabian peninsula, see ibid., 6.32.
28. This observation is indebted, yet again, to V. Nutton (2013), p. 5.
29. Pliny the Elder, *Natural History*, 7.52, tr. Bostock.
30. Apuleius, *Apologia*, tr. H. E. Butler, 19.
31. Apuleius, *Apologia*, 19, 4, ed. and tr. C. P. Jones.
32. Ibid., 19, 5.
33. Ibid., 19, 6–7.
34. Ibid., 19, 8–9.
35. Pliny the Elder, *Natural History*, 26.8.
36. Clement of Rome, First Epistle to the Corinthians, XXV–XXVI, ANF, vol. 1.
37. Origen, *Contra Celsum*, II.16, tr. Chadwick.
38. Ibid., II.55.
39. Celsus, *De Medicina*, 2.6.18, tr. W. G. Spencer.
40. Apuleius, *The Golden Ass*, II.28.
41. Ibid.
42. Ibid., II.29.
43. Origen, *Contra Celsum*, II.55.
44. Plutarch, *The Cleverness of Animals*, 973e–974a, tr. Harold Cherniss and William C. Helmbold; discussed in Winkler (1980), pp. 174–5 and also in the fascinating Bowersock (1997), p. 114, to whom this observation is much indebted.
45. Quoted in Macarius, *Apokritikos*, 4.24, in R. M. Berchman (2005), fr. 210.
46. Ibid.
47. Codex Theodosianus, 9.17.4.
48. S. Tilg (2010), p. 61.

49. Matthew 27:62–4, ESV.
50. John 20:1–2.
51. Chariton, Callirhoe, 3.3, tr. G. P. Goold.
52. Mark 16:2–5, ESV.
53. Tilg (2010), pp. 59–65.
54. Cicero, *Letters to Atticus*, 5. XII.15, tr. D. R. Shackleton Bailey.
55. Cicero, *Letters to Atticus*, vol. 3, XII.36, tr. E. O. Winstedt.

Chapter Three: The Falsehoods of the Magicians

1. Pliny the Younger, *Letters*, III.5.10–13. Like an audiobook of antiquity, the slave could be paused and asked to go back to reread a bit that the listener missed – though this irritated Pliny immeasurably when people did it, as he considered it a waste of time.
2. See D. Favro (1992), p. 73; on the heights of buildings and the darkness, see Strabo, *Geography*, 5.3.7; for Nero (naturally) brawling in the streets in disguise, see Suetonius, *Nero*, 26.
3. B. D. Shaw (1984), pp. 9–12.
4. For the rich man and the poor man, see Juvenal, *Satire*, 3.83–9; for the dripping arches, see Juvenal, *Satire*, 3.11.
5. In some ways. There is evidence that there was also an increased tendency to eating out later and going out later. For a different discussion of dark and light in Rome, see Dossey (2018).
6. For the pale shades, see, for example, Propertius, *Elegies*, 4.7.1–2; also, Horace, *Epistles*, 2.2.209.
7. On figs, see L. Watson (2003), p. 200, and M. Johnson (2012), pp. 5–44, to whom this paragraph is indebted.
8. Horace, *Satires*, 1.8.16; see also discussion in Johnson (2012), pp. 13–21. For discussion of the location, see T. P. Wiseman (2016), pp. 131–55.
9. Horace, *Satires*, 1.8.
10. Horace, *Epodes*, V.
11. CIL vi 19747, quoted in Johnson (2012).
12. Pliny the Elder, *Natural History*, 28.20, tr. Bostock.
13. Codex Justinianus ix, 16, 7 (8), on the Cornelian law concerning assassins (6 February AD 374), quoted in C. Pharr (1932), p. 288.
14. On attempts to redefine magic by arguing this point, see R. L. Gordon (2017), pp. 122–3. On the correlation between spice and India and magic, see E. A. Pollard (2013), pp. 1–23.
15. Table VIII, 1a in Johnson et al. (2012), p. 11.

16. Pliny the Elder, *Natural History*, 28.4.19 (*'defigi quidem diris deprecationibus nemo non metuit'*).
17. Pliny the Elder, *Natural History*, 37.14, tr. Bostock.
18. See, for example, Tacitus, *Histories*, V.13.1.
19. Paulus, quoted in M. Smith (1981), p. 75.
20. Ibid. See also Pharr (1932), p. 280.
21. Acts 19:17–19, ESV.
22. Such as the Philoponoi: the *Life of Severus* discusses the zeal with which they did this; see an analysis of their actions and the truth of the account in D. Rohmann (2016), chapter 3.
23. For the prohibition of all magic, see Pharr (1932), p. 269 and p. 294. For the changes in book prohibitions brought about by Christianity, see D. Rohmann (2016).
24. H. D. Betz (1996), p. xli.

Chapter Four: Serpent's Blood and Eye of Ape

1. A. D. Nock (1929), p. 219.
2. *Greek Magical Papyri*, V.70–90 (triangle), VII.300 (circle), II.165–75 (headless human), II.150–65 (dung beetle).
3. Chant: *Greek Magical Papyri*, III.572–5.
4. Ibid., IV.2346–50.
5. Ibid., I.222–31 (turning invisible), I.100–30 (solidifying rivers and seas).
6. Nock (1929), p. 228.
7. Ibid., p. 219.
8. *Greek Magical Papyri*, I.222–4.
9. Ibid., I.9–10.
10. Ibid., II.1–64.
11. Ibid., IV.915–20 (cumin), III.390–5 (cardamom), II.70–80 (nightshade and bayberries), VII.995–1000 (figs), III.1–164 (cinnabar ink and drowned cat), IV.2000–5 (serpent's blood and soot), I.247–9 (peony and eye of ape).
12. For storax, sage, frankincense and myrrh, see ibid., IV.2870–80; for asphodel and wild garlic, see *Papyri Demoticae Magicae*, xiv 966–9; for myrrh, garlic and gall of gazelle, see *Papyri Demoticae Magicae*, xiv 961–6.
13. *Greek Magical Papyri*, I.247–62.
14. Ibid., IV.2875–6.
15. Ibid., XCV.14–18 (epilepsy), XCIV.17–21 (daimon possession), VII.209–10 (swollen testicles); for stopping the flow of blood from a woman, see *Papyri Demoticae Magicae*, xiv 961–5; for a pregnancy test, see *Papyri*

Demoticae Magicae, xiv 956–60; for an erection, see *Papyri Demoticae Magicae*, lxi 58–62.

16. *Greek Magical Papyri*, IV.467–8 (restraining anger), VII.149–54 (bug-free house), VII.423–8 (winning at dice).
17. Ibid., I.247–62 (invisibility), III.479–83 (foreknowledge), VII.505–28 (meeting one's own daimon), IV.86–7 (guarding against demons), IV.1227–64 (driving out daimons, among others), VI.1–47 (meeting a god (Helios)), XII.14–95 (making a god obey your command).
18. Betz (1996), p. xlv.
19. *Greek Magical Papyri*, XIa.1–40.
20. Ibid., IV.1227–35.
21. Ibid., IV.3007–86.
22. Betz (1996), p. xlv.
23. Ibid., p. xlvii.
24. Ibid., p. xlviii.
25. E. A. Wallis Budge (1971), p. x.
26. Ibid., pp. x–xi.
27. Ibid., p. xi.
28. Ibid., p. x.
29. Ibid.
30. Betz (1996), p. xliii.
31. Origen, *Contra Celsum*, I.68, tr. Chadwick.
32. P. Schäfer (2007), p. 55.
33. Origen, *Contra Celsum*, I.28, tr. Chadwick.
34. Quoted in E. S. Drower (1962), p. 443.
35. Justin, *Second Apology*, VI, ANF, vol. I.
36. *Pistis Sophia: A Gnostic Gospel*, 1.25, tr. G. R. S. Mead.
37. Augustine, *City of God against the Pagans*, X.9, tr. R. W. Dyson.
38. Augustine, *City of God*, X.9, tr. D. S. Wiesen.
39. Augustine, *City of God*, tr. Dyson, X.9.
40. Origen, *Contra Celsum*, II.49, tr. Chadwick.
41. 'Benighted fools': Eusebius, *Reply to Hierocles*, 4; for superficiality, see 4.1; for illusions, see 2.2.
42. M. Smith (1981), p. vii.
43. Ibid., p. 6.
44. Ibid., p. vii
45. Ibid., p. 7.
46. P. Lond, 122, quoted in Nock (1929), p. 231, n. 5.
47. *Greek Magical Papyri*, I.100–110.
48. Ibid., I.120–125.
49. Ibid., I.105–115.

50. Lucian, *Philopseudes*, 12–13, tr. Harmon.
51. Mark 5:9–13, ESV.
52. Lucian, *Philopseudes*, 16, tr. Harmon, discussed in M. Smith (1981), p. 56ff.
53. Lucian, *Philopseudes*, 16, tr. Harmon.
54. Lucian, *Philopseudes*, 16, tr. H. W. Fowler and F. G. Fowler.
55. Lucian, *Menippus*, 6, tr. Harmon.
56. Ibid., 7.
57. Ibid., 9.
58. See, for example, Tillotson (1820), p. 443.
59. Philostratus, *Life of Apollonius of Tyana*, VIII.7,10, tr. C. P. Jones.
60. Jerome, *Tractatus de Psalmo* 81 in R. M. Berchman (2005), fr. 93.
61. Or, in Greek, *magos* and *magoi*.
62. Matthew 2:1, KJV.
63. Ebony staff: *Greek Magical Papyri*, I.335–6; *Greek Magical Papyri*, IV.2115–16.
64. T. F. Mathews (1999), p. 54.
65. Mathews (1999), p. 57ff. See also D. J. Cartlidge and J. K. Elliot (2001), p. 60, who note, of images of Jesus performing miracles, that, 'In these scenes he is often holding a wand, a virga. Thus, Jesus is also a *magos*.'

Chapter Five: The Product of Insanity

1. See G. D. Dunn (2007), pp. 467–84, for an outline of the ancient debate and for an overview of the modern debates about whether or not what is being referred to was Mary's hymen. The debate is complicated, both theologically and biologically (since fitting modern ideas of physiology onto ancient ones rarely goes well).
2. Luke 2:7.
3. Matthew 1:25, ESV.
4. Shoemaker (2008), p. 499, who notes that it formed a 'regular part of Christian worship'; see also Horn (2018) on its importance in the Caucasus.
5. The figure of 140 comes from Shoemaker (2008), p. 499; the languages are from Elliott (2009), p. 48.
6. Shoemaker (2008), p. 499.
7. For the lack of the ox and the ass in the Bible, see D. J. Cartlidge and J. K. Elliott (2001), pp. 18–19; for Giotto and mosaics, see ibid., p. 23ff.
8. Klauck, quoted in Shoemaker (2008), p. 498. See also Cameron (1994), p. 98, who notes that 'generations of preachers dwelt so often and so lovingly' on such texts.
9. *Protoevangelium of James*, 17:3, tr. Elliott.

10. Ibid., 19:2–3.
11. *Protoevangelium of James*, 18:3, tr. Walker. The exclamation is an ancient incantation formula of great force.
12. *Protoevangelium of James*, 20:1, tr. Elliott.
13. *Protoevangelium of James*, 20:1, tr. M. R. James.
14. The matting, seats and stone are, of course, Larkin's in 'Church Going'.
15. Epiphanius, *Panarion*, Book I, 31.1, referring to the Valentinians; Epiphanius, *Panarion*, Book I, 24.1, referring to the Basilidians.
16. Epiphanius, *Panarion*, Book I, 30, 2 and 30.3, 2.
17. Ibid., 44.2, 1.
18. Extract from the *Latin Infancy Gospel*, in the Arundel Manuscript, Schneemelcher (ed.), p. 466.
19. See Irenaeus, *Against the Heresies*, III.19 for similar; the quotation is from Epiphanius, *Panarion*, Book I, 27.2, 2.
20. Epiphanius, *Panarion*, Book I, 27.2, 2.
21. Basil of Ancyra, The Synodal Letter of the Council of Ancyra, in A. Radde-Gallwitz and E. Muehlberger (eds.) (2017), p. 148.
22. Origen, *Contra Celsum*, I.39, tr. Crombie.
23. Origen, *Contra Celsum*, I.28, tr. Chadwick.
24. Tertullian, *De spectaculis*, 30.
25. P. Schäfer (2007), p. 22.
26. Ibid. See also M. Smith (1981), pp. 26–8, for further discussion of the same point from a Christian perspective.
27. Quoted in Schäfer (2007), p. 24.
28. Epiphanius, discussed in M. Smith (1981), pp. 60–1.
29. Matthew 1:25, ESV.
30. See K. Rahner (1975), pp. 892–8, for a summary of developments.
31. For doors, see Augustine, Sermon 247.2; for fence and seal, see Ambrose, Epistle LXIII, 33. Such euphemisms, combined with a certain vagueness of ancient biology, can make it hard to know precisely what is being discussed, and there are those who argue that this debate is not in fact over the question of Mary's hymen, but about the more general shape of her vagina after birth. But whatever the precise body part such ancient authors had in mind, the point remains: what is being discussed is the fleshly proof of virginity – or otherwise.
32. Aëtius, *Libri medicinales*, 16.17, quoted in K. Hopkins (2018), p. 70.
33. From Saint Ephrem the Syrian, *The Harp of the Spirit*, tr. S. Brock (1983), p. 62ff.
34. Discussed in Cartlidge and Elliott (2001), pp. 82–4.
35. *Protoevangelium of James*, 13:1, tr. Elliott.
36. Ibid., 13:2–3.

37. *Protoevangelium of James*, 13:2–3, tr. M. R. James.
38. The Ethiopic *Liber Requiei Mariae*, 5, 4–6, tr. Shoemaker, quoted in S. J. Shoemaker (2009), pp. 7–8.
39. Ibid.

Chapter Six: What Would Jesus Do?

1. *Infancy Gospel of Thomas*, Greek A, 4.2, tr. Elliott.
2. Ibid., 5.1.
3. *Infancy Gospel of Thomas*, Greek A, 5.1, tr. James.
4. *Infancy Gospel of Thomas*, Greek A, 5.2–3, tr. Elliott.
5. *Infancy Gospel of Thomas*, Greek A, 14.2, tr. Elliott.
6. Ibid.
7. Ibid.
8. Ibid., 7.2.
9. Ibid., 14.3.
10. See W. Elzey (Winter 1975), p. 466.
11. Sheldon (2016), p. 1108.
12. Sheldon, in ibid., pp. 1110–11.
13. Ibid., p. 1101.
14. For chameleon comparison, see T. F. Mathews (1999), p. 115; for Greek god, see L. M. Jefferson (2014), pp. 100–1, who is wary of Asclepius similarities; Mathews (1999), pp. 69–72, who considers them more pronounced; also see F. Flannery (2017), pp. 409–10. For Jesus' breasts, see D. J. Cartlidge and J. K. Elliott (2001), pp. 64–8, and their observation that much that is considered uncomfortable is dismissed as gnostic. For width, see Epiphanius, *Panarion*, Book I, 19.4, 1.
15. *Acts of Thomas*, 12, tr. Elliott.
16. Epiphanius, *Panarion*, Book I, 26.8, 1, tr. Williams.
17. *Acts of John*, 93, tr. Elliott.
18. Clement, *Stromata*, 6.72.1, quoted and translated in P. Ashwin-Siejkowski (2010), p. 99.
19. See Epiphanius, *Panarion*, Book I, 20.1, 1, tr. Williams; Tertullian, *Against All Heresies*, I.I.
20. Papias, quoted in Eusebius, *History of the Church*, III.39.4, tr. G. A. Williamson.
21. B. M. Metzger (2009), p. 262.
22. Luke 2:33, KJV. See also A. Globe (1980), pp. 52–72.
23. Quoted in Macarius, *Apokritikos*, 2.12 in R. M. Berchman (2005), fr. 169.
24. Luke 24:1; Matthew 28:1–7; Mark 16:1; John 20:1.

25. Matthew 28:2–3; Mark 16:5; Luke 24:4; John 20:12.
26. B. D. Ehrman and Z. Pleše (2014), p. xii.
27. Origen, *Homilies on Luke*, 1.2.
28. Clement, *Stromata*, VI.9, ed. Schaff.
29. Fragment 3, quoted in G. Quispel (1996), p. 346. One of the reasons that fasting was considered a sacred act by some in the ancient world was because, soon, such 'shameful and repulsive' excretions cease (discussed in Quispel (1996), p. 348).
30. G. K. Chesterton (2007), p. 176.
31. Mark 11:14, ESV.
32. B. Russell (2004), p. 19.
33. Matthew 10:34–6, ESV.
34. Luke 6:24–6, ESV.

Chapter Seven: On Sardines and Resurrections

1. Acts 8:9–11, KJV.
2. For 'craft of Satan', see *Acts of Peter*, V, tr. M. R. James.
3. *Acts of Peter*, VIII, tr. M. R. James.
4. Ibid., IX.
5. Ibid., XII and IX, respectively.
6. Ibid., XII.
7. Ibid., XIII.
8. Ibid.
9. W. Hone (2003), p. 10.
10. Ibid., p. 73.
11. Hone quoted in J. Marsh (1998), pp. 29–31, to whose book this section is indebted.
12. Ibid., p. 30.
13. Hone quoted in J. Marsh (1998), pp. 43–4.
14. The title is that of a reprint, with foreword by Hancock (1863). See M. R. James (2004), pp. xiv–xx, for a typically Jamesian sniff at the work.
15. All quoted in J. Marsh (1998): 'mischievous and malevolent' (Archdeacon Butler), p. 46; 'most dangerous . . .' etc., p. 44; 'Systematic disregard', 'deep and desperate malignity', 'notorious infidelity' (all quoted by Hone), p. 48.
16. Archdeacon Butler, quoted in Marsh (1998), p. 47.
17. Hone (1820), p. 58; p. 82.
18. Ibid., p. xv.
19. James, M. R. (1924), p. xv.

20. Hone (1820), xv.
21. *Acts of John*, 60, tr. M. R. James.
22. Matthew 19:24, KJV.
23. *Acts of Peter and Andrew*, 16, tr. M. R. James.
24. Ibid., 16–18.
25. Ibid.
26. The story doesn't quite say that he finally gives his wealth away – there is a baptism that intervenes – but it is the clear implication of verses 18–23.
27. *Acts of Peter*, 28, tr. Elliott.
28. Ibid.
29. For 'schlock', see J. A. Fitzmyer (1980), p. 123, quoted in H. Koester (1980), p. 106. See also B. M. Metzger (2009), p. 77, who disdains the Nag Hamamdi texts as 'tedious and verbose'.
30. 'Preposterous' in Berchman (2005), p. 211; 'the absolute stupidity of it all', p. 206; 'obscurity and stupidity', p. 197; 'no one is so uneducated or stupid', p. 212. 'Drunken' in Origen, *Contra Celsum*, VI.37.
31. Porphyry, in Macarius, *Apokritikos*, 3.4, in Berchman (2005), fr. 177.
32. Ibid.
33. Ibid.
34. B. Russell (2004).
35. Origen, *Contra Celsum*, VI.51, tr. Chadwick.
36. Ibid., VI.54.
37. Ibid.
38. Ibid., VI.50.
39. Mark 9:43; see also Mark 9:45 and Mark 9:47, all KJV.
40. Mark 9:48, KJV.
41. D. J. Kyrtatas (2009), pp. 282–3.
42. There is a list given in the superb article by Kyrtatas (2009), p. 288.
43. *Apocalypse of Peter*, 23–5, tr. Elliott.
44. *Apocalypse of Paul*, 38 (for whoremongers); 39 (for virgins and unguents), tr. M. R. James.
45. The words are from the so-called 'Gelasian Decree', for a discussion on which, see the typically brisk F. Crawford Burkitt (1913), pp. 469–71. The Latin comes from von Dobschütz (1921).
46. Kyrtatas (2009), p. 288.
47. From Bremmer (2007), p. 314, and Kyrtatas (2009), passim.
48. See, for example, Kyrtatas (2009), p. 288: 'In fact, it is the Apoc. Pet., not the New Testament, which introduces us to what we have come to recognize as Christian hell.'

Chapter Eight: Fruit From a Dunghill

1. Pliny the Elder, *Natural History*, 36.105–8, tr. Eichholz.
2. For men sweating in togas, see Quintilian's image of a sweaty orator, *Institutio Oratorio*, XI.3; for the carts and the pots on the slaves' heads, see Juvenal, Satire III.250–9.
3. For the smell of drying lakes, see Strabo, 17.1.7; for dead animals, see Martial, 6.93.
4. For fullers' jars, see Martial, 6.93.
5. For cinnamon and lavender, see Martial, 6.55; 3.55.
6. For fresh breezes, see Strabo, 17.7, tr. Roller, with slight alteration for modernity.
7. *Expositio totius mundi et gentium*, VIII, tr. J. Rouge.
8. For transport types, see L. Casson (1954), pp. 101–2, but also passim.
9. *Expositio totius mundi et gentium*, VIII.
10. Epiphanius, *Panarion*, Book I, 26.3, 3–5, tr. Williams.
11. Ibid., 26.1, 1–2. Epiphanius refers to the location of this as being 'the city'. For the fact that the city is Alexandria, see Williams (2008), xiii and Benko (1967), 112. While it suited ancient writers to represent Alexandria as a sink of iniquity, it seems at least possible if not probable that Epiphanius was conflating (mis)information on different gnostic sects here.
12. Ibid., 26.17, 8.
13. Ibid., 26.17, 4.
14. Ibid., 26.3, 3.
15. Ibid., 26 passim.
16. Ibid., 26.17, 6.
17. Ibid., 26.4, 1.
18. Ibid., 26.4, 1–3.
19. Ibid., 26.4, 3.
20. Epiphanius, *Panarion*, Book I, 26.4, 3, tr. Williams, with small emendation in that '*agape*' has been translated as 'love' for ease of understanding of those who are unfamiliar with the term '*agape*'.
21. Ibid.
22. Acts 9:1, KJV.
23. Acts 9:3–4, KJV.
24. The calculation is that of Ronald Hock, quoted in W. Meeks (1983), p. 16, to which excellent book this paragraph and the next are much indebted.
25. W. Meeks (1983), p. 17.
26. From the fascinating B. D. Shaw (1984), pp. 3–52.
27. Meeks (1983), p. 17.
28. *The Digest of Justinian*, 39.4.16.7, tr A. Watson.

29. The king was Herod Agrippa, quoted in the excellent Casson (1954), p. 102.
30. T. Hardy, 'The Roman Road'.
31. Statius, *Silvae*, IV.3.40–44, tr. Shackleton Bailey.
32. Ibid., IV, prologue.
33. Ibid., IV.3.36–9.
34. B. Ward-Perkins (2006), p. 100, to whose splendid and readable book this paragraph is much indebted.
35. Pliny the Elder, *Natural History*, XII.41, tr. Bostock.
36. Ward-Perkins (2006), p. 95. And, as Ward-Perkins points out, immediately after Rome fell, they fell back down to levels closer to those of prehistoric times.
37. Ibid., p. 90–2.
38. Procopius, *The Secret History*, 30.2ff, tr. G. A. Williamson; for the estimate see P. Sabin et al. (2007), p. 9.
39. See Suetonius, *Galba*, 22. Such systems were for the use of the most privileged of the Empire; but even ordinary people were assumed to be able to travel far, and fast: if you were summoned to court Roman law expected you to turn up and to, if necessary, travel 20 miles a day to get there; if you did not, the case would automatically go against you. See Ausonius, Epistles, XVI.11–15.
40. Juvenal, Satire III.69–71, tr. P. Green.
41. Varro, quoted in Aulus Gellius, *Attic Nights*, VI.16, tr. Rolfe.
42. Ward-Perkins (2006), p. 89.
43. Juvenal, Satire XV.109–13, tr. Green.
44. This observation is indebted to N. Hirschfeld (1990), p. 25.
45. This came from a discussion with Tim Whitmarsh about a forthcoming book he is writing on this era.

Chapter Nine: Go Into All the World

1. *The Periplus of the Erythraean Sea*, 20; 55, tr. W. H. Schoff.
2. All from Cosmas Indicopleustes, *The Christian Topography*, tr. J. W. McCrindle: for unicorn, see Book XI.335; for pepper tree, see Book XI.336; for dolphin meat, see Book XI.336.
3. Ibid., Book XI.339.
4. Ibid., Book III.178. Though, what Cosmas meant by Persia and what modern readers understand by the term are likely to be quite different.
5. Matthew 24:14, quoted in Ibid.
6. Cosmas Indicopleustes, *The Christian Topography,* III.178, tr. J. W. McCrindle.

7. Mark 16:15, ESV.
8. See, for example, D. Scott (2008), p. 63.
9. Jenkins (2008), p. 63.
10. A. S. Atiya (1968), p. 261. This paragraph is indebted to Atiya's magnificent book.
11. The conclusion is that of Atiya (1968), p. 240: 'It is no exaggeration to contend that, in the early Middle Ages the Nestorian Church was the most widespread in the whole world.'
12. Peter Frankopan's lovely book – *The Silk Roads* (2016) – is one modern attempt to redress the balance. Other thoughtful scholars have, to their credit, been pointing this out for decades. The scholar F. Burkitt made a similar point in his 1899 lectures, 'Beyond the Roman Empire'.
13. Atiya (1968), p. 13.
14. Jenkins (2008), pp. 52–3.
15. See A. A. Barrett (1991), pp. 11–12.
16. Strabo, *Geography*, 4.5.1–4, tr. D. W. Roller.
17. See B. Bawer (2001), pp. 685–92.
18. *The Book of Enoch*, 8.1–2, tr. R. H. Charles.
19. Or at least according to Epiphanius, anyway. Epiphanius, *Panarion*, Book I, 37.1 and 37.6.5.
20. Ibid., 37.1 and 37.6, 8.
21. Ibid., 37.5, 8.
22. Ibid., 27.6, 9–10.
23. Ibid., 28.1, 1–2.
24. They are also attested in the work of an earlier Syrian writer, and mentioned in a later law outlawing them (Codex Theodosianus, 16.5.65.2) and other places. They were known by many other names, including the Phibionites. On Epiphanius' broad spectrum of names, see S. Benko (1967), pp. 103–19.
25. Epiphanius, *Panarion*, Book I, 26.4, 3.
26. Ibid., 26.9, 6–9.
27. Ibid., Book II, 43.1, 4.
28. See R. S. Kraemer (1992) and V. Burrus (1991), pp. 229–48.
29. Echoes of which can be heard in Pliny the Younger's letters to Trajan. See Pliny the Younger, *Letters*, X.96.
30. Epiphanius, *Panarion*, Book I, 26.5, 4.
31. See B. M. Metzger (1980), p. 27. The whole of the chapter, which is titled 'Names for the Nameless in the New Testament', is fascinating.
32. Ephraem, Madrash 1.18, quoted in W. Bauer (1972), pp. 29–31.
33. John 14:26, as discussed in the very old, but very elegantly written, F. Crawford Burkitt (1899), pp. 37–8.

34. Quoted in S. H. Moffett (1998), p. 53.
35. Burkitt (1899), pp. 61–2.
36. Aphraates, quoted in ibid., pp. 38–9.
37. *The Gospel According to the Hebrews*, quoted in Origen, *On John* 2.12, tr. Elliott.
38. Solomon, *Odes of Solomon*, Ode 19, tr. J. R. Harris. Almost everything about these odes is debated, but that they were originally composed in Syriac seems likely, and a date of the second century is probable.
39. For the hymn, see Moffett (1998), pp. 52–3; for the music, see W. Dalrymple (1997), pp. 175–6.
40. Atiya (1968), p. 55.
41. D. Brakke (1994), p. 401.
42. See ibid., p. 407.
43. *Acts of Thomas*, 1, tr. Elliott.
44. For the modern location of this kingdom, see R. E. Frykenberg (2008), pp. 94–5, to whom these paragraphs are much indebted. The modern translation offers 'carpenter'; in truth, 'builder' would be more accurate.
45. *Acts of Thomas*, 2–3, tr. Elliott.
46. Ibid., 11.
47. Ibid., 12.
48. Ibid.
49. Brown (1982), pp. 49–51, quoted in Frykenberg (2008), p. 99, n. 10.
50. G. F. Snyder (2003), pp. 60–1, who also discusses the possibility that certain things may be considered to be crosses (or have been argued to be).

Chapter Ten: In Eden

1. W. Thesiger (2007), p. 60.
2. Ibid., p. 23.
3. Ibid.
4. Ibid.
5. Quoted in E. S. Drower (1962), pp. 441–2.
6. Quoted in ibid., p. 443.
7. Quoted in ibid., p. 442.
8. Quoted in ibid., p. 441–2.
9. G. Russell (2015), p. xix.
10. Herodotus, *The Histories*, 1.1, tr. A. de Sélincourt.
11. H. G. Snyder (2013), p. 184.
12. For this date, see P. Piovanelli (2003).

13. *Book of the Cock*, tr. M. R. James. For a discussion of the history and transmission of this text, see Piovanelli (2003).
14. For the history of the Western 'discovery' of the *Book of the Cock*, see Piovanelli (2003), p. 428.
15. Quoted in R. E. Frykenberg (2008), p. 1021, n. 15, to whom these paragraphs on Thomas Christians are much indebted.
16. *Jesus Messiah Sutra*, 3, tr. Saeki, quoted in the fascinating D. Scott (1985), p. 92.
17. *Jesus Messiah Sutra*, 87, tr. Saeki, quoted in Scott (1985), p. 93.
18. For a roundup of Prester John and the background to his letter, see K. Brewer (2015), pp. 1–12.
19. For date, see ibid., p. 3.
20. Ibid., p. 68.
21. Ibid.
22. Ibid., p.72.
23. Ibid., p. 71–6.
24. Ibid., p. 82, taking Brewer's suggestion of 'centaurs' for 'archers'.
25. Lobo, *Voyage to Abyssinia*, quoted in the fascinating P. Jenkins (2008), p. 147, to whom this and the next observations are indebted.
26. From Korschorke, Ludwig and Delgado (eds.) (2007), p. 28.
27. Marco Polo, *The Travels of Marco Polo*, tr. R. E. Latham.
28. This observation is indebted to S. Lieu (1980), p. 71.
29. Marco Polo (1982), tr. Latham.
30. Ibid.
31. Lieu (1980), p. 79. See also S. Lieu et al. (2012), pp. 25–52 and 208–211 and S. Lieu (2023), pp. 329–60.
32. Klimkeit (1993), p. 16.
33. Ibid., p. 264, Ten Commandments for Auditors.
34. Ibid., p. 266.
35. Ibid., p. 267.
36. Discussed in ibid., p. 7; quotation from ibid., p. 181.

Chapter Eleven: The Birth of Heresy

1. Quoted in *Historia Albigensis*, tr. W. A. Sibly and M. D. Sibly, p. 64.
2. Ibid.
3. Ibid., p. 84.
4. Chanson de la Croisade, 18.430–40, quoted in Z. Oldenbourg (2000), p. 114.
5. The figure of 15,000 is from the Chanson; the hour comes from *Historia Albigensis*, p. 90.

6. Quoted in Oldenbourg (2000), p. 114.
7. The not wholly reliable number is from *Historia Albigensis*, p. 91.
8. Ibid.
9. Ibid., p. 90.
10. Ibid., p. 91.
11. Caesarius, 5.XXI, tr. H. Von E. Scott and C. C. Swinton Bland.
12. Ad extirpanda, quoted and translated in Prudlo (2019), p. 97.
13. C. Murphy (2012), pp. 4–5, to whom this is much indebted. These were afternoon meetings; there were others in the mornings.
14. Ibid.
15. The full sentence of the Inquisition is quoted in Russell (2017).
16. The observation is indebted to Kynaston (2007), p. 242.
17. It is in the middle form that it means 'choose' – as in, 'I take for myself'. So, strictly speaking, the first-person singular is *haireomai*. But that is more of a mouthful.
18. I am, here and in this entire paragraph, indebted to the hugely interesting M. Simon (1979), p. 110.
19. Simon (1979), p. 115.
20. This observation is indebted to Simon, ibid.
21. Ignatius of Antioch, *Trallians* 6, tr. Grant.
22. Epiphanius, *Panarion*, Book I, 1–2 (poison); Codex Theodosianus, 16.5.20 (polluted contagion), 16.5.64 (criminals); Augustine, *Sermo ad Caesariensis plebem*, 8, quoted in B. D. Shaw (2011), p. 330 (whore); Epiphanius, *Panarion*, Book I, Proem I.2,3 (frauds, tramps, wretches). Both *Panarion* and the Theodosian Code provide a wealth of other mouth-filling insults to hurl at heretics. This paragraph is much indebted to Shaw.
23. The following are all from Epiphanius – chosen because he provides the supreme example of the genre. Epiphanius, *Panarion*, 26.1, 1 (swarms of insects), 38.8, 6 (dung-beetles), 26.5, 1 (swine), 27.33, 3 (wolves), 27.5, 1 (wild beasts).
24. Epiphanius, *Panarion*, passim, but especially: 26.3, 8 and 21.7, 2.
25. Augustine, Sermo 5.1, in Shaw (2011), p. 339.
26. Optatus, *Against the Donatists*, I.III, tr. Vassall-Phillips.
27. *Irenaeus: Against the Heresies II*, pp. v–vi.
28. The famous account of the Bacchic scandal is, of course, Livy's, see *The Early History of Rome*, 39.8. This list and discussion are indebted to J. A. North (1979), pp. 85–6.
29. Edict of Diocletian, AD 302, tr. Hyamson (1913), rev. S. Lieu, quoted in Lieu and Gardner (2004), p. 116.
30. Roman writers were apt to launch into long and contemptuous descriptions of foreign religions. The reliably cantankerous Roman writer

Juvenal, for example, satirized women who would at one moment become a frenzied acolyte of Cybele, the Mother of Gods; then head off to Egypt to get water to splash around in the temple of Isis; then visit a Jewish soothsayer or an Eastern fortune-teller. See Juvenal, Satire VI.508–91.

31. Herodotus, *The Histories*, III.38, tr. A. de Sélincourt.
32. Origen, *Contra Celsum*, V.34, tr. Chadwick.
33. Symmachus, *Memorandum*, 3.8–10, quoted in Lee (2000), p. 116–17.
34. John 14:6, ESV.
35. Julian, *Against the Galileans*, Book I.115, tr. W. C. Wright.
36. Ibid.
37. Chrysostom, Homily 1, in First Timothy, 2, quoted and discussed in the superb D. Rohmann (2016), p. 87.
38. Plato, *Apology*, 21d, tr. H. N. Fowler.
39. Epiphanius, *Panarion*, Book I, 4.2,8, tr. Williams.
40. Tertullian, *De Praescriptione Haereticorum*, 9.4, quoted and discussed in Simon (1979), p. 115.
41. Prudentius, *The Divinity of Christ*, tr. H. J. Thomson, pp. 203–4.
42. Gregory Nazianzen, *Oration*, 5.28, translated in Rohmann (2016), p. 59. The observation is Rohmann's.
43. Ibid., Book I.
44. Julian, *Against the Galileans*, 230A–239E, tr. Wright.
45. Origen, *Contra Celsum*, 3.12, tr. Chadwick.
46. Ibid.
47. Augustine, *De utilitate ieiunii*, 7.9: *'et illi sub multis falsis non habent divisionem, nos sub uno vero non tenemus unitatem'*, Patrologia Latina *XL*, ed. Migne (1844).
48. Ammianus Marcellinus, *The Later Roman Empire*, 22.5, tr. W. Hamilton.
49. All Codex Theodosianus: (feral) 16.5.7.3; (insanity) 16.5.18, but also passim; (contagion) 16.5.56, but also passim.

Chapter Twelve: On Laws

1. Virgil, *The Aeneid*, I.279, tr. H. Rushton Fairclough.
2. Horace, *Odes*, II.11.
3. Pliny the Younger, *The Letters of the Younger Pliny*, I.6, tr. J. B. Firth.
4. Horace, Satire 1.2, 114–19, cited in C. Williams and M. Nussbaum (2010), p. 33.
5. Augustine, *Confessions*, tr. F. J. Sheed: 10.35 (sunlight), 9.8 (thirst). This observation is indebted to Peter Brown and his wonderful *Augustine of Hippo: A Biography* (2000).

6. Augustine, Ep. 7.3,6, tr. NPNF, vol. I; the bowl point is indebted to Lane-Fox's biography.
7. Augustine, *Confessions*, 2.3, tr. Sheed.
8. Ibid., 8.7.
9. I wrote about this first in an *Economist* article, 'To understand the Roman Empire, read Pliny the Younger', 29 January 2022.
10. Codex Theodosianus, 9.12.1.
11. Ibid., 9.15.1.
12. Ibid., 9.24.1.4.
13. Ibid., 9.24.1.5, interpretation.
14. Ibid., 9.9.1.
15. Ibid., 9.30.1–3 (horses), 10.21.1–2 (colours), 15.7.11 (gems). For fabrics, see below.
16. Ibid., 14.10.4 (hair), 14.10.3 (trousers).
17. Ibid., 10.21.2.
18. The law is ibid. 15.7.12: 'actresses of mimes and other women who acquire gain by the wantonness of their bodies shall not publicly wear the dress of those virgins who are dedicated to God.'
19. In tone, topic and status, it should be noted that these laws are a breed apart from bread prices and slave beatings – not quite civil law, they are something else again. On the separation of the laws of Book 16 from the rest of the code, see Shaw (2011), p. 223. The licence imagery is frequently used, but originated with MacMullen.
20. Eusebius, *Life of Constantine*, tr. A. Cameron and S. G. Hall (Oxford: Clarendon Press, 1999), I.28.2.
21. Panegyric of Constantine, IV.21.4, tr. C. E. V. Nixon and B. Saylor Rodgers.
22. Hal Drake (particularly in his 2017 book *A Century of Miracles*) is characteristically excellent on this, both at summing up the (endless) controversies over it and in suggesting a sensible way to understand it.
23. Suetonius, *The Twelve Caesars*, Augustus, 95, tr. Graves.
24. *Historia Augusta*, 18.25, tr. D. Magie, rev. D. Rohrbacher.
25. Though the information about its celebration comes later, from the Chronography (or 'calendar') of 354. See S. Hijmans (2003) for a discussion of when it started to be celebrated on that date.
26. Tertullian, referenced in R. M. Jensen (2000), p. 42.
27. See ibid., pp. 42–3.
28. *Historia Augusta*, 17.3.4, tr. Magie. For a hugely entertaining account of this supremely eccentric emperor, see Harry Sidebottom's *The Mad Emperor.*
29. J. H. Saleh (2019).

30. See A. D. Lee (2005), p. 172: 'There can be no doubt that Constantine's pronouncements from 324 onwards sometimes indicated a more critical attitude against traditional religions.'
31. Codex Theodosianus, 16.5.1.

Chapter Thirteen: The Breeds of Heretical Monsters

1. Eusebius, *The History of the Church from Christ to Constantine*, 10.1, tr. G. A. Williamson.
2. Ibid., 10.9.
3. Ibid.
4. Ibid.
5. Codex Theodosianus, 16.5.5.
6. Codex Theodosianus, 16.5.34.
7. Fines, varying according to social rank, stipulated in ibid., 16.5.52.
8. Ibid., 16.5.53; for a discussion of the tone of the law, see P. Brown (2015), pp. 638–9.
9. Codex Theodosianus, 16.5.21.
10. Novels of Theodosius, 3.1.4.
11. Codex Theodosianus, 16.5.9.
12. Ibid., 16.5.13.
13. Ibid., 16.5.15.
14. Ibid., 16.5.34.1.
15. Ibid., 16.5.34.1.
16. Ibid., 16.1.3 (malicious subtlety), 16.6.3 (madness, but there are many other examples), 16.8.1 and passim ('feral' and 'nefarious' Jews). This book does not deal with the Christian Church's vicious attitude to Judaism in these years – not because it was not vicious, but because it would deserve an entire book to itself.
17. Ibid., 16.4.1, 16.4.3.
18. Ibid., 16.5.6.1, AD 381.
19. Hopkins (2017), p. 442.
20. Novels of Theodosius, 3.1.9–10.
21. Julian, letter to a priest, tr. W. C. Wright.
22. G. E. M. de Ste. Croix (2006), p. 201, gives the example of the (then) current edition of the *Oxford Dictionary of the Christian Church*.
23. Ibid.
24. Vermaseren (1956–60), quoted in Lee (2005), p. 161.
25. For this being the earliest 'Eleousa', as this image is called, see Werner (1972), p. 5.

26. B. D. Shaw (2011), p. 223. For 'juggernaut', see King (1969), p. 54, paraphrased in Shaw.
27. Codex Theodosianus, 16.10.4.
28. Eusebius, *Life of Constantine*, III.54ff, tr. Cameron and Hall.
29. Codex Theodosianus, 16.10.4.
30. Novels of Theodosius, 3.1.8.
31. See Brown (2015), p. 657: 'A thousand persons might be initiated every year at Easter in any large city.'
32. This paragraph and its observation is indebted to Brown (2015), p. 657, referencing Dialogue of Palladius concerning the Life of St John Chrysostom, IX.
33. Codex Theodosianus, 16.5.25.
34. Ibid., 16.5.29.
35. Ibid. See discussion in the lucid M. R. Salzman (1993), p. 375ff. Also, her observation about how little the Code has been used as a method of studying conversion.
36. Russell, B., 'Free Thought and Official Propaganda' in Russell (2000), p. 359.
37. Codex Theodosianus, 16.5.56, also issued in AD 410.
38. Ibid., 16.5.54.
39. Codex Justinianus, 1.5.4.
40. Ibid.

Chapter Fourteen: Like Grains of Sand

1. J. Doresse (1950), p. 435. See the detailed analysis in J. Robinson, *The Nag Hammadi Story* (Leiden: Brill, 2014), to whom these paragraphs are indebted: p. 13ff (for graves); pp. 28–9 (for animals and properly cut tombs).
2. Doresse, quoted in Robinson (2014), p. 9.
3. *The Life of Saint Pachomius and His Disciples*. Pachomian Koinonia, tr. A. Veilleux, vol. 1, p. 15.
4. For a discussion of this and the role of the holy man in these years, see P. Brown (1971), pp. 80–101.
5. *Rules of Pachomius*, I, tr. Schodde, p. 682.
6. Ibid., I, pp. 682–3.
7. Ibid., I, p. 683.
8. Ibid., II, p. 684.
9. Ibid., II, p. 684.
10. Ibid., II, p. 685.
11. Ibid., III, p.686.

12. Ibid., II, p. 685.
13. Ibid.
14. Or such, anyway, are the figures given by ibid., I, pp. 680–1.
15. Robinson (2014), pp. 35–6 (for the traditional telling of this story, including the date), pp. 95–7 (for the dating of one of the codices). On what the men were digging for (sabakh) and its use – and the tendency of disrupting sites when digging it up – see A. T. Quickel and G. Williams (2016), pp. 89–108. For criticism of the tale, see N. Denzey and J. A. Blount (2014), pp. 399–419.
16. Described by Robinson (2014), p. 35.
17. Opinion differs on how many there were. Some think twelve, others thirteen. Doresse originally reported eleven complete books and two part books: see Doresse (1950), p. 70. Robinson comes to the distressing conclusion that 'it will be prudent to continue referring to the discovery as consisting only of thirteen codices, and to mean by this twelve codices': Robinson (2014), p. 39.
18. Doresse (June 1950), pp. 70–1.
19. This is indebted to Pagels' superb summary: E. H. Pagels (2006), p. 14. The whole book is a wonderful read.
20. *The Gospel of Thomas*, prologue, tr. M. Meyer.

Chapter Fifteen: On the Other Origin of the World

1. Genesis 1:1–3, ESV.
2. Isaiah 45:5, ESV.
3. Exodus 20:3, ESV.
4. Exodus 20:5, ESV.
5. Isaiah 6: 1–3, ESV.
6. Genesis 1:1–25, KJV.
7. *On the Origin of the World*, Yaldabaoth Creates Heaven and Earth and Produces Sons, 100.29–101.23, tr. M. Meyer.
8. Ibid., Yaldabaoth Boasts that He is God, 103.2–32.
9. Ibid.
10. Ibid.
11. Ibid., Yaldabaoth Is Distressed About His Mistake, 107.17–108.5.
12. E. M. Yamauchi (1987), p. 428. See also M. W. Meyer (2009), p. 137; E. H. Pagels (2006), p. 17.
13. *The Nature of Rulers*, Eleleth's Story of Creation (93,32–95,13), tr. Meyer.
14. Ibid.

15. Ibid. See discussion in D. Brakke (2010), p. 61: 'their craftsman god is ignorant and even malicious.'
16. *Secret Book of John*, Yaldabaoth's World Order, 10,19–13,13, tr. Meyer.
17. Genesis 2:17, KJV.
18. Genesis 3:3, KJV.
19. *Testimony of Truth*, Midrash on the Biblical Snake, 45,23–49,10, tr. Meyer; date from Meyer (2009), p. 616.
20. *Testimony of Truth*, Midrash on the Biblical Snake, 45,23–49,10, tr. Meyer.
21. Cf. *Paradise Lost*, IX.529–31.
22. *Testimony of Truth*, Midrash on the Biblical Snake, 89,17–90,12, tr. Meyer.
23. *Secret Book of John*, The Creation of Eve, 22,28–23,35, tr. Meyer.
24. Ibid., The Creation of Adam, 15,1–19,10, passim.
25. See the wonderful discussion of this in the superb and lucid Pagels (2006), p. 71ff.
26. *Secret Book of John*, The Fall of Sophia, 9,25–10,19, tr. Meyer.
27. *On the Origin of the World*, Jesus the Word, 125,14–32, tr. Meyer.
28. *Secret Book of John*, Barbelo Appears, 4,19–6,10, tr. Meyer.
29. *On the Origin of the World*, Eve Gives Adam Life, 115,30–116,8, tr. Meyer.
30. Ibid., Song of Eve, 114,4–24.
31. Pagels (1976), p. 293.
32. *Apocalypse of Peter*, Others, Who are Martyrs, Bishops, and Deacons, Are Dry Canals, 78,31–79,31, tr. Meyer. N.44 on the page suggests that this is directed against 'the profession that salvation comes only through the church – i.e., the emerging orthodox church.'
33. Ignatius, Epistle of Ignatius to the Ephesians, VI in ANF, vol. 1.
34. Ibid., V.
35. P. Brown (2015), p. 661.
36. H. Jonas (1992), p. xxxi.
37. *The Nature of the Rulers*, 93,32ff, tr. Meyer.
38. Jonas (1992), p. xxxi.

Chapter Sixteen: To Unweave the Rainbow

1. James Joyce, *A Portrait of the Artist as a Young Man*, pp. 91–5.
2. Obituary, *The New York Times*, 11 March 1893.
3. Obituatry, *The Critic*, vol. 19, 1893, p. 170.
4. Plutarch, *On the Delay of the Divine Justice*, 22, tr. Peabody.
5. Ibid.
6. Ibid.
7. Ibid.

8. Ibid.
9. Virgil, *The Aeneid*, VI.557, tr. H. Rushton Fairclough.
10. Plato, *Phaedo*, 112e, and 113a–c, tr. D. Gallop. They would then be re-born.
11. Ibid., 112a–114c.
12. Lucian, *True History*, 93, tr. F. Hickes.
13. Plutarch, *On the Delay of the Divine Justice*, 22, tr. Peabody (1885).
14. Ibid., p. xiv.
15. Ibid., p. xv.
16. Ibid.
17. W. James, *The Varieties of Religious Experience*.
18. R. MacMullen (1981), p. 206, n. 16. See also M. Smith (1981).
19. Vielhauer (1975), p. 282, quoted in Koester (1990), pp. 25–6.
20. Clement, *Stromata*, ANF, 2.1.
21. Ibid., V.5.
22. Virgil, *Eclogues* IV.I.16, tr. H. Rushton Fairclough.
23. Epist. 53, chap. 7, quoted in E. Bourne (1916), p. 393.
24. Or rather, in a splendidly Ciceronian praeteritio, he said that he wasn't going to comment: '*Taceo si quid divinius ac sanctius* (*quod credo equidem*) *adhaeret istis auguriis*': Keble, quoted in Bourne (1916). It wasn't just Virgil: schoolboys were taught that the final words of Cicero were *Causa causarum, miserere mei*. It is a sadness that Cicero never knew this; his response would have been one to savour.
25. Y. I. Finkel (2014), pp. 2–3. Finkel writes that he has often wondered if the cause of this might have been a minor epileptic response to the discovery.
26. S. Dalley (2008), p. 3.
27. Genesis 2:7, ESV.
28. *Atrahasis*, I.OBV, tr. Dalley.
29. Genesis 1:26, KJV.
30. *Atrahasis*, II.V.i; cf. *Atrahasis*, II.SBV.iii and iv, tr. Dalley.
31. *Gilgamesh*, Tablet XI.i.
32. Genesis 6:5–7, KJV.
33. *Atrahasis*, III.OBV.i–ii, tr. Dalley.
34. *Gilgamesh*, Tablet XI.ii.
35. For Noah being righteous, see Genesis 6:9, ESV; for details of the boat, see Genesis 6:14–21, ESV.
36. *Gilgamesh*, Tablet XI.iii; Genesis 7:4; *Atrahasis*, III.OBV.iii, tr. Dalley.
37. Dalley (2008), p. 7.
38. Genesis 6:9.
39. Justin, *Second Apology*, VII, ANF, vol. 1.
40. Origen, *Contra Celsum*, IV.41, tr. Chadwick.

41. Berossus, quoted by Alexander Polyhistor, in *Cory's Ancient Fragments of the Phoenician, Carthaginian, Babylonian, Egyptian and Other Authors* (1876).
42. Ibid.
43. Caesar, *The Gallic War*, 6.17, tr. Edwards.
44. Symmachus, *Relat*.3.10 in Lee (2015), p. 122.
45. The inscription dates to 9 BC and is quoted in H. Koester (1990), pp. 3–4.
46. L. Kreitzer (1990), p. 213. Though Augustus' numen was worshipped (rather than him himself) during his lifetime, full deification took place only after his death in AD 14.
47. Justin, *Dialogues*, 69.3, in Edelstein and Edelstein (1945), T.95.
48. For Asclepius as a demon, see Sozomen, *Ecclesiastical History*, II.5; for Asclepius as a beast, see Tertullian, *Ad Nationes*, II.14, in Edelstein and Edelstein (1945), T.103.
49. Eusebius, *Life of Constantine*, III.56, tr. Cameron and Hall.
50. Justin, *First Apology*, 1.66, ANF, vol. 2.
51. Vermaseren (1956–60), quoted in Lee (2005), p. 161.
52. Justin, *First Apology*, 1.66, ANF, vol. 2.
53. Tertullian, *De Praescriptione Haereticorum*, 40.2–4, ANF, vol. 3.
54. Augustine, Homily 7, John i.34–51.
55. The analogy is a little longer than that, and is superb. For the full quotation, see A. D. Nock (1964), p. 58 (who is nodding to Cumont).
56. Eusebius, *Life of Constantine*, III.55.5–56, tr. Cameron and Hall.
57. Huetius, *Demonstratio Evangelica*, in the detailed summary in M. Dzielska (1986), p. 203, to which this paragraph and the following are much indebted.
58. Discussed in Dzielska (1986), 200–201. The innocence of his life was, wrote Godeau, one more ploy.
59. Louis-Sébastien Le Nain de Tillemon (1702), p. 2.
60. Pierre Jean-Baptiste Legrand d'Aussy (1807), p. xxxiv; censorship and Bastille dungeons quoted in Dzielska (1986), p. 208.
61. G. Bowersock (1970), pp. 20–1.
62. The famous footnote is in Gibbon, *The History of the Decline and Fall of the Roman Empire* (vol. 2), chapter XI, p. 87, n.70.
63. Dzielska (1986), p. 58.
64. Ibid., p. 182.
65. Keats, 'Lamia', Part 2, lines 231–5 and 237.

Chapter Seventeen: St Augustine and the Spider

1. Pliny the Elder, *The Natural History of Pliny*, 11.28, tr. J. Bostock and H. T. Riley.
2. Aristotle, *Historia Animalium*, vol. IV, V.27.
3. Lucretius, *De Rerum Natura*, 1.931–2, tr. W. E. Leonard.
4. Ibid., 3.381–95.
5. Augustine, *Confessions*, X.35, tr. R. S. Pine-Coffin.
6. Ibid.
7. T. E. Mommsen (1942), p. 227.
8. Ibid., quoting Petrarch using the term in its old sense – on that occasion, of Cicero.
9. See ibid., p. 227.
10. R. MacMullen (1990), p. 143.
11. Ibid., p. 144.
12. Ibid., pp. 145–6.
13. Ibid., p. 155.
14. John Malalas, *The Chronicle of John Malalas*, Book 1.1–6, tr. E. Jeffreys.
15. Gregory of Tours, *History of the Franks*, I.1–10, tr. L. G. M. Thorpe.
16. Bede, *A History of the English Church and People*, 1.2 and 1.4, tr. Leo Sherley-Price. It's best not to press Bede too closely on dates or Roman history. Or, indeed, names.
17. Bede, *The Reckoning of Time*, 47, tr. F. Wallis.
18. Augustine, *City of God*, tr. M. Dods (1913), contents.
19. Ambrose, On the duties of the clergy, 20.
20. Plutarch, *Moralia*, vol. 2, tr. F. C. Babbitt: On Having Many Friends, 2; On Eating Meat, 3; Advice to Bride and Groom, 16.
21. Ibid., 16.
22. Plutarch, 'Whether Land or Sea Animals Are Cleverer', 18, tr. H. Cherniss, W. C. Helmbold.
23. Aristotle, *On the Heavens*, 13.297a–14.298a, tr. W. K. C. Guthrie.
24. Plato, *Timaeus*, 63a, tr. Bury.
25. Pliny the Elder, *Natural History*, 2.LXV, tr. H. Rackham.
26. Ibid., 2.LXIV–V.
27. For whether (or not) these were more widely accepted as the Roman Empire became Christian, see the discussion in McCrindle (2010), p. 108, who concludes that: 'Although the idea of inhabited Antipodes seems to have been generally endorsed in the ancient world, in Christian circles it found less favor and was largely rejected from the patristic period right up to the rise of scholasticism.'

28. Cosmas Indicopleustes, *The Christian Topography of Cosmas, an Egyptian Monk*, Prologue I, tr. J. W. McCrindle.
29. Ibid., Book IV.186.
30. Ibid., Book IV.191.
31. Ibid., Book VI.265.
32. Ibid., Book I.117.
33. Lactantius, 'Divine Institutes', III.XX–XXI, ANF, 7.
34. Ibid., III.XXVI.
35. Augustine, *The City of God against the Pagans*, XVI.9, tr. R. W. Dyson.
36. Ibid.
37. Ibid.
38. Ibid.
39. Ibid.

Chapter Eighteen: To Extirpate the Adversaries of Faith

1. The underlying heretical basis of the dispute was over the treatment of bishops in the wake of Athanasius. See the *Collectio Avellana*, document 1, 1 – a document to be treated with some suspicion.
2. Ammianus Marcellinus, *The Later Roman Empire,* 27.3, tr. W. Hamilton.
3. The 'Cadaver Synod' is described and discussed in Nash (2019), pp. 18–21.
4. Blood: see A. Wiseman (1965), pp. 219–26.; milk and prostitutes: G. Noel (2016), pp. 70; 161.
5. See the superb Rapp (2013), p. 5ff, for a description of the evolution of the role of bishop.
6. For the list of perks, see Augustine, Epistle 23.3, who characteristically disavows this glitter; for the rioting, there are numerous sources, but a good starting guide is G. Fowden (1978), pp. 53–78; Gregory Nazianzen, Oration 42, 7. He goes on, the gold 'which you did, in part pour forth like water, in part treasure up like sand.'
7. Nazianzen, Oration 42, tr. Browne and Swallow.
8. Augustine, Epistle 23.3.
9. The comment was allegedly addressed to Damasus himself. Quoted in E. D. Hunt (1985), p. 191, n. 32.
10. Ammianus Marcellinus, 27.3, tr. Hamilton.
11. Ibid.
12. Codex Theodosianus, 16.2.42.
13. Chrysostom, First Letter to Pope Innocent, quoted in M. Gaddis (2005), p. 275.

14. *Collectio Avellana*, document 1, 2–7.
15. Ibid.
16. Ammianus Marcellinus, 27.3, tr. Hamilton.
17. As Averil Cameron has put it: 'The term the "peace of the church", used by Christians to denote the ending of persecution, is something of a misnomer in light of the violent quarrels which followed during the rest of the fourth century and after.' See Cameron (2008), p. 538ff.
18. Julian, Epistle 41, tr. W. C. Wright; 'slaughtered' etc. in *Against the Galileans*, I.206, tr. W. C. Wright.
19. Ibid.
20. Habetdeum, GCC 3.258, quoted in B. D. Shaw (2011), p. 147.
21. P. Brown (2015), p. 642.
22. *Passio Maximian*, 5, tr. M. A. Tilley.
23. Ibid., 12–14. For whether this was a true story or whether it is too close to a well-known formula, see Shaw (2011), pp. 176–8.
24. Discussed in Shaw (2011), p. 160, to whom these paragraphs are indebted.
25. Eusebius, *Life of Constantine*, II.60.1. Discussed in A. D. Lee (2005), p. 173. See also H. A. Drake (2002), who presents an always nuanced and interesting view of Constantine.
26. Epiphanius, *Panarion*, Book I, Proem II.3.4.
27. *Life of Rabbula*, 40, tr. R. Phenix and C. Horn.
28. Ibid., 41.
29. Ibid., 27.
30. Ibid.
31. Ibid., 40, 41.
32. W. Bauer (1972), p. 27.
33. Ibid., p. 26.
34. Ibid., p. 28.
35. *Life of Rabbula*, 41, tr. Phenix and Horn.
36. Ibid.
37. Ibid., 42.
38. See, for example, Augustine, Letter 185.9.35: 'As to the charge that they bring against us, that we covet and plunder their possessions, I would that they would become Catholics, and possess in peace and love with us, not only what they call theirs, but also what confessedly belongs to us . . .' And so on.
39. Augustine, *De Hares*, 87, quoted in Shaw (2011), p. 310.
40. Ibid.
41. Ibid.

Chapter Nineteen: That no Memorial be Left

1. For date and place, see M. A. Tilley (1996), p. 77.
2. *Passio Marculi*, 2, tr. Tilley.
3. Ibid.
4. Ibid., 1.
5. Ibid., 4.
6. Ibid., 5.
7. Ibid.
8. Ibid., 11.
9. Ibid.
10. G. E. M. de Ste. Croix (2006), pp. 201–2.
11. A similar point has been made by academics to explain the widespread amnesia towards early Christian attitudes to 'pagan' religions. I discuss this in my first book, *The Darkening Age*.
12. Ovid, *Tristia*, II.207.
13. C. Murphy (2012), p. 102.
14. R. Vose (2022), p. 173.
15. Eusebius, *Life of Constantine*, I.46, tr. Cameron and Hall.
16. Ibid., III.66.1–3. The 'letter' underplays this slightly; it was a piece of imperial legislation.
17. It was more complicated than this, but, for a simple summary, see Socrates, *The Ecclesiastical History*, 1.5. The Church took the opposite view.
18. According to *Parastaseis syntomoi chronikai*, 39, quoted in R. Lim (1995), p. 148, n. 209.
19. Another Epistle of Constantine in Socrates, *Ecclesiastical History*, 1.9, translated and discussed in D. Rohmann (2016), pp. 34–5.
20. Ibid.
21. Epistle of Constantine, in Socrates, *Ecclesiastical History*, 1.9, translated and discussed in Rohmann (2016), pp. 34–5.
22. Novels of Theodosius, 3.1.8, but using the slightly more poetic translation that Pharr offers on p. 10 of his introduction, *The Theodosian Code and Novels: And the Sirmondian Constitutions* (1952).
23. Tertullian, *Apology*, 40, tr. T. R. Glover, G. H. Rendall.
24. Lucretius, *On the Nature of Things*, V.828–31, tr. W. H. D. Rouse.
25. Novels of Theodosius, 3.1.1.
26. Novels of Theodosius, 3.1.8.
27. On how what happened next in the empire was related to the old imperial role of ensuring *pax deorum*, see Drake (2007), p. 421, who concludes that 'ironically this failure to break with political thought is what opened the door to conversion!'

28. Codex Justinianus, 1.5.8.12, tr. Rohmann, quoted in Rohmann (2016), p. 100.
29. The law is that of Theodosius II and Valentinian III, but contained in Codex Justinianus, 1.5.16.3, quoted and discussed in Rohmann (2016), p. 101, to whom this paragraph is indebted.
30. Codex Theodosianus, 16.5.66.
31. Rabbula, Collection of Canons, 3.3.1.10 and 3.3.2.50, tr. R. Phenix and C. Horn.
32. Sozomen, *Ecclesiastical History*, III.15, tr. C. D. Hartranft.
33. Eusebius, *The History of the Church from Christ to Constantine*, 8.2, tr. G. A. Williamson.
34. *Acta conciliorum oecumenicorum* 1.54, quoted in M. Gaddis (2005), p. 306.
35. Stephen of Ephesus, quoted in ibid.
36. Tilley (1996), p. viii.
37. *Passio Marculi*, 12, tr. Tilley.

Epilogue

1. Marco Polo, *The Travels of Marco Polo*, tr. R. E. Latham: robbers, p. 65; concubines, p. 122; rain in India, p. 267.
2. Ibid., p. 58.
3. All from Marco Polo, *The Travels*, tr. N. Cliff, pp. 29–31.

Index

About the Author

Catherine Nixey is a journalist and author. She currently writes for *The Economist*. Her writing has previously appeared in *The Times* and the *Financial Times*, among others. She lives in England with her husband. Her first book, *The Darkening Age*, was published in 2017 and was an international bestseller, and won a Royal Society of Literature Jerwood Award.

ABOUT

MARINER BOOKS

Mariner Books traces its beginnings to 1832 when William Ticknor cofounded the Old Corner Bookstore in Boston, from which he would run the legendary firm Ticknor and Fields, publisher of Ralph Waldo Emerson, Harriet Beecher Stowe, Nathaniel Hawthorne, and Henry David Thoreau. Following Ticknor's death, Henry Oscar Houghton acquired Ticknor and Fields and, in 1880, formed Houghton Mifflin, which later merged with venerable Harcourt Publishing to form Houghton Mifflin Harcourt. HarperCollins purchased HMH's trade publishing business in 2021 and reestablished their storied lists and editorial team under the name Mariner Books.

Uniting the legacies of Houghton Mifflin, Harcourt Brace, and Ticknor and Fields, Mariner Books continues one of the great traditions in American bookselling. Our imprints have introduced an incomparable roster of enduring classics, including Hawthorne's *The Scarlet Letter,* Thoreau's *Walden,* Willa Cather's *O Pioneers!,* Virginia Woolf's *To the Lighthouse,* W.E.B. Du Bois's *Black Reconstruction,* J.R.R. Tolkien's *The Lord of the Rings,* Carson McCullers's *The Heart Is a Lonely Hunter,* Ann Petry's *The Narrows,* George Orwell's *Animal Farm* and *Nineteen Eighty-Four,* Rachel Carson's *Silent Spring,* Margaret Walker's *Jubilee,* Italo Calvino's *Invisible Cities,* Alice Walker's *The Color Purple,* Margaret Atwood's *The Handmaid's Tale,* Tim O'Brien's *The Things They Carried,* Philip Roth's *The Plot Against America,* Jhumpa Lahiri's *Interpreter of Maladies,* and many others. Today Mariner Books remains proudly committed to the craft of fine publishing established nearly two centuries ago at the Old Corner Bookstore.